Undoing Apartheid

Critical South

The publication of this series is supported by the International Consortium of Critical Theory Programs funded by the Andrew W. Mellon Foundation

Series editors: Natalia Brizuela, Victoria Collis-Buthelezi and Leticia Sabsay

Leonor Arfuch, *Memory and Autobiography*
Paula Biglieri and Luciana Cadahia, *Seven Essays on Populism*
Aimé Césaire, *Resolutely Black*
Bolívar Echeverría, *Modernity and "Whiteness"*
Diego Falconí Trávez, *From Ashes to Text*
Malcom Ferdinand, *Decolonial Ecology*
Celso Furtado, *The Myth of Economic Development*
Eduardo Grüner, *The Haitian Revolution*
Premesh Lalu, *Undoing Apartheid*
Karima Lazali, *Colonial Trauma*
María Pia López, *Not One Less*
Pablo Oyarzun, *Doing Justice*
Néstor Perlongher, *Plebeian Prose*
Bento Prado Jr., *Error, Illusion, Madness*
Nelly Richard, *Eruptions of Memory*
Silvia Rivera Cusicanqui, *Ch'ixinakax utxiwa*
Tendayi Sithole, *The Black Register*
Maboula Soumahoro, *Black is the Journey, Africana the Name*
Dénètem Touam Bona, *Fugitive, Where Are You Running?*

Undoing Apartheid

Premesh Lalu

polity

Copyright © Premesh Lalu 2023

The right of Premesh Lalu to be identified as Author of this Work has been asserted in accordance with the UK Copyright, Designs and Patents Act 1988.

First published in 2023 by Polity Press

Polity Press
65 Bridge Street
Cambridge CB2 1UR, UK

Polity Press
111 River Street
Hoboken, NJ 07030, USA

All rights reserved. Except for the quotation of short passages for the purpose of criticism and review, no part of this publication may be reproduced, stored in a retrieval system or transmitted, in any form or by any means, electronic, mechanical, photocopying, recording or otherwise, without the prior permission of the publisher.

ISBN-13: 978-1-5095-5282-5
ISBN-13: 978-1-5095-5283-2 (pb)

A catalogue record for this book is available from the British Library.

Library of Congress Control Number: 2022937711

Typeset in 10.5 on 12pt Sabon
by Fakenham Prepress Solutions, Fakenham, Norfolk NR21 8NL
Printed and bound in Great Britain by TJ Books Ltd, Padstow, Cornwall

The publisher has used its best endeavours to ensure that the URLs for external websites referred to in this book are correct and active at the time of going to press. However, the publisher has no responsibility for the websites and can make no guarantee that a site will remain live or that the content is or will remain appropriate.

Every effort has been made to trace all copyright holders, but if any have been overlooked the publisher will be pleased to include any necessary credits in any subsequent reprint or edition.

For further information on Polity, visit our website:
politybooks.com

For
John Mowitt
Qadri Ismail
Rashieda Nkunkumana
Lolo Mkhonto
Saliem Patel

Contents

Acknowledgements	viii
1 Introduction: Apartheid's Double-binds	1
2 Apartheid's Mythic Precursors	33
3 The Return of Faust: Rats, Hyenas and other Miscreants	67
4 Woyzeck and the Secret Life of Apartheid's Things	102
5 Post-Apartheid Slapstick	137
6 The Double Futures of Post-Apartheid Freedom	162
Notes	192
Select Bibliography	209
Index	219

Acknowledgements

This book is the product of conversations with colleagues, graduate fellows, visiting scholars and researchers at the Centre for Humanities Research (CHR) of the University of the Western Cape over more than ten years. I hope that traces of our discussions will be found in the pages of *Undoing Apartheid*, and that this work serves as an acknowledgement of the generosity and collegiality for which the Centre at UWC is known. I thank my colleagues at the CHR for their patience in the making of this long-overdue work. The book responds to the CHR's inaugural question of the meaning of post-apartheid freedom, especially through sustained projects on aesthetic education, the becoming technical of the human, and communicating the humanities.

I am especially grateful to those who read and commented on earlier drafts. They include Jesse Bucher, Jacob Cloete, Seelan Naidoo, Debjani Ganguly, Adam Sitze, Monika Mehta, Ian Baucom, James Chandler, Jane Ohlmeyer, Michael Neocosmos, John Noyes, Christoph Marx, Maurits van Bever Donker, Ross Truscott, Heidi Grunebaum, Aidan Erasmus, Valmont Layne, Lauren van der Rede, Fernanda Pinto de Almeida, Emma Minkley, Gary Minkley, Thozama April, Crain Soudien, Pumla Gobodo Madikizela, Daryl Hendley, Pamela Scully, Tim Campbell, Sipho Dlamini, Ben Nolan, Anaïs Nony, Ali Ridha Khan, Reza Khota, Qadri Ismail, John Mowitt, Shamil Jeppie, Marissa Moorman, Jon Soske, Jean Allman, Dan Magaziner, Warren Crichlow, Kass

Acknowledgements *ix*

Banning, Carina Ray, Tejumola Olaniyan, Gary Candasamy, Nicky Rousseau, Riedwaan Moosage, Bianca van Laun, Binyam Sisay Mendisu, Surafel Wondimu, Timothy Murray, Ranjana Khanna and Srinivas Aravamudan. Basil Jones, Adrian Kholer, Jane Taylor, Siphokazi Mpofu, Luyanda Nogodlwana, Sipho Ngxola, Janni Younge and Aja Marneweck provided me with a much-needed education in puppetry arts. Helen Moffett's careful reading of the entire manuscript deserves special mention, as do Chumisa Fihla and Retha Ferguson for the making of the cover artwork. Iona Gilburt believed in this book in ways that made its completion possible and Julie van der Vlugt offered invaluable editorial support in the final stages. Patricia Hayes, the SARChI Chair in Visual History and Theory in the CHR, has been an invaluable interlocutor over many years. I wish to especially thank my research assistant, Kiasha Naidoo, for her insights, thoughtfulness, and philosophical commitments.

A three-month writing fellowship at the Trinity Long Room Hub Arts and Humanities Research Institute at Trinity College, Dublin provided much-needed respite from the demands of directing a humanities centre and access to the necessary library resources to think about race and apartheid in a global frame. An early attempt to provide a synthesis of the present book at the invitation of Dianna Shandy at the Macalester College Kofi Annan Centre inspired me to refine the argument, so too colleagues at the Dahlem Centre for the Humanities at Freie Universität Berlin, ICGC at the University of Minnesota and the Africa Institute in Sharjah. I also wish to thank members of the Advisory Board of the Consortium for Humanities Centres and Institutes for giving me an opportunity to learn from a truly trans-hemispheric humanities exchange.

This book benefited enormously from the guidance of Leticia Sabsay, Natalia Brizuela and Victoria Collis-Buthelezi, editors of the Critical South Series, and Judith Butler and Penelope Deutscher, convenors of the Andrew W. Mellon-funded International Consortium of Critical Theory Programmes, for unwavering support for my work. John Thompson and Julia Davies at Polity Press offered much-needed guidance and facilitated the publication process.

Ajay Lalu, Jaymathie Lalu and Hansa Lalloo, and my daughter, Kiera Lalu, have been unflinching in their support of my meandering scholarly pursuits. For Kiera, my most incisive interlocutor, I hope this serves as a gesture of friendship across the generations. Finally, this book is an effort to make sense of Jayantilal Lalu's many cautions about what he called apartheid's acts of daylight robbery.

I dedicate this book to two exceptional educators, John Mowitt and Qadri Ismail, as well as three formidable critics of apartheid, Rashieda Nkunkumana, Lolo Mkhonto and Saliem Patel, from whom I have had the good fortune to learn in the heady days of the student struggles of 1985.

1

Introduction

Apartheid's Double-binds

Come with me; for my painful wound
Requires thy friendly hand to help me onward.
                                    Sophocles, *Philoctetes*

Tragedy Strikes

This book tracks the sporadic two-centuries-long emergence of a sentient subject of modernity, in the hope that it might render an image of the perceptual habits formed by apartheid's mythic core, particularly that mythos expressed as an extreme tautology of race lodged in the banality of the everyday. This mostly neglected feature of a system of racial oppression now foreshadows a reckoning with apartheid's aftermaths, imbricated as they are with a techno-modernity of our contemporary world. It certainly weighs on the need to unlearn habits and attitudes formed under apartheid, and the necessity to re-enchant the desire for post-apartheid freedom. But more is needed. The terrain of sense-perception served as a specific site of apartheid's attention, a site where we discover its double-binds. These, as it turns out, were experienced as a condition of race, not once, but twice – as grand apartheid and as petty apartheid. While grand apartheid is plotted in a familiar architectonics that combines metaphors of architecture and social engineering, the seemingly

2   Undoing Apartheid

intractable and elusive character of petty apartheid, which mostly goes unnoticed, may yet teach us something about an enduring and persistent problem of race and modernity. Unless rethought and extended beyond, this deceptively benign strand of petty apartheid is likely to bring a long-brewed idea of race full circle.

The blockage was revealed at the very point where attempts were made to undo apartheid's oppressive grip on everyday life. Apartheid, as a project that tilted sentience towards ever-more mechanical forms of life, appeared to have wedged itself in the circuits of sense and perception, leaving little room for manoeuvre or escape, and even less for desire.

This difficulty dawns for the reader who takes to the streets of the pages of Richard Rive's novel, *Emergency Continued*.[1] Here the gathering storm of protest fuels an urgent debate about the competing exigencies of liberation and education during the dying days of apartheid. As Andrew Dreyer, a college lecturer and lead protagonist, puts pen to paper in a bid to describe a political impasse, he is confronted by a feeling of sheer exhaustion at his own futile efforts to overcome apartheid. The year is 1985 and the setting the edges of Cape Town, in a racially separated zone cursed with the name of the last British governor in South Africa, Athlone, in the aftermath of large-scale forced relocations under the dreaded resettlements of the Group Areas Act of 1950. Fearful of becoming cogs in the apartheid machine, students on the Cape Flats join a country-wide boycott of formal schooling in light of the draconian emergency regulations imposed on everyday life.[2] Like Dreyer, they brush up against a barrier of indecision, weighing the tactical implications of the difference between the entrenched structures of apartheid and its everyday constraints in delaying the onset of freedom. Despite his weariness about the effectiveness of a schools boycott, Dreyer the teacher asks whether there may be more at stake in the debate about liberation and education as a means of achieving the desire for post-apartheid freedom than the students imagine.

Rive brings us face-to-face with the threat of the eternal returns of race that plague the students in his novel. Beyond the standpoints that education avails, the reader is compelled to reflect on what has become of the promise of education against the backdrop of a revolting city – both a city in revolt and one that produces sensations of nausea. Contrasted with Rive's much

Introduction 3

earlier novel, *Emergency*,[3] about the experience of the generation of nationalist opposition in 1960, *Emergency Continued* takes us to the heart of the street fighting in 1985 in order to ask what has remained unresolved in critiques of apartheid. The limitations of the schools boycott are placed alongside an earlier struggle, of the generation of the Mandelas and the Sobukwes, which culminated in a state of emergency being declared in 1960. In contrast to the struggles that tested the limits of apartheid's legality in *Emergency*, in *Emergency Continued* a generation of students stumbles on a more discreet form of violence enacted in everyday life, and which places under threat all desire for the future.

In the much later sequel, the reader is presented with a raging disagreement about liberation and education when competing claims made on the image of freedom are cut short by a surreal act of state violence that rapidly gained notoriety as the Trojan Horse massacre. Images of a trap set for protesting students soon found expression in a popular ancient myth. As the language of the streets seeps into the classroom of the teachers' training college in Athlone, the beleaguered Dreyer, who is presented as both a failed writer and a disillusioned former anti-apartheid activist, is forced to come to terms with the fact that education is not immune from the mythic incursions that apartheid enacts upon psychic life. His waning belief in the efficacy of politics to offer a solution for life under an oppressive system leads him to ponder whether education might offer the only hope for overcoming apartheid. As the anxieties produced by that which returns through mythic infiltrations of the everyday intensify, he realizes that the students are trapped in a zone of indecision, albeit not of their own making.

Figuring out the difference between two states of emergency, the text turns its attention to the contradictory impulses expressed through competing political slogans – 'liberation before education' and 'education before liberation' – that surfaced, exposing the unanticipated generational tension brought about by apartheid's conflicting orchestrations. When his activist son, Bradley, rejects the façade of normalcy surrounding education in an unmistakably abnormal society of permanent emergency, Dreyer has little option but to reckon with the disavowed political views he once embraced in his youth. References to Dreyer's failure as a writer explain blockages of desire that multiply with successive states of emergency. He nevertheless commits himself to preserving something from the vestiges of an education system on the brink of collapse rather than risk a decision that might exacerbate an already debilitating intergenerational conflict.

The uncertainty of what was to come, in contrast to what was to be overcome, is the generative spirit behind *Emergency Continued*, a title that expresses immediate trepidation about a future beyond apartheid constituted by endless collisions. Rive's novel confronts the unceasing threat of the return of myth in the streets in which the story unfolds. This premonition relayed fears of the abrupt foreclosures of mythic violence before a resolution to the disagreement about liberation and education could be reached. Dreyer searches for ways to nurture the educational sentiment in the itinerant worldliness of students that precedes the onset of such violence, but with little success. Although the students' movement is premised on the demand for an education unencumbered by the designs of state power, state power ultimately distracts from the pursuits of education.

Sooner or later, the embattled educator must reckon with the drift towards permanent emergency. While crediting the students with this discovery, he also cautions that the hitherto discrete script of race, which they have resolutely identified as the target of their militancy, has also been constituted as a source of superstition and paranoia that threatens the partitioned city from within, and which must be confronted through conscientious study. *Emergency Continued* extends a hand of friendship across the generational divide in the hope of tempering perpetual internal strife among those most harmed by the banality of apartheid. The promissory statement of the text lies in a mostly untapped resource for relinking education to politics and life, albeit from the shards of memory lodged in the crevices of the divided city. Amidst the ruins of apartheid's permanent emergency, Rive is concerned with generational feuds over fragments of memories.

If the generation of 1985 identified a psychopathology shaped by apartheid's rationality that had been overlooked by Mandela and Sobukwe's generation in the 1960s, Rive would have his readers believe that the former risked something far greater than their predecessors did. If they insisted on revolt at the expense of study, they risked squandering their accidental discovery of a symptom otherwise overlooked in the critique of the meaning

Introduction

of race under apartheid. The concern about an intergenerational conflict that would outlive apartheid reflected an anxiety about the intensification of oppression in which the expansion of technological resources in everyday life produced a masochism of speed and a claustrophobic constriction of space.

The novel does not present a yearning for a return to normalized education, which under apartheid was anyway inconceivable, but a search for a form of education that points towards an exit from the constraints of apartheid that the students stumbled upon in the course of their struggles. It expresses resolute confidence in education as necessary for ensuring a redemptive end to apartheid. This is exemplified by the way in which the text works as a chronicle foretold, in which the search for an educational outlet was foreclosed by the Trojan Horse massacre. Refusing to pit education against the demands of liberation, Rive believes that a pursuit of knowledge that draws on the confrontation with mythic constellations in everyday life may be a critical resource for a future beyond apartheid. In places like Athlone, a dumping ground for apartheid's racial policies of forced removals and Group Areas demarcation in which the novel is set, education required the additional resources of intuition to evade surrender to apartheid's determinations of a fateful destiny.

The tenor of Rive's novel emulates a life of anticipation on the outskirts of the city, where intuition had become a habituated form of surviving the drudgery of everyday life. The quality of anticipation was widespread. Exactly a year before the massacre of 1985, for example, students at a local school staged Jean-Paul Sartre's *The Trojan Women* a mere stone's throw from where Rive's literary foray was set. Randi Hartzenberg, an art teacher at a local Athlone school, was inspired by Sartre's 1965 adaptation of the Euripides play, upon which he happened in a local library while searching for traces of the struggle against apartheid in France's colonial wars in Vietnam and Algeria. Besides serving as a commentary on political anxiety about the threat of violence, the production of Sartre's play in Athlone foretold an impending collision in which manifestations of the unconscious in everyday life brushed up against the edifice of a divided city. Yet an educational sensibility prevailed as dreams of a post-apartheid future were wrapped in the garb of an ancient myth, this time to decry the lingering effects of war on those who had fallen prey to acts of colonial and imperial deception;

6   Undoing Apartheid

later, in Rive's novel, the warning is of uncanny returns. As everyday life collided with an oppressive and suffocating racial formation, the myth of the Trojan Horse revealed something hitherto unanticipated and dangerously virulent in the content of apartheid's violent rationality.

In 'Study and Revolt', Adam Sitze encourages us to follow Rive in asking what to do with the idea of 'school' – and *scholē* – that seems to have been a specific site of indecision and intensification under rule of the permanent emergency of apartheid.[4] Perhaps the students' movement evinced a desire for a mode of schooling that restored an interval which could avert the threat of being overwhelmed by the rapid expansion of technological resources against the backdrop of political constraint. Both study and revolt were appropriate methods of staving off such a fate, even if they offered different prospects for charting a destiny unmoored from apartheid's stifling racial formations. Through nuances of competing temporalities, *Emergency Continued* permits the reader to explicate the dangers unforeseen by the students preoccupied with their indecision about education and liberation in the months leading up to the Trojan Horse massacre. That which is unforeseen, however, also proves to be a feature of apartheid that had not been grasped by the earlier generation of Mandela and Sobukwe. As successive generations emerged from prison, they ignored a caution that showed not only how myth had seeped into education, but that myth signalled a deeper crisis for the ideal of post-apartheid freedom. Rive's *Emergency Continued* ends on a note of disenchantment as Dreyer and Bradley face a future of indeterminate intergenerational conflict. The disenchantment Rive seems to have intuited would be one result of the counterintuitive model of education bequeathed by apartheid, which would stultify any desire for post-apartheid freedom.

Beginnings

This work, *Undoing Apartheid*, is motivated by the need to escape Rive's quandary by arguing that only an aesthetic education attuned to a desire for post-apartheid freedom can properly prepare for a future beyond apartheid, especially with regard to an apartheid of the everyday, known as petty apartheid.

Introduction

Understood as an operation of racial interpellation that traps certain life forms in a near-mechanical existence by blocking pathways to the enchantments of freedom, the aftershocks of petty apartheid would be felt long after apartheid had been laid to rest, thwarting desire and bedevilling creativity wherever it left a trace. The question then, as now, is how to re-enchant the desire for freedom against the backdrop of a racial modernity that took shape under the sign of petty apartheid.

A brief caveat followed by a proposal for how best to proceed is necessary at this point. Since petty apartheid has at best proven elusive to critical currents of theories of the state in South Africa, and while it is mostly unavailable as a trace in the archive, the work of unravelling its effects may be best apprehended in the patterns of everyday life formed in repertoires of object theatre. A key aspect of object theatre is its reliance on mnemotechnic objects – instrumentalities of communication used to record, recall and replay – that offer a rare glimpse of the psychic breach orchestrated in the guise of petty apartheid. But object theatre is not simply beholden to the scripts which it enacts. It is rather an exemplary model of aesthetic education, drawing us towards the realms of *techne*, or the work of crafting that is not reducible to a distinction between a world of contingencies and necessity, but a way of knowing in which things can be otherwise. Where a racial modernity is pressured by a yearning for a future beyond it, object theatre may very well marshal the resources of an aesthetic education towards outwitting the uncanny returns of race.

What is needed is a form of education capable of surpassing the circular causality of race that paradoxically destines modernity to return to a partitioned fate. A model of political education that seeks mastery over this wretched predicament, or one which proceeds via methods derived from anthropology and history to recollect that which has been forgotten, will no longer suffice for the task of undoing apartheid. The double-bind of apartheid's discursivity solicits a twofold approach. While training the senses on the attractions of the object, where the consiliences of the arts and sciences that resulted in a modern concept of race are made available for scrutiny, it simultaneously calls attention to how the object might be put to work in the interests of a viable concept of reconciliation endowed with a truth content and capable of overturning apartheid's sordid rationality. If race, as I argue, came to signify the drift towards mechanized life in modernity, apartheid's end must necessarily be scripted in a manner that releases the energies appropriated to the technical circuits that sustained a facile and psychically debilitating orchestration of a racial modernity.

Fortuitously, on the cusp of a much-vaunted transition to democracy in South Africa, the quagmire of a racial modernity resurfaced in three theatrical works – two by William Kentridge and the Handspring Puppet Company, and a third written by Jane Taylor – that thematized the human and technological entanglements of petty apartheid. *Faust*, *Woyzeck* and *Ubu Roi* were originally conceived by Johann Wolfgang von Goethe, Georg Büchner and Alfred Jarry respectively, at times when the human condition seemed imperilled by uncertainty regarding the rapid expansion of technological resources in the nineteenth and early twentieth centuries. This European hermeneutics of theatrical suspicion, I argue, paralleled the proliferation of origin myths of race that ensued with the abolition of slavery. With, we should add, one significant difference that resurfaced on the eve of the demise of apartheid: as Europe turned its back on the figure of the slave in 1834, from the vantage of the Cape Colony, the slave bore witness to an afterlife inscribed in a signifier of race that disparagingly degraded life into elementary parts.

Faustus in Africa, *Woyzeck on the Highveld* and *Ubu and the Truth Commission* compositely brush up against the demand to de-constitute a modern configuration of race as it suffused an emerging field of experimental psychology, or psychotechnics, that presumed a disaggregation of the apparatus of sense-perception.[5] The garnering of a theatrical response to this inheritance reclaims an element of surprise directed at the task of making history, rather than merely recording or recalling the past. Harnessing figurative and literal references to labour, discipline and power, in their South African incarnations *Faustus*, *Woyzeck* and *Ubu* disclose subjectivities embroiled in a turbulent struggle between human and machine that belies the otherwise calm appearance of the co-evolution of object life in modernity. Whether in fears of displacement of the human by technology (*Faustus*), the depletion of sensory resources (*Woyzeck*), or the collisions of unrequited love in ideals of truth and reconciliation (*Ubu*), each revolves around a contradiction of instrumental reason that came to pass as petty apartheid. Thematization of the

Introduction 9

human and machine thus refracted via the medium of a theatre of objects in a South African setting helps to craft an image of localized life in a struggle to stave off the overwhelming technological reorientations underway in the world.

To bring about a twist in the tale of fate, the works under discussion here exploit an indecision about apartheid's place in the co-evolving story of the human and technology. They confront those anxieties regarding an enlightenment in which the slide into mechanized forms of life unfolded as a story of an incremental racialized modernity. The audience is encouraged to reconsider the problem not at the level of grand design of political programmes, but in intricate mechanisms and techniques that threaten to overwhelm life at its most individuated encounter in a changing world. This is achieved by deftly assembling elements of myth and machine that held sway in the shifting relation between subjects and objects – in a bid to flip object life into a renewed scene of freedom.

To the extent that this book conjures up an image of freedom to which the medium of theatricality aspires, it is similarly committed to asking whether the enigmatic charm of theatrical objects might help to re-enchant the desire for post-apartheid freedom. This is tantamount to asking whether the Trojan Horse offers to art, politics and writing what Monique Wittig, in a ground-breaking essay from 1984, saw as a necessary process of questioning with which to reimagine freedom. Wittig elucidates how event, metaphor and memory thrive in the shadows of the Trojan Horse, yet remain beholden to the seductions of instrumentalities of war upon which oppression ultimately pivots.

> The horse built by the Greeks is doubtless also one for the Trojans, while they still consider it with uneasiness. It is barbaric for its size but also for its form, too raw for them, the effeminate ones, as Virgil calls them. But later on, they become fond of the apparent simplicity, within which they see sophistication. They see, by now, all the elaboration that was hidden at first under a brutal coarseness. They come to see as strong, powerful, the work they had considered formless. They want to make it theirs, to adopt it as a monument and shelter it in their walls, a gratuitous object whose only purpose is to be found in itself. But what if it were a war machine?[6]

What, indeed, if the arrival of the post-apartheid evokes memories of a Trojan Horse that turns out to be little more than

10 Undoing Apartheid

a war machine with which we have come to make a premature peace? The motif of the Trojan Horse describes the seemingly inescapable arc of human attitudes to technological objects: from trepidation to gradual accommodation. To paraphrase Wittig, what if this war machine requires a detour where the shock of words produced by their association, disposition and arrangement now calls for a work of turning raw material into something else – perhaps another perspective of freedom? Wittig lays forth a plan for gathering the aesthetic resources of myth and tragedy – where myth harbours the conditions of violence, and tragedy serves as a pathway to self-definition in modernity. Her plan enlivens the possibilities of rereading figurations of race in *Faustus in Africa*, *Woyzeck on the Highveld* and *Ubu and the Truth Commission* from which aesthetic resources may be diverted towards the productive work of re-enchantment. If the *aesthetic* in aesthetic education leads to a piecing together, Wittig's injunction to unlearn assumes an equally potent educational function that ought to be clarified. The pertinent question is whether it is possible to remake post-apartheid freedom from the shards of images remaining after the violence constelled by the Trojan Horse of petty apartheid.

Taking seriously the diminutive descriptor, a strand of racial thinking that surfaced as a trait of petty apartheid in South Africa emulated a dangerously simplistic response to a complex problem arising from the nineteenth-century Promethean shifts in distributions of energy between humans and machines that accompanied a revolution in thermodynamics. Briefly, the first law of thermodynamics laid the foundation for a principle of energy conservation to determine the place of the human in a nexus of nature and technology. In the 1860s, an attempt to violate a second law of thermodynamics by introducing an imaginary mediator, Maxwell's demon, established a precedent to redistribute entropic energy towards an extreme ordered state. The violation of this second law, while failing to live up to the expectation of perpetual motion machines, nevertheless affected contentions about the distribution of energy across the spectrum of the human, nature, information and technology: as the source of a metabolic rift (Marx and Engels), as transforming labour into a perfect machine (Sergei Podolinsky), or as a sensory-energetic loop resulting in active sensing (Wilhelm Wundt).[7] Petty apartheid seems to have reductively settled on the

Introduction 11

informational dynamic of sense-perception derived from Wundt, whose studies into nerve mechanics in the bonds of individual and group psychologies found expression in a working out of a twentieth-century category of race with which South Africa was to become synonymous.

Apartheid, by this account, strategically combined technology (the architectonic implementation of scientific knowledge) with a machinery (stratagems, abilities, instruments of power, or tricks) to transfer indelibly the mythic precursors of race to a near-automated form of life.[8] The many architectural and engineering metaphors used to describe its power somehow fail to account for this level of technical and mechanistic existence. Focus on the level of apartheid's architectonics has meant that the process of corralling disorderly intensities of racial feeling and attitudes into a system of communication and control by the state project of apartheid has been overlooked. Much like the science of cybernetics established after World War II, which resulted in the invention of automated machines inspired by discoveries of machine control over the unpredictable qualities of human speech, an apartheid of the everyday ordered race, conscripting its signifier in the transmission of messages between human and machine, in an overarching technology of power.[9]

With all the trappings of a repressed mythic inheritance that bound human subjection to machines, petty apartheid was tantamount to a Trojan Horse dispatched to conjure a feeling of unceasing strife, requiring a tautological stoking of the flames of civil war by means of everyday provocations to justify the enforcement of *stasis*, a future collapsed into a recurring present. This prohibitive and constraining circular causality took on the characteristics of a self-perpetuating circuit in which race served as a standing reserve of energy that could be relied on to propel and modulate the exercise of power.[10] The result was a convenient state fiction about sensory aphasia, a belief premised on a false problem of the assumed dissonance of images and words against which the orders of race were mapped and enforced. The ability to outwit the political sophistry of apartheid hinges on where precisely we apprehend the effects of race in this tautology. Rather than begin with the presumption of a master plan, I suggest that we begin elsewhere: at the point where a post-apartheid future encounters the remains of race in everyday life.

Unlearning Apartheid's Sophistry

The lifting of the burden of apartheid in South Africa was tinged with irony as celebrations of the dawn of democracy unfolded a stone's throw from an official archive of the unfulfilled promises made to emancipated slaves in the Cape Colony in 1834. Crowds gathered at the Grand Parade in Cape Town to welcome Mandela and his peers – once banished to an island prison – at the very site where slaves rejoiced upon hearing news about their pending freedom. Yet the gut-wrenching cries of racial torment (from which there had been little respite over the subsequent centuries) threatened to punctuate the euphoria surrounding the birth of democracy in South Africa at the closing of the Cold War. Fortunately, what might have passed as fear of history repeating itself – in which a desire to exit the rule of race amounts to naught – was momentarily suspended by the vista of a new horizon.[11] Scenes of exuberance arising from an animated and vocal *demos* warded off the dark clouds of history and pointed towards a future beyond apartheid.[12]

Chris Ledochowski's painterly portrait of Nelson Mandela on the balcony of the City Hall at the Grand Parade in Cape Town set the stage for aligning hope and history. Painting and photograph comingled through a shared idiom in a makeshift arena against the backdrop of Table Mountain, a garrison city beneath it, offset by the dwindling fortunes of Victorian architecture. It was a scene that evoked mixed feelings of *déjà vu* and future memories, in defiance of the strictures of time and space.

And so it came to be that by stepping out of the confines of prison and into a theatrical arena, Mandela's arrival was met with the thunderous welcome of the postcolonial world that so eagerly awaited a renewed promise for the future. Amidst the jubilation of those gathered to celebrate the dawn of freedom, an unmistakably discordant note could be heard, as if to proclaim: *Nomen est omen* – your destiny is in your name. If there is a lesson that apartheid teaches, it is that its name, like those of slavery and colonialism, bears traces of the formation of race that would not simply disappear with a triumphalist reception of post-apartheid freedom.

Scars etched in the edifice of a divided city, formed over centuries of racial anguish, summoned long-repressed memories

Introduction 13

of offence from which the *demos* hoped to emerge as Mandela passed *en route* to his much-anticipated appearance at the Grand Parade. The burden of the past was laid bare before him: here, a reminder of the public rehanging of a deceased girl, Sara, following her suicide at the Dutch Slave Lodge in 1672;[13] there, the home of the British colonial governor, Sir Benjamin D'Urban, where the plot to attack the Xhosa king, Hintsa, was hatched in 1834.[14] And once, in that same place where a vast sea of people now gathered to welcome Mandela, an unidentified photographer captured an image of an inverted Jan van Riebeeck protesting the 1952 Tercentenary Celebrations of the fictional founding of the Cape of Good Hope.[15] Mandela appeared to be stepping into a theatre of the world – one rich in irony and contradiction – rather than onto a stage of world history. While abjuring apartheid and contemplating the long walk to freedom (later the title of his famous autobiography), the *demos* awaited the first words of a returning hero, as if in a redemptive scene drawn from the ancient genre of tragedy.

Outrage over Mandela's unjust imprisonment was projected onto a *demos* in fact and fiction. The long walk to freedom welcomed improvisation in making history. A refusal to allow his tormentors any role in preparing the journey to the centre of the city of Cape Town extended an already lengthy wait for the arrival of a long-lost hero. When he finally made an appearance, the longstanding ban placed on his image and voice, hiding him from public view for twenty-seven years, confounded anticipations and expectations. And in a moment of mild comic relief, a frantic search ensued for spectacles required to deliver a speech for which the world waited with bated breath. All was forgiven, especially since Mandela came bearing long-awaited news about racism's last word – apartheid. Yet, in the shadow of the garrison city, questions abounded: among racism's permutations, which script of race would be the last word signalled by apartheid? Would the wake of apartheid signal an end to the bifurcation of rural and urban labour along the lines of race and ethnicity? Or was apartheid's eulogy performed over the psychic wreckage of everyday life unevenly borne by a racially designated population?

As Mandela looked towards the future with borrowed lenses, a gift of theatre from a distant land, written to mark the occasion of his release, plotted possible pitfalls that lay in wait along the walk to freedom, returning us to a theatrical

14　　Undoing Apartheid

engagement with the seepage of myth into reason. Irish poet Seamus Heaney's play *The Cure at Troy* restages a Sophoclean tragedy from ancient Greece to lay bare the trials and tribulations facing Mandela's pursuit of a rhyme of hope and history.[16] Hints of optimism notwithstanding, the longing for a promised tidal wave of justice was interwoven with a cautionary tale about the dangers ahead if the wound of partitioned states was left to fester. Doubling as a celebration and a plea, Heaney's adaptation of a play from the fourth century BC begs forbearance in the face of the turbulence accompanying transitions in two such states of partition – Ireland and South Africa – at the end of the twentieth century.

The verses of *The Cure at Troy* express a commitment to re-enchant freedom, not by proclamation, but by encouraging and nurturing educated choices. We gather this much from how an eviscerated Philoctetes – the wounded hero of Sophocles' original play – is summoned to temper expectations of freedom for the purposes of the equally important task of remaking the self and the *demos*. This considerably delicate undertaking is performed against a sparse backdrop. A minimalist setting allows for a meditation on the conflicting demands for a cure for a wound, and the desire for a release from the solitude of suffering. Why a gift in the form of a play about a wounded wretch to inspire confidence in the tasks of re-enchanting freedom?

As the story goes, during a lull in the siege of Troy, we meet a Greek archer, Philoctetes, on the island of Lemnos, where he had been abandoned by his fellow warriors after developing a reeking and festering wound from a snakebite. Although overcome by self-doubt, Philoctetes nevertheless possesses the weapon necessary for victory in the war against Troy. This leads a calculating Odysseus and a younger warrior, Neoptolemus, himself willing to forego an abiding commitment to truth in the interests of loyalty to the Greeks, to trick the wounded outcast into surrendering the divine bow needed for victory over the Trojans. Philoctetes' expectation of being freed once he surrenders his bow leads to puzzlement about the true meaning of the archer's desire for freedom.

Taking a leaf from *The Cure at Troy*, meaningful resolution to conflict can only be reached by attending to a festering wound. After all, when partition is stealthily rationalized as a basis for peaceful coexistence as in apartheid's 'separate but equal'

Introduction 15

doctrine or its fanciful justification as a project of 'good neighbourliness', it often masks a deeper wound. Strangely enough,
while the world wished to be rid of the stain of past conflict with
the onset of an era of globalization, and as proclamations about
the end of apartheid proliferated, the scars of petty apartheid on
the memory of those who lived with its worst excesses remained
or continued to be inscribed. This is not to suggest that petty
apartheid could or can ever be entirely detached from grand
apartheid. The instabilities of race specific to the former were
corralled by the sophistry of a master narrative that claimed
to have established political peace – *stasis* – through partition.
With growing weariness surrounding the political sophistry
that advocated partition as a strategy to guard against civil
war, a peace brokered to thwart civil war among the subjects of
partition was ironic at best.

Beneath the veneer of peace, qualities of race drawn from the
past appeared to be converging with expansions in technological
resources that promised a new world order in the present.[17]
Fresh contradictions arose in the place of older unresolved ones,
placing even greater constraints on transcendent political claims.
Ultimately, the residual effects of myths that co-evolve with
machines cannot be simply transcended – only unlearned in the
process of forging newer prognoses for subjectivity. Unlearning
is called for because disenchantment inevitably builds when the
myth on which partition rests is folded into technology, prohibiting easy exit from its hold over a repertoire of communication
and control in which modern subjectivity is ensnared. This is
particularly the case when we heed the subjective constraints that
accrue in the cobbling together of petty apartheid.

Petty apartheid, as suggested earlier, will only ever be undone
through a process of unlearning and a simultaneous process
of learning to learn. It is perhaps in the gift of a story about
a wounded Philoctetes that we discover a key to unlock the
promise and potential of education specific to the aesthetics
necessary for simultaneously unlearning and learning to learn.
In Sophocles' play about an outcast hero, a language about
education necessary for avoiding the pitfalls of a deceptive *stasis*
makes available points of departure that extend the search for
resolution to conflict while guarding against political sophistry.
In short, Heaney lays out the terms for negotiating the deceptive
plots of partition, garnering the mythic precursors of race and

16 Undoing Apartheid

harnessing the method of education necessary for averting a slide towards recurring conflict and war.

The Cure at Troy belongs to the theatre of expectation, or what Samuel Weber calls the rise of theatrocracy in ancient Greece, disparagingly referred to as a 'government' of spectators. A theatrocracy eludes the grids of intelligibility of both history and anthropology in its anticipation of the subjectivity that freedom names. Consider, for example, Weber's crisp definition of this much-maligned political offshoot of ancient theatre:

> Theatrocracy, which replaces aristocracy and is not even democratic, is associated with the dissolution of universally valid laws and consequently with the destabilisation of the social space that those laws both presuppose and help maintain. The rise of theatrocracy subverts and perverts the unity of the *theatron* as a social and political site by introducing an irreducible and unpredictable *heterogeneity*, a multiplicity of perspectives and a cacophony of voices. The disruption of the *theatron* goes together, it seems, with a concomitant disruption of theory, which is to say, of the ability of *knowledge* and *competence* to localise things, keep them in their proper place and thus contribute to social stability.[18]

We should be careful not to reduce this formulation to mean mere freedom. Rather, the novelty of freedom lies in the conviction to think ahead, to think the absurd, when passions and politics are misaligned. Effectively, theatrocracy makes available a model of education for uncertain times, akin to the decision by Heaney to deliver a lesson about a future unencumbered by sectarian violence in the form of *The Cure at Troy*. Instead of storming the citadel, Weber notes that theatrocracy enables itinerant choruses that sidle up to the altar, issuing seductive, contagious and hypnotic strains that disrupt the injunction to know one's place.[19] By extension, Heaney's gift to Mandela evokes a similar sentiment. Bearing the burden of history both as tragedy and farce, it is difficult to ascertain whether behind the voice that cut into the late afternoon sun in Cape Town, inviting the *demos* to join in the long walk to freedom, we would hear echoes of a wounded Philoctetes, a guilt-ridden Neoptolemus or a plotting Odysseus. Amidst the euphoria, a chorus similar to that encountered in Greek tragedy could be heard – welcoming Mandela with jubilant cheers in lieu of an end to threats of war. Returning home, it would appear, proved to offer welcome, if

Introduction

17

momentary, relief from the experience of exile or banishment. In verse inspired by Mandela's release, strains of hope of a world beyond the violence of partition are conveyed by a chorus of three women reflecting on the blindness of three men:

> Human beings suffer,
> They torture one another,
> They get hurt and get hard.
> No poem or play or song
> Can fully right a wrong
> Inflicted and endured.
>
> The innocent in gaols
> Beat on their bars together.
> A hunger-striker's father
> Stands in the graveyard dumb.
> The police widow in veils
> Faints at the funeral home.
>
> History says, don't hope
> On this side of the grave
> But then, once in a lifetime
> The longed-for tidal wave
> Of justice can rise up,
> And hope and history rhyme.
>
> So hope for a great sea-change
> On the far side of revenge.
> Believe that further shore
> Is reachable from here
> Believe in miracle
> And cure and healing wells.[20]

Nothing stirs postcolonial passions quite like the rituals surrounding the theatrical repertory of overcoming oppression, especially when the stage is set for an angst-ridden tale about an abandoned wretch with a festering wound.[21] Eclipsing the hero's welcome, the curious theatrical tale of a wounded archer with a divine bow and poisoned arrows delivers a gift that doubles as an act of generosity and trickery. Heaney finds in the occasion an opportunity to distinguish sophistry from cure, beyond the genuine expressions of joy to welcome the return of an outcast hero. Philoctetes' mistrust of the promise of freedom that

18   Undoing Apartheid

doubles as a cure for his wound is placed alongside the trickery of Odysseus, who is determined to ensure victory at any cost. Could it be that by invoking the figure of Philoctetes amidst promises of peace in a partitioned world at the end of the Cold War, Heaney looks askance at the prospect of success, pondering whether the conceit of freedom reveals that the half-true rhyme of hope and history is inevitably deceit?

Notwithstanding Heaney's view that 'poetry tends to evolve a little ahead of what is actually happening', or Eugene O'Brien's qualification that his work be read as 'a poeticized thinking that opens up hitherto unseen and unexpected aspects of philosophy and history',[22] *The Cure at Troy* curiously delimits the possibility of righting a past wrong through poetry, play and song.[23] Rather, the medium of theatricality works niftily to craft pathways out of the impasse of the threats of recurring violence. Theatre is where a message of 'hope' is prepared in the wake of history's sea-change, when the pain and stench of a festering wound thwarts the desire for a future 'on this side of the grave'. *The Cure at Troy* thus makes available the memory of theatre to negotiate a passage through deception and pathos out of which a different future will have to be crafted. Heaney offers Mandela a gift about the interplay of myth and tragedy in everyday life in order to prepare for the arrival of a future that ought not to be mistaken for a 'chronicle foretold'.

What precisely to hold onto in *The Cure at Troy* in order to make a hopeful future? Perhaps we are to discover in it the inspiration for a discourse on education adequate to the task of re-enchanting freedom. Or, as it pertains to the demands to quell the thirst for civil war, Heaney may be cautioning Mandela about the dangers lurking in political rationalizations obscured by characters such as Odysseus. After all, the latter acts as a master journeyman whose capacity for intentional deception, more than lying or falsehood, knows no bounds. In *The Cure at Troy*, the force and consequence of deception reflect the mercenary relationship that Odysseus forges with those under his tutelage, foreclosing possibilities of an education allied to the desire for freedom. The dramatic purpose served by inserting a youthful Neoptolemus between the deceptive oratory of Odysseus and the battered sensibility of Philoctetes leads to the affixing double-bind that overwhelms plans to exit a cycle of violence and recurrent generational conflict. An education oriented towards

Introduction   *19*

the everyday that strives to remake a concept of freedom beyond the bounds of tradition and national resonance may be the only hope of reaching Heaney's proverbial other shore. As we learn from experiences of apartheid, such an endeavour soon brushes up against the limits of deception and sophistry. Tucked away in the gift of a Sophoclean meditation on freedom and education, Philoctetes is left uncertain about whether a humanistic or technically expedient education might potentially re-enchant his search for freedom.

Wounded Education

In *The Cure at Troy*, Philoctetes underscores the tasks of sensing freedom by emphasizing educated resolution when working to overturn plots born of deception. Heaney thus tellingly passes the decision to choose between loyalty and desire to a youthful Neoptolemus. He is possibly the only reliable subject of education, given the care taken to weigh options. Beguiled by Odysseus, Philoctetes is at pains to win over his youthful visitor by soliciting empathy for his festering wound and his desperate yearning for release from isolation.

The Cure at Troy provides an abiding metaphor for a paradox that bedevils anticipations about a future that will prove inconceivable without an aesthetic education. As the chorus fêtes the rhyme of hope and history, Heaney's Philoctetes remains rightfully reticent, fearful of being deceived by Odysseus, desperate to escape the trap posed by hope and history. In responding to the *aporia*, Heaney leans towards Neoptolemus as he follows in the missteps of a wounded Philoctetes, whose debilitating sore causes him to stumble in the pursuit of freedom. The young Neoptolemus is thereby persuaded of the importance of unlearning tradition, while learning to learn from circumstances of which nothing can be known in advance.

Heaney grafts an ethical conundrum onto an expedient narrative made up of lies, tricks, deceit and intrigue. This serves to reinforce a predicament of enforced *stasis*, on the cusp of a widely hailed political change in states where partition was used as a cynically deceptive justification for allegedly quelling the threat of civil war. The adaptation of Sophocles' *Philoctetes* lays bare the political choices in such states by means of a 'deception

20 Undoing Apartheid

plot'. In *The Philosophical Stage*, Joshua Billings hints at the complexities of the Sophoclean tragedy adapted by Heaney to delineate the choices available in a world where intrigue is the order of the day. Sophocles' *Philoctetes*, Billings notes, 'encompasses a quasi-reality from which there appears to be no escape, and which renders trust between individuals nearly impossible'.[24] The dynamics of the play provide a fitting mix of metaphor and realism to explore some of the more difficult aspects of escaping the violence of partition.

A distinguishing feature of a 'deception plot' is the wager between the demands of education and freedom, or, more precisely, the education necessary to unlearn the trappings of sophistry, which amounts to a mere expectation of admiration and affection in return for absolution. Politics emulates an educational principle of unconditional trust in this particular resolution to conflict. While education generally assumes a measure of trusteeship, Heaney seems to be asking: to whom is one to entrust an education that would allow for freedom to begin anew, in a novel way capable of reaching beyond a world of mere appearances? This question can be answered only with great difficulty in an environment filled with intrigue, requiring a way to rework intentional deception through the skills of art and *techne* – as happens in the medium of theatre – to trick the senses into believing that another destiny is possible.

The work of theatre as education for another destiny enacted by the wounded is easily sustained alongside Simon Goldhill's claims that plays like Sophocles' *Philoctetes* placed the audience on stage, making the *demos* integral to the tragedy.[25] Goldhill notes how Neoptolemus is exemplary of the educational meditations in Sophoclean tragedy. More than weighing in on elite and public morality, Heaney's version of Sophocles' *Philoctetes* points beyond the exigencies of the immediate to the reasoned choices facing one as educationally unseasoned as Neoptolemus. In the exchange between the older archer and novice soldier, we encounter a discourse about an education best suited for meaningful, as opposed to an expedient, freedom. While Odysseus is a purveyor of education once reserved for elites, Philoctetes offers an education that harnesses the sensibilities permeating the streets.

Heaney's careful use of the chorus implicitly questions the effectiveness of an education in the meaning of freedom that

Introduction 21

occludes the passions of a theatrocracy. If freedom is indeed infused with the choices we make about education, he finds in Sophocles' *Philoctetes* an educator who, despite his isolation, is more acutely tuned into everyday life and thus better prepared for a cure, where cure (from *curare*) amounts to seeking the sources of freedom beyond the strictures of the aristocracy and the immediate demands of the *demos*. With one notable difference: whereas Odysseus offers an education in freedom that demands patriotism, strictly disavowing any questioning of possible deception that might be entailed in an education imbued with sophistry, Philoctetes offers Neoptolemus an education that excites the senses, in which freedom lies ahead without guarantees, in a form that cannot be known in advance, and for which trust is an unfolding labour.

Considering that his language is preceded by howls of agony, Philoctetes is undeniably a better teacher to Neoptolemus than Odysseus. His mark of distinction relies on connecting education to the speculative realm of freedom, as opposed to those forms of speculation that direct youth to the endpoints of obedience and war. Enveloped in a cloud of suspicion, Odysseus proclaims mastery over Neoptolemus, with the bland words of a blunt command resulting from 'a nightmare of the loosening of scruples brought about by war'.

> I can see the whole thing in my head
> So all you need to do is listen
> And do the things I tell you.

With the skill of a great orator and bolstered by tradition, Odysseus implicates Neoptolemus by instructing the latter to stealthily retrieve Philoctetes' bow. When Odysseus instructs Neoptolemus thus, he notes that 'arguments wouldn't work, no more than force', as if to expect from the offer of education an exchange of mastery for unquestioning loyalty, affection and admiration. However, upon meeting the elusive Philoctetes at his cave, Neoptolemus discovers that education may be modelled not only in relation to tradition, but also the unconscious elements of experience upon which one stumbles. In the end, though, Philoctetes has to come to terms with the fact that experience is no match for tradition, and that the cure for his wound lies in restoring his reputation in a national frame – even as he knows that he has been betrayed by the Greeks, whom he has come to hate. Between Odysseus' pedagogy of trickery, where cunning holds sway over experience, and Philoctetes' search for a cure, Heaney's gift comes to Mandela with the reminder that we should also teach what we don't know; that is, we start from the wound of knowing that we know nothing.

As Philoctetes' festering wound causes him to stumble onto stage, an education in freedom beckons us to behold the performativity that is underway, wading through the moral and political abyss of time. To Neoptolemus, Philoctetes offers an education, shorn of mastery, about what might be shared in the idea of freedom. This pedagogy is oriented towards that in which nothing certain is really known in advance, other than seductions of poetic desire. While Philoctetes discovers an interlocutor as opposed to a disciple in Neoptolemus, the youthful charge is set on the path of an education with the potential to ensure generational continuity, unlearning the mastery of tradition and learning to learn from self-discovery.

The burden of Philoctetes' education is twofold: bearer of a symptom of the past and a supplement for the future – much like the subject *qua* subject of race coded by sensibilities formed by earlier disappointments of slave, colonial subject and, more recently, the subject of partition, in the pursuit of the desire for freedom. Through the poet's encouragement, we might set to work on deciphering the names given to race, forged from forfeited futures of slave emancipation, and the education necessary for transcending the characteristics of seemingly unending oppression.

Theory and Theatre

Affirming theatre as a site for making history, rather than merely functioning as a ruse for talking about history, consider the productivity of the medium of theatricality in assembling fragments of images to craft a sense of freedom in a world where the lessons of tragedy have been replaced with myth. What sense might theatre make of the chaotic experience of apartheid? To receive *The Cure at Troy* on this side of the grave, from a place expectantly awaiting the outcomes of a transition from centuries of war and violence, avails, as Heaney puts it,

Introduction 23

a 'double-take of feeling'. It signals a theatrical technique of delayed reaction or delayed surprise, much like a scene from Freud's uncanny returns, which unsettles the ontologies of modernity. Similarly, this theatrical technique alerts us to what passes and what threatens to return under the sign of apartheid. A double-take brings us to the point of seeing apartheid in its iterability.

Under apartheid, the mythic was destined for a theatrical treatment because it substituted the redemptive aspects of tragedy with the dogma of religious justification. Apartheid's returns belonged to a repetition of such mythic performance that found an outlet in violence. Weber provides an explanation for apprehending this form of power when he argues that in Sophocles' Theban plays '"myth" designates a network of reference that has no simple beginning or end, and therefore cannot be taken in at a single view or single sitting'.[26] Even as it replicates myth, theatre grants us access to the elusive elements of mediation in constituting relations between the human and technical props of memory. In keeping with Weber's mediational reading of theatricality, theatre combines with theory to forge an assemblage of images of the repressed aspects of experience. It encourages us to make the most of the shared root of theory and theatre from the Hellenic *theasomai* – to behold – as though asking that the pitfalls of the deceptive plots of sophistry be heeded, and simultaneously exceeded.

Circling back to Weber's earlier definition of theatrocracy and the streets of Rive's text, the contestations over the understandings of apartheid make for very difficult theatrical representation.[27] Between structure and agency, the vocal *demos* became too conveniently available as a basis for merely symbolic or moral alternatives, without consideration for what may have been elided and lost with such necessary acts of solidarity in constituting an image of freedom. Unfortunately, what was missed by this availing of notions of agency and subjectivity to modes of disciplinary reason downplayed the aesthetic functions of theatrocracy in the critique of apartheid. If theatrocracy exposed the limits of disciplinary reason in breaching a limit set by apartheid, there was always a question about how effective theatre might prove to be in exploding myth. After all, this is also the medium of theatricality that best lays bare the mythic underpinnings of apartheid's entrenched authority and

24   Undoing Apartheid

the contestations that surrounded it in the everyday. But which idiom of theatricality best helps us to decipher the rituals of its exercise of power in the form of petty apartheid?

At face value, apartheid invokes a semblance of Walter Benjamin's explorations of the rise of German *Trauerspiel*, where tragedy's redemptive ends are displaced by the most banal and ridiculous expressions of heroism, redeployed in the chaotic onset of an uncertain modernity. To the extent that it described apartheid, Elizabeth Stewart's caricature of the seventeenth-century German form of *Trauerspiel* solicits comparison with apartheid:

> The *Trauerspiel*, naively thinking of itself as restoring tragedy, actually perverts and dislocates it: instead of a trial ending in a decision and sentencing as happens in tragedy, the *Trauerspiel* presents courts where no decision can be made because everyone and everything is equally fallen, equally guilty, equally doomed to a hollow grave. Instead of the decisive oedipal action that charac-terizes tragedy, here we have mainly chaotic schemes, machinations and deals.[28]

Perhaps the baroque qualities of apartheid proved more enduring. It takes hold as a trace of the baroque in the converging themes of myth and nostalgia that shaped sectarian nationalism rapidly transformed into the cultural bedrock on which apartheid rested. Unfortunately, the critique of apartheid is predominantly focused on an architectonics upon which Hendrik Verwoerd, frequently identified as the architect of apartheid, plotted the circumstance of power in keeping with a *Trauerspiel*. In keeping with Deborah Posel's critique that South Africa's Truth and Reconciliation Commission (TRC) 'made for good theatre but bad history', the focus on the grand design of apartheid persists because the theatrical motif of *Trauerspiel* was left intact with apartheid's unbundling.[29]

To counter this tendency, Posel insists that we focus on the realms of complex negotiation (such as those formed around influx control measures) through which apartheid was sustained. The caution about over-emphasizing apartheid's grand design should not be lost to us. Neither should we lose sight of its often forgotten theatricality, through which it codified life. To the extent that we can say apartheid unfolds as a *Trauerspiel*, its master plan was supplemented by a street plan for infiltrating the

Introduction 25

fluctuations of sense-perception. The theatre of the everyday called Verwoerd into a different role: that of a laboratory technician, as opposed to architect, administering stimuli measured through frequencies of surprise, shock or empathy to determine psychological vulnerabilities in individuals and collectives. This was a version of Verwoerd who applied well-honed skills in psychological experiments of numbing, exciting and determining the psychic responses of the human sensorium. Executed as petty apartheid, a disciplinary schooling resulted in dispensing with the soul – central to Greek tragedy – on empirical grounds to lay claim to a brand of psychology that emphasized the investigation of physiological makeup of conscious events. In the inaugural schema of *Völkerpsychologie* (loosely, ethnographic psychology), which Verwoerd seems to have encountered as a doctoral student at Stellenbosch University in 1917 and, later, as a researcher in Leipzig in 1927,[30] the myths of ancient Greece may have superseded so-called primitive perception, but proved less advanced than a scientifically measured consciousness. The emergent disciplines of the mind could claim a unique understanding of everyday life by proving that science had the capacity to measure behaviour and determine sensory responses by technical means. To mark apartheid's performativity as a variation of *Trauerspiel* is to encounter a stalled dialectic of a master plan and a street plan.

Bookended by the end of slavery in 1834 and the end of apartheid in 1994, Faustus, Woyzeck and Ubu give answers to the sense of entrapment in a stalled dialectic towards which apartheid's *Trauerspiel* leads. *Faustus in Africa* tells a story about the search for escape from colonial entrapment in which the shift from the life of the mind to the life of the senses, or from cold reason to the emotions, is interrupted by the way technology sways myth to the ends of nihilism. *Woyzeck on the Highveld* tells of how an embattled sense of suffering driving the European imagination of the nineteenth century resulted in short-circuiting the distinction between sense and perception, opening room for mythic configurations of technology in the making of the modern subject. And *Ubu and the Truth Commission* explores how weak forms of love induce collisions between the human and machine orchestrated by apartheid. What beckons us in each is the mnemotechnic prosthesis of the puppet as an object caught between materiality and immateriality that mediates our

26 Undoing Apartheid

encounter with object life, or life lived as an object. The puppet keeps watch over the becoming technical of the human, resisting the slide into mechanized life that took shape as the racial logic of petty apartheid.

Unlike the racial configuration of fascism, petty apartheid bound the individual's struggle over fate and destiny to extended metaphors of multi-racialism and bureaucratic processes articulated in taunting formulations of 'good neighbourliness'.[31] The deployment of metaphor created the impression of order notwithstanding the morass of administrative chaos and bureaucratic bungling that often left the subject with little choice but to surrender to a prescribed fate. There was little room to breathe in the suffocating enclosures of a tragi-comic display of endless state planning and control over everyday life; but this level of intervention also shifted the horizon of hope, considering the psychic vulnerability that petty apartheid projected on the scene of the everyday.[32]

This is where the evocative appeal to reckon with a wound might take on an altered meaning. Historically, the response pointed to the expedient use of race to enfold an often unwitting subject into processes of capitalist extraction. In South Africa, this would come to mean sustaining a critique that viewed grand apartheid as a politically effective strategy for ensuring structures of accumulation and state power. The neglect of petty apartheid in this prioritization has largely diminished the need to address the question of freedom, other than as a means to a political end or as an end in itself. Yet, by failing to follow through on a reckoning with petty apartheid, the grounds of freedom are too easily conceded to an entrepreneurial spirit where human faltering is completely privatized and accordingly judged.

At its most basic, petty apartheid was distinguished from grand apartheid's social engineering by the way it set to work on affecting relations of sense and perception in everyday life. Often mistaken for inconvenience or humiliation, this minor discourse of race parodied studies on sensory responses triggered by instrumentalities of communication and control. These studies established patterns of images formed in the spaces of free time, cultural institutions and leisure, which were mobilized towards the prescriptions of a society of control. An infinite repertoire of experiments on *mentalités*, of approximations to determine shared community outlooks, robbed the vocabulary of freedom

Introduction 27

of its potency by ultimately restricting it to a measure of the capacity to work and consume. Dispersed across individuated and collective parts, petty apartheid was a wound inflicted on the life-affirming aspects of sense-perception in the guise of a narrative aimed at obscuring the contradictions and instabilities of the lived experience of race. Its ruse could thus not be transcended, only challenged through equally petty acts of transgression that invariably invoked the ire of the law. This aspect of apartheid that has largely passed unnoticed, presumably because it is viewed as mere trickery and therefore unworthy of sustained critique, is precisely where the passage to the post-apartheid was blocked. Petty apartheid is that which repeats insistently, during and after the struggle against apartheid, threatening to erupt in ever-more virulent forms of mythic violence and war.

Critiques of apartheid too glibly dismiss petty apartheid for its presumably minor role in entrenching racial subjection. The archive of apartheid would have us believe that petty apartheid – controlling populations through the selective and uneven modernization of everydayness, and influencing interpersonal relations – was a failed dimension of state power, eventually jettisoned to augment cosmetic changes during the period of reform in the 1980s. By contrast, grand apartheid – associated with a partitioning of populations into ethnically defined homelands and racially designated Group Areas – is often seen as the apartheid of consequence, upheld by means of defined politico-juridical structures in the service of ideological claims. Highlighting the difference between these divergent intensities of power, Aletta Norval and Jamie Miller, two prominent scholars of apartheid's discourse, identify the gradual loosening of the grip of petty apartheid in the 1970s and 1980s.[33] But the withdrawal from this supposedly minor manifestation of apartheid's discourse masked a protracted working out of a modern concept of race that now haunts a nascent public sphere.

The archive of apartheid rule obscures more than it tends to reveal about the intricate workings of state ideology, disciplinary reason and discourse. This is because the archive, by virtue of its constitution, understates the orchestration of an exercise of power that permeated everyday life. Petty apartheid, as an example of this obscured domain of population control, proved more consequential than has initially been assumed. It targeted the links between sense and perception, or individual and group psychologies, in an overall effort to corral the psychopathologies of the everyday to ends that would continue to burden the afterlives of apartheid. The problem relates to the quotient of race borne by the exercise of a lesser script when measured against its grander proclamations. This was not an arbitrary equation, as is often assumed. Rather, petty apartheid was the product of a disciplinary project that sought to measure psychic responses to stimuli brought about by technologies of communication and control. It was a technique born out of a scientific enquiry called experimental psychology, or, as it was more aptly named, psychotechnics, that emerged in Europe in tandem with life philosophy in the early twentieth century. A failure to account for petty apartheid now imperils the sense of freedom that was called into being in 1994, and for which the abolition of slavery in 1834 provided an iterative warning.

The inability to find a rhyme between hope and history in this deceptive political narrative leads to an all-too-easy dismissal of an intractable problem of the disciplinary and psychic dimensions of apartheid. The establishment of a truth commission to deal with the human rights violations of apartheid proved no match for uncovering the meaning of this infinitely more surreptitious and intricate form of power. While the commission prioritized the legal foundations that upheld apartheid's rationalization, it appeared somewhat tentative in tackling the affective dynamics of apartheid's banality.[34] As a consequence, the TRC is frequently suspected of insufficiently reckoning with apartheid's past, especially when the latter is placed alongside the festering wound of partition in twentieth-century postcolonial formations across the world.

The time to reconsider the presumably banal and lesser-known dynamic of petty apartheid, often scorned and ridiculed as an ineffective and absurd form of power, may be upon us, especially as the sun sets on the promises of the TRC's model of transitional justice. As its ambitions are tempered by global shifts that bring newer forms of mythic violence into view, the fate and destiny prescribed by petty apartheid survives as a lesson, offering us a different and wholly unexpected view of the workings of race that apartheid bequeaths to the world as a biopolitics of the future. We have few options but to gather together the remains of tragedy to revisit the myths of partition that came to be recalibrated under this minor sign of apartheid.

Introduction 29

That much we learn from Heaney, who knew all too well that while tragedy momentarily rekindles a yearning for freedom, it is soon burdened by the weight of history. Likewise, the medium of theatricality may keep alive a sense of freedom implicit in the genre of tragedy, if only to entice us to find ways to escape the ever-present pull of the mythic undercurrents of the past.

Setting to Work

Restating the problem of race that passes under the sign of petty apartheid demands that we revisit Rive and Heaney's rejoinders to the debate on education and liberation, if only that we might behold forms of life that potentially undo the strictures of race. Both strain to hear the chime of freedom beneath the din of the becoming technical of the human, much like the colligations of human and technology explored in the theatrical works by Kentridge, Taylor and the Handspring Puppet Company that bridge the divide between the end of slavery and the end of apartheid. Beyond thematizing the mythic precursors that shaped petty apartheid in theatrical iterations originally conceived at the end of slavery, Faustus, Woyzeck and Ubu were reincarnated to answer to a desire specific to the arrival of a post-apartheid future. Collectively, they provide a glimpse into the making of a modern concept of race that accompanied shifting relations between human and machine in the wake of slavery's abolition, colonialism and apartheid, leaving little room for plotting an escape. It is this very mechanistic figuration of the ontology of the slave extending into modern forms of subjectivity in the European imagination that effortlessly settled in a singular name: apartheid.

To this end, Kentridge assembles the sensory field and a perceptual apparatus wrenched apart in everyday life under apartheid, making available a specific aesthetic modality for relating subjects to objects. In this way, he helps us to discern the strands of modernity from which apartheid was cobbled. Overcoming apartheid is thereby shown to be infinitely more complex if race is located in a longer genealogy of modernity. To give effect to this task, kinetic prostheses designed and performed by the Handspring Puppet Company, in styles akin to the Bunraku and Bambara puppetry traditions from Japan

30 Undoing Apartheid

and Mali respectively, are set against moving images, sound designs and projected charcoal drawings that reveal their erasures in the process of composition. The deployment of the puppet mediates the relationship between materiality and immateriality, remediates the intricate ways in which the senses are mobilized, and at times demobilized, in the interplay of myth and reason, and is an intermediate mnemotechnic means for the exchange of messages and information between the human and the machine.

Among these, the most crucial for the purposes of my argument relates to how the puppet is deployed as a kinetic object to animate life actualized by machines in narratives of the co-evolution of human and technology, thereby revealing the traces of modernity that apartheid later gathered under the doubling of the sign of race. The puppet therefore does not merely represent, but educates about how we are to read the emergence of a modern concept of race accreted in petty apartheid. Thus conceived, exiting apartheid will depend not only on education modelled on ruptures and breaks. Rather, it will require an openness to stumbling on the co-extensive assemblages of the human and technology, where the manipulation of an invisible hand can be seized and directed away from the inevitable endpoints of collision.

Messenger puppets of ill-repute – the grimacing hyena in *Faustus in Africa*, the cocky rhino in *Woyzeck on the Highveld*, and conniving Niles the Crocodile, along with the scheming three-headed dogs-of-war puppets from *Ubu and the Truth Commission* – compel the viewer into the role of an accomplice in the trappings of a political impasse. A careful re-enactment of the drama of fate and destiny invites us to engage in a reassemblage of the parts that apartheid took apart through its archetypal gift of perpetual war. In the end, the three theatrical works compose an image of the predicament of race while directing our attention to the resource of an aesthetic education necessary for undoing apartheid.

Thus implicated, the gift of theatre is an invitation to overturn the meaning conveyed in the ultimate of message-bearing gifts: the Trojan Horse, which has, albeit unequally, served modernity in its colonial and postcolonial guises. Kentridge and the Handspring Puppet Company return us to the prosthetic prior to its appearance as a deceptive war machine. In the constellation

Introduction 31

of puppet and performer, theirs is an invitation to see if it is at all possible to reshape the human condition if, or when, sense and perception are connected through the movement of objects and images of human and animal forms. The three productions linking the story of the elusive parts of apartheid in the pages that follow reveal the dangers, pitfalls and possibilities that Heaney discloses to Mandela on the long walk to freedom – encountered on either side of the devastating nineteenth- and twentieth-century experiences and constructions of race – as each looks towards a further shore that is yet to be reached.

Thinking Ahead

Rive's beleaguered lecturer, Andrew Dreyer, would have surmised that a political education focused on the history or anthropology of apartheid would prove inadequate to draw his students from the temptation to monumentalize the Trojan Horse. He knows full well that it would return them to the very form of *stasis* to which they were destined by apartheid, and from which they sought release when first they confronted its deceptive plot. As Dreyer sets out to affirm their discovery of a discrete form of race that folded its mythic precursors into a war machine and entered the city in 1985, bringing death and mayhem to the streets of Athlone, he himself is drawn into the space of theatrocracy bearing a message of hope in education. But he understands that this is a form of education which must turn its back on sophistry in the interests of attending to the instruction of the wounded, even when the odds are that the latter will be no match for a deceptive plot. Urging his charges not to squander their discovery of how race has been oriented towards the machinic, they too, following Wittig, must find a detour around the shock of words and images produced by their association, disposition and arrangement, to turn raw material into something else, something new. As they confront the aftermaths of the Trojan Horse massacre, the students will have to find a pathway to study what lies behind their suspicion about the shock and horror internal to the ordinary mundanity of a version of race in everyday life. They will have to study how their fate and destiny are bound up with that of Faustus, as an incarnation of immaterial labour; Woyzeck, a subject who is sensed before being capable of sensing; and Ubu, who cautions them about collisions with machines if the relationship to technology is not rethought and the idea of freedom is not re-enchanted. In short, they will need to learn to sense post-apartheid freedom from within the belly of the beast.

Exit Heaney.

2
Apartheid's Mythic Precursors

If there's fire on the mountain
Or lightning and storm
And a god speaks from the sky

That means someone is hearing
The outcry and the birth-cry
Of new life at its term.

Seamus Heaney, The Cure at Troy

Leonard Thompson's *Political Mythology of Apartheid* recapitulates a longstanding historiographical preoccupation with the mythic sources of a racial order charted against an antithetical course of scientific and liberal reason in studies of the South African past.[1] Harking back to a time after World War II when it was not uncommon to proclaim causal links between religious precedent and racial ideology, scholarly interest often presupposed that the rise of the idea of race in South African politics was sustained by far-fetched mythic claims rooted in Calvinist doctrine. The controversy surrounding how best to explain the origins of a racial order is often also an attempt to overturn what is seen to be the religious odyssey of an Afrikaner nationalism that later cohered in the system of apartheid. In this repertoire of critique, the myth underpinning apartheid has generally been pitted against the truth of history

34   Undoing Apartheid

and anthropology, thereby reducing apartheid to an aberration of reason.

Questions of how Afrikaner nationalism is related to apartheid as a technology of power often neglect to ask whether myth had anything to do with sustaining apartheid's most intensely rationalized power. Like the fate that awaited reason, apartheid too reveals that myth had a devastating and far-reaching claim on the future. This claim to futurity was exacerbated by a tendency in myth to draw sustenance from the very science of the limits of reason, or what we might call the substrate of metaphysics.

If the mythic holds sway in the story of apartheid, it is not simply because Afrikaner nationalism elects to narrate its own emergence by repeatedly deploying familiar tropes of the 'fall of Man' and God's partisan attitude towards a chosen people.[2] Rather, myth was also a site for reworking historical precedents in the story of progress to provide justification for a nationalist historiography: the British abolition of slavery in the Cape Colony in 1834, which coincided with claims of losses suffered during the Sixth War of Dispossession and the alleged beheading of the Xhosa king Hintsa by the British (who conveniently accused the king of practising slavery), that compelled an arduous mass exodus of Afrikaner frontiersmen into the interior by the will of God.[3] Ironically, the critique of the political mythology of apartheid ends by reasserting many of the premises of Afrikaner nationalist historiography as it seeks to reaffirm liberalism's morality in the story of the abolition of slavery. A religious iconography specific to Afrikaner nationalism is thus viewed as regressive when compared to the political morality associated with the abolition of slavery, leaving little room to consider whether abolition discreetly propelled a nationalist mythology into an unforeseeable future of race.

Eluding the charge of apostasy, Afrikaner nationalism was very much a product of the accommodations established between a nascent scientific discourse and a fledgling public sphere in the wake of the abolition of slavery in the nineteenth century. A foray into the mythic precursors of apartheid's political rationality therefore inevitably finds its way back to 1834, on the cusp of the abolition of slavery, where the uncertain dance of myth and reason resulted in a series of missteps into the future. By this account, the exodus from the Cape that ensued, with the British abolition of slavery, generated an origin story of Afrikaner nationalism endowing myth with a futural character that rivalled the claims made for reason.

While the political mythology of apartheid has occupied historians and anthropologists in separate quests to pinpoint its origins, the uncertainty about whether race belongs to myth or to reason nevertheless confounds the critique of apartheid. The resultant indecision leads to a profoundly schizophrenic critical attitude aimed at an equally schizophrenic object. To caricature the debate, race is often assigned an origin that is irrational and mythic, while class is seen as a consequence of a more affirmative technoscientific discourse located in a belated peripheral development of capitalism. With a few exceptions, revisionist historiographies, predicated on what in South African criticism is referred to as the race/class debate, mostly reworked this script for much of the latter half of the twentieth century. In so doing, they indirectly reinforced a foundational fiction of Boer and Briton, or more precisely, a regressive, autochthonous Afrikaner nationalism and a progressive, worldly (albeit complicit) liberalism, that, in a Marxist synthesis, pitted the rise of a *volkskapitalisme* against prevailing imperial interests.

The urgency to elaborate what precisely is implied by the term 'post-apartheid' now compels us to rethink earlier critical attitudes and their premises by admitting to the shortcomings of an abiding historicism in the race/class debate, where reason is viewed as the ultimate arbiter of the provocations engendered by mythic appeals to race. The work of undoing apartheid can no longer entirely depend on a critical apparatus that presupposes the distinction between myth and reason. Rather, an elaboration of the meaning assigned to the 'post-apartheid' obliges a return to the intellectual ferment generated by the abolition of slavery, which resulted in a struggle between myth and reason out of which a renewed idea of race was formed. The messy confluence found expression in an aesthetic practice that linked one technical system (slavery) to another (industrialization). It is here that we first glimpse how myth and reason collude to create what later came to be known as petty apartheid, and which ultimately conferred on apartheid the qualities of a modern political technique of governmentality.

To make sense of petty apartheid, I propose a genealogy of race which directs us to the mythic charge running through the abolition of slavery that spurred and surpassed a nineteenth-century scientific revolution. Enabled by the abolition of slavery, this scientific revolution, buoyed by political realignments in the 1830s, assumed an authority to adjudicate reason's relationship to myth. Unfortunately, electing to narrate the career of reason at the expense of the figure of the slave, the professionalization of science faltered in its efforts to rein in the mythic. Over time, science seemed unable to contain myth, leaving the latter to gather the excess of race and redirect the temporal flows of modernity in the aftermath of Atlantic slavery. Petty apartheid, I suggest, must be understood against the backdrop of a scientific faltering in this quest that allowed myth to appropriate reason to its course.

The Limits of Reason

In the story that science tells about its emergence as a distinguishable field of disciplinary enquiry, John Herschel, Charles Babbage and William Whewell, three pre-eminent Cambridge scientists at the heart of the revolution in physics, mathematics and calculating machines, are hailed as luminaries in the professionalization of science. They are credited with instituting an agonistic method drawn from analytical mathematics, which paved the way for the hegemony of the physical sciences amidst the apparent incoherence that afflicted natural philosophy in the early 1800s. The shift in method that they collectively and independently championed revolutionized science. Less known is that they also inadvertently activated a latent mythos of race festering in the lacunae formed by the end of slavery and the unprecedented expansion of industrial technologies.

Scientific biographies seldom explicitly acknowledge the political forces that shaped research agendas and intellectual attitudes. As one of the Cambridge three who settled briefly in a slaveholding society at the Cape between 1834 and 1838, the biography of Herschel highlights his supportive private attitude towards a liberal humanitarian course, but claims that it did not translate into an advocacy of science, which, as far as possible, sought to steer clear of explicit political standpoints against the backdrop of empire through which scientific exploration was authorized. He is said, according to Steven Ruskin, to have loathed colonial officialdom, and to have held strong pro-abolitionist

Apartheid's Mythic Precursors 37

and humanitarian sentiments allied to Thomas Pringle, a poet and pressman who advocated against colonial plunder of the Xhosa in the southeast of the Cape Colony.[4] Similarly, William Ashworth notes that Herschel's project doubled as 'a mission to enculturate and map the southern skies'.[5]

The need for public credibility of science that Herschel professed along with his Cambridge interlocutors was undoubtedly on the side of liberal and progressive courses of abolition and humanitarianism (the latter associated with the 1835 Aborigines Commission in Britain). Ironically, these attitudes placed science in a favourable relation to the prospecting impulse of empire. Herschellian science, governed by the expanded possibilities of collecting empirical evidence by aligning scientific and public interests, deferred an added responsibility to an emerging profession of filtering the excesses derived from a public sphere. A generalized scientific sensibility provided for expansion capable of apprehending the world through attention towards component parts overseen by disciplinary specialization in an overall model of theory construction. Science was in step with the time, and its confidence enabled it to negotiate a complex array of tensions involving state, capital and a nascent public sphere.

Notwithstanding these fleeting references to political choices made in the name of science, in accounts of the lineages of scientific communities and the refinement and professionalization of methods to which such communities dedicated themselves, the cultural and political milieux for scientific exploration are seldom disclosed. We have yet to ask whether the movement towards the abolition of slavery and the accompanying expansion of the European colonial project had any bearing on the nature of the scientific revolution attributed to Herschel, Babbage and Whewell in the 1830s. This is not inconsequential given that their interest in the philosophy and history of science coincided with the great push for the abolition of slavery. The failure to be scrupulous about political and cultural interests also rendered science available for appropriation by such interests. Ruskin tells us that in the case of Herschel, despite efforts to shield his scientific endeavour from being overtly associated with imperial interests, he was nonetheless claimed as a scientist of empire. Regardless of such appropriation, Herschel's mockery of scholasticism should perhaps be viewed as an attempt to orient science towards the general public interest while guarding against drawing too much attention to scientific abstraction. This is borne out by Herschel's leadership of the South African Literary and Scientific Institute (LSI) upon his arrival at the Cape in January 1834.[6] Beyond making science public, the society, we learn, avoided any talk of slavery for fear of antagonizing local Afrikaner sensibilities, even though the abolition of slavery was the very source for pursuing research interests supported by a nascent public sphere. By circumventing contests between state and the public sphere, science established the parameters of reason as the domain proper to its competencies. Ultimately, balancing the demands of professionalization and orienting enquiry towards public interests divulges the extent to which the tensions of empire were nevertheless refracted through the theoretical and methodological emphases of scientific enquiry.

Beyond scientific biography with its overly celebratory tone of individual discovery and invention, the political stakes of science were more systematically, albeit less explicitly, set forth in several methodological treatises on the foundations of reason consolidated through the physical sciences. These treatises included Babbage's *Reflections on the Decline in Science* (1830), Herschel's *A Preliminary Discourse on the Study of Natural Philosophy* (1830), Mary Somerville's *The Connexion of the Physical Sciences* (1834) and Whewell's *History of the Inductive Sciences* (1837). Along with specifying the principles and processes of the inductive sciences, a newly conceived scientific method established the ground rules for adjudicating what qualifies as the exercise of reason.

Herschel, in particular, set his sights on managing error as constitutive of the field of scientific discovery. He pursued a scientific method that affirmed truth and reason, while leaving error to autocorrection, and professed confidence in opening science to public interests beyond the guild of professional scientists and institutional sanction. Scientific success did not need to disqualify speculation. Herschel reckoned that the invention and operation of the calculating machine that had been advanced by his colleague Babbage, together with the proper communication of method, would in future be sufficient to curtail wild speculation. The telescope, similarly, functioned as that instrument which retained access to Newton's mechanics while evading the error that seeped in with his optics. The assurance that a carefully plotted method would result in autocorrection contributed to

Apartheid's Mythic Precursors

expanding the horizon of scientific research while simultaneously affirming its jurisdiction over the exercise of reason.

Rather than validation of theory in which the *particular* was used to justify an *a priori* universal, Herschel unmoored a level of the empirical from disciplinary insecurities with the assurances of a requirement of *vera causa*, or first truths. This was a means of bringing experience into relation with the search for true causes by making the former integral to hypothesis formation. The truth of a hypothesis resided in the quality of the experience at its inception. Theory, by extension, existed principally to curtail wild speculation and to create altered conceptions from existing facts.

A few years later, Whewell extended the work of hypothesis through a process he called 'colligation'. It entailed bringing together a number of facts – connected phenomena presented to the senses – by 'superinducing' upon them a fundamental conception that unites the facts and renders them capable of being expressed as a general law. The result was a description of a phenomenon that was more than the sum of the facts according to Whewell, that allowed for an interpretation of the facts in a different light.

Conscious of the fact that natural philosophy had become fragmented, Whewell was driven by a determination to inaugurate the study of science as a theory-driven discourse, calling science the 'idealization of facts'. This was not just an idealization given over to a 'divine mind', but one that depended on the mediation of, and adjudication at the institutional site of, the university, where a paradigm backed by a definitive scientific method could be established through a revised consensus. Steven Fuller notes that Whewell held that the natural sciences reverse-engineered the design of God's clockwork universe.[7] Whewell's *History of the Inductive Sciences* (1837) was inspired by a search for a shared method of enquiry premised on establishing an academic authority that could validate alleged discoveries within a unified natural order. The text advocated a level of institutionalization and professionalization to address the fragmentation of a science hitherto conducted as an amateur pursuit.

If there is a coincidence of this vocabulary in Charles Darwin's *On the Origins of Species*, it is because of a reliance on Whewell and his contemporaries, Herschel in particular, on a scientific method that could be communicated to the state

40   Undoing Apartheid

and public sphere. Darwin, we learn, also carefully studied texts such as Babbage's *Reflections on the Decline in Science* (1830), and, as noted above, Herschel's *Preliminary Discourse* (1830), both of which record an expansive history of scientific discovery and invention that led to a unified methodological field.

Ultimately, Herschel and Whewell's setting forth of the rules of verifiable method in scientific explanation converged in the idea of consilience, directing science to explain the unexpected and surprising outcomes of hypothesis formation as it shifted across distinct spheres of scientific enquiry. Both emphasized the importance of an element of surprise as central to their inductive method, a serendipitous discovery of interconnections which Whewell named 'consilience of inductions' – literally a jumping together of distinct branches of knowledge to produce an unexpected unifying result. Beyond its purely scientific ambition, consilience speaks of a shared endeavour in which the convergence of evidence from differing fields of study produced an unprecedented discovery through another. While Whewell and Herschel turned to the skies to find an example of consilience across the physical sciences, another fate of the human – race – emerged as an unacknowledged feature of a consilience across the physical and human sciences. And while science accrued reason by virtue of consilience, the end of slavery seemingly paved the way for a consilience of inductions from which a modern concept of race was born through surreptitiously linking one technical system, slavery, with another, industrialization. It would be through the link between slavery and industrialization that myth would reappear to challenge the securities that a unified science formed around reason.

The methodological blindspot in the inductive sciences of the Cambridge scientists was telling. The alignment with abolitionist and humanitarian sentiment fell short of holding onto the image of the slave as the grounds from which to renegotiate a contract with metropole and colony, instead allowing science to fall prey to a deeply racialized public sphere. It was this lapse in reason that exposed science to the mere expedience of popular sentiment. Overly confident about the discovery of a comprehensive scientific method, the advocates of the scientific revolution were perhaps too youthful to fully grasp the political implications of their revolution. The identification of science with method that distinguishes between theory and hypothesis, where theory is verifiable, and hypothesis, a refutable instrument of first causes, not only dispensed with the figure of the slave, but also created an environment, in both Europe and the colonial world, in which science proved susceptible to a mythic content. Late in Herschel's text, the distinction between theory and hypothesis is brought into sharp relief, with difficulty: 'the liberty of speculation which we possess in the domain of theory is not like the wild licence of the slave broke loose from his fetters, but rather like that of a freeman who has learned the lesson of self-restraint in the school of just subordination'.[8] Note the displacement of the slave in this formulation. By making common cause with a fledgling bourgeois and contested settler public sphere, the reconstituted scientific method thoroughly miscalculated the extent to which the end of slavery had become the grounds for mythic constructions of a futurity of race.

With, or perhaps because of, the end of slavery, a pursuit of a unified study of science inspired Whewell and Herschel to seek refuge in a metaphoric *deus ex machina* – a theatrical mechanism that brought God to the stage of the drama between 'human' and 'nature' to deal with the unanswerable questions of causality. Their many disagreements notwithstanding, Whewell and Herschel concurred on a few fundamental principles of scientific investigation indispensable for its enhancement. Both agreed that astronomy, given its universality, was the queen of the sciences, with mechanics being the god that allowed astronomy to rule by divine right.[9] Neither had sympathy for Hegel or Schelling's speculative metaphysics, which established *a priori* the totality of all knowledge discovered or discoverable in 'the Absolute'. In both Whewell and Herschel, there is a thread of theological thinking in which God is the ultimate arbiter in the intertwining of 'human' and 'nature', responsible for ensuring that they are perfectly designed for each other, so that God's universal agency is the only origin of any efficient force.[10] Ironically, the overarching theological thinking among British scientists instituted some distance from the secularizing authority of the state. Instead, science connected to popular sentiment, from which a fledgling nationalist sentiment in turn drew inspiration.

As scientists debated the relative importance of deductive and inductive methods, Herschel and Whewell seemed conscious of the competing appeals that the state, capital and the public sphere made on science. Their specific methodological interventions set in place the institutionalization of science as the model of consilience for unifying knowledge by elevating reason as the ultimate arbiter of deliberation. Yet, the inductive sciences also shaped a discourse that was forward-looking rather than simply a record of past errors, making room for both novice and expert. Its most lasting consequence related to the confidence it developed in attending to disaggregated parts, allowing for a unity of knowledge to emerge through a process of validation of collected data that helped to establish patterns and images. We would be correct to see a shape of the racial foundations of a modern university and state as also a deliberative public sphere on the horizon of this search for a newfound unity of knowledge.

Whewell and Herschel consolidated a revolution in science that had begun with Francis Bacon, the originator of a distinct scientific method of induction in eighteenth-century natural philosophy, while simultaneously consolidating the requirements of professionalization. The working out of an identifiable method for launching a disciplinary specialization in science was strongly aligned to popular precedent, when the young Herschel located his endeavours in direct relation to the rise of bourgeois Victorian culture in nineteenth-century Britain. Thus, a development from within an emerging field of astronomy related scientific enquiry to the altered circumstances of an industrial revolution, which it indirectly helped to foster. Science and empire were not merely derivative of each other but were constitutive of a world picture in the wake of the abolition of slavery and in the rise of industrial capitalism. Scientific curiosity gained traction alongside the novelty of discovery in the age of empire. It is in Herschel's method that we gain access to the complete miscalculation of scientists in their confidence that reason could ward off irrational sentiment. A method attuned to the shifting political dynamics that had come into existence with the rise of the factory system in Europe would invariably be tested against the elements that had reshaped sentient life in the accelerations of industrial expansion. These elements were sense, sensation and perception. This is the point at which the reason of the inductive sciences would prove to be no match for the myths that had formed around the abolition of slavery.

Apartheid's Mythic Precursors   *43*

Science Meets its Match

In a rare contemporary critique of Herschel, Joseph Agassi reflects on the fault line in the former's philosophy of success with a direct bearing upon the attachments of myth to scientific progress. This barely noticeable aspect of scientific method, I suggest, facilitated an assemblage of race and enabled it to thrive beyond the specialization of disciplinary enquiry.[11] According to Agassi, Herschel desired non-dogmatism on the part of students of science, at least so that reason might be afforded an opportunity to contest the mythic, magical and irrational tendencies of *a priori* beliefs formed through habit and association. These irrational tendencies were attributed almost entirely to the intrusion of sense and sensation in the making of scientific hypotheses. Agassi notes that an emergent scientific method of the 1830s distinguished between eliminating prejudices of the senses and the complete mistrust of the senses in the naïve sensationalism of *apriorism*. In essence, the scientific method set out to destroy unconscious judgements by appealing to the strict use of the senses themselves.[12] A scientific attitude to sensation, both in the form of a naïve sensationalism, in which experience misleads, and a sophisticated sensationalism, which gives scope to the idea that mathematics and theoretical science are admirable structures produced by the imagination, was necessary if science was to live up to the expectation of altering the prevailing picture of the world.[13] The task of science was to remain both wary of and open to the information relayed through the senses.

Herschel argued that 'the sensible impressions made by external objects upon us depend on circumstances and therefore we must be careful; we must lay confidence in our observations only to a limited degree at first, correcting them appropriately before being certain of them'.[14] In other words, the senses needed to be subjected to scientific interpretation before their experiential worth could be evaluated and admitted into scientific theory. Herschel understood induction by enumerating a simple principle: 'we can only regard sensible impressions as signals conveyed ... to our minds ... which receives and reviews them, and by habit and association, connects them with corresponding qualities ... of objects; just as a person writing down and comparing signals of a telegraph might interpret

44 Undoing Apartheid

meaning'.[15] The only way to preserve an element of sensationalism, then, was to bring it under the sway of objects that could be controlled. This is how Agassi puts it once he has cleared the space to tell us that science is not naïve realism, and that while it might explain the world picture to us, its aim is to ultimately change the picture:

> But why do people observe? Why do they not simply imagine facts? My first answer is that they do, in all earnestness, try to imagine facts, but that their imagination is ludicrously less informative than the imagination of experimental investigators. Not only is the imagination of the author of *Arabian Nights* infinitely inferior to that of Jules Verne; when a cinematic version of a science-fiction novel of Verne is done nowadays, its script-writers have to improve upon his imagination – by using what men of science present, rightly or wrongly, as observed facts! Facts are stranger than fiction. Fiction is a very poor substitute for observation![16]

Verne's *From the Earth to the Moon* (1865) provides an example of how science had extended the realms of the imagination, beyond the fictional qualities of the *Arabian Nights*, in which a naïve sensationalism was thought to operate as an *apriorism*. Stated differently, in the *Arabian Nights*, the world picture is considered plausible because it is conceived as fictional. In Verne's novel, the world picture, although fictional, is plausible because it is backed up by observation and scientific calculation. The point that Agassi makes, however tainted with Orientalism, is a finer one about how the science of success ceded the ground of metaphysics, only to emerge as a more pronounced imaginary structure.

The provisional surrender of scientific authority to popular belief sets a dangerous precedent for the future of reason. Verne spells out the implications when he places the practical and honed science of astronomy against the imaginary and fantastical in his novel. The president of the Baltimore Gun Club, Barbicane, prefaces his bold plan to launch a projectile to the moon by recalling, among other similar fictional accounts, the 1835 rumour that John Herschel, while at the Cape, had discovered life on the moon (to which I shall return), and concluding, 'I have now enumerated ... the experiments which I call purely paper ones, and wholly insufficient to establish serious relations with the Queen of the Night.' Such 'paper'

Apartheid's Mythic Precursors

endeavours of the imagination, while intriguing, fell short of establishing actual communication with the 'Queen of the Night'.[17] For Verne's gun club, the prospects for the discovery of hitherto undiscovered frontiers of science in reaching the moon are instead formed around advances in ballistics and communication, honed during the American Civil War (1861–5). With exultant expectations about this great experiment, Verne creates a vivid image of members of the club fervently applauding their president's assertion that they should strive to be the Columbuses of this new world.

Crucial for our purposes is that a paradigmatic shift in science in the 1830s, which sought to guard the autonomy of scientific reason while holding onto strands of theological thinking, inadvertently opened the door to mythic precursors in processes of 'hypothesis formation' and inductive method. The discourse of science seemed secure in its knowledge of its independence, assured that science would be unaffected by the tensions of empire. A revised method allowed for greater emphasis to be placed on the professional adjudication of the processes and results of inductive reasoning that transformed the nature of scientific enquiry. In other words, science proceeded both from facts and idealism, and it was the question of which sources of idealism were permitted that decided the debate between Whewell and Herschel. Compared to Whewell's insistence on theory extracted from concrete contexts as the foundation for science as systematic knowledge, Herschel believed in a science that was founded on a balance between inductive and deductive methods, but with a gradual affirmation of the former.[18] What was repressed in the version of the scientific revolution thus inaugurated relates to its indebtedness to the concept of freedom – a concept that had been brewing in the philosophical forays into an aesthetics of myth, where the figure of the slave functioned as a source of speculation and anxiety about the fate that awaited the proletarian classes of Europe.

If modern conceptions of race emerged from the afterlife of slavery, we might trace the transfer at the crossroads of circa 1834, in the ascendancy of astronomy and the rise of an apocalyptic sublime that entertained eccentricities of catastrophic futures and flaming skies. In the cross-hatching, and in the absence of the figure of the slave to watch over the scene, the possibility for myth to eclipse reason presented itself from

46   Undoing Apartheid

the very sources over which science believed it prevailed. Two examples of this process by which myth mapped itself on the career of science delineate the afterlife of slavery around which a modern idea of race was forged. Francis Danby's painting *The Opening of the Sixth Seal* and the story of the Great Moon Hoax respectively offer us a view of how a consilience of inductions was at the heart of forging a modern concept of race, to which scientific reason would be conscripted.

The Eclipse of Reason

Francis Danby's 1828 pro-abolitionist painting bears witness to a modern idea of race that was forged out of the ruins of slavery and oriented towards an expansion of technological drives. In Danby's vast, intricate and ever-darkening canvas, a theme of biblical revelation offsets a representation of the future that awaited the freed slave, depicted through images of a kneeling slave and an unshackled slave with arms outstretched towards the heavens. The painting reaches towards an uncertain future, as if untethered from glib proclamations about the triumph of reason over myth claimed in the liberal discourse about the abolition of slavery. Danby's painting instead rehearses the struggle between myth and reason against the backdrop of a shift from slavery to industrial capitalism, with strokes of anarchical mysticism.

At first glance, the eye is drawn towards two noteworthy elements that combine, soliciting responses to a frightful but equally promising phase in the passage of modernity: the motif celebrating the abolition of slavery standing over a fallen sovereign crouched over moribund symbols of authority, and a bolt of lightning breaching the chasm between heaven and earth, striking a cliff with vengeful force. The more obvious appeal of the work as depicting the wrath of God, to which the Irish writer James Joyce was subjected in his youth, complements troubling futuristic scenes of chaos woven into the texture of the painting. Locked in the evocation of apocalyptic art, Danby aims to provoke a strong sensory response to draw attention to the tension between the rational and religious drives behind slave emancipation and the tumultuous consequences that follow for the pain that was wrought in the process.

Apartheid's Mythic Precursors 47

While feelings of apocalypse dominated the painting's early reception, later commentaries emphasized how the work combined advocacy for the abolition of slavery with concern about the displacements effected by a dramatically altered world picture in the aftermath of slavery. The placement of the emancipated slave slightly ahead of a kneeling slave, facing the opening of heaven, calls for a reading of the painting that is not restricted to the apocalyptic. Similarly, the lightning charge running through *The Opening* takes us from the event of abolition to a crafting of the world picture focused on an earthly reckoning with speculation amidst premonitions of a static future. To this end, the work provokes a jarring sensory disorientation, which accounts for its unprecedented public reception and its entanglement in defining a market in art, effectively signalling the onset of a mythic eclipse of reason.

Given its thematic concerns, the artwork is surprisingly absent from the index of postcolonial art history. Brendan Rooney, curator of the National Gallery of Ireland, weaves an intriguing narrative of the circulation and circumstances pertaining to a work that is spectacular in scale and, when set against its time, unprecedented in political implication. For Rooney, Danby's painting marks a departure from the pictorialization of the Book of Revelation through the inclusion of an emancipated slave at the centre of the composition. The painting makes much of the biblical reference contained in the title, conveying aspects of the painting's apocalyptic sensibilities:

> And the heaven departed as a scroll when it is rolled together, and every mountain and island were moved out of their places. And the kings of the earth, and the great men, and the rich men, and the chief captains, and the mighty men, and every bondman, and every freeman, hid themselves in dens, and in the rocks of the mountains. And said to the mountains and rocks, Fall on us, and hide us from the face of Him that sitteth on the throne, and from the wrath of the Lamb. For the great day of his wrath is come, and who shall be able to stand? (Revelation 6:14–17)

However, as Rooney suggests, the painting departs from conventional claims made in the name of Christianity, but also science, about the motive for abolition. Ultimately, the freed slave is granted primacy in determining the aftermath of the chaos brought about by the struggle between myth and reason. In

48 Undoing Apartheid

Danby's work, it is the freed slave that can stand, that *must* stand, and face the God from the sky. A broadsheet accompanying the exhibition of the painting in Bristol from 1835–6 quotes Danby's reflections on the freed slave as a 'poetical representation of freedom of the oppressed' to emphasize the symbolic references to the abolitionist movement. To convey this ideal of freedom, Danby ventriloquized the poetics of the work as an idiom of 'mankind that descends into disarray, an earth that is rent while a king slumps over worthless symbols of his sovereignty'. By extending the biblical reference from which the painting derives its title, a commonplace punitive religious metaphor is pitted against the bolt of artistic electricity that potentially recharges the most critical aspects of the abolitionist cause. Read in relation to the artist's abolitionist sympathies, *The Opening* yearns for a deeper meaning of freedom following the abolition of slavery.

Danby's dramatic representation portends an unrecognizable world in the wake of the abolition of slavery and the promise of a scientific revolution in communication (the lightning from the sky, to which I shall return). *The Opening* functions as a judgement aimed at instilling fear in the upholders of slavery and anticipates a break in representations of the natural order in which the signification of the slave proved indispensable. This helps to explain its vast viewership in the 1830s as the abolitionist movement gained prominence among a metropolitan intelligentsia and the bourgeois public sphere. Attesting to the painting's provocation as a statement on slavery, Rooney tells how in May 1843, while the work was on display in the industrial town of Rochdale in England, two men entered the exhibition space and mutilated the canvas by excising the unshackled slave at the centre of the piece. In its current display in Dublin, Rooney draws attention to the seam where Danby restored the work, returning the figure of the emancipated slave to the scene from which it had been excised. Extrapolating from Rooney's narration, we might say that the excising and suturing of the slave into the canvas, beyond the intention of either artist or saboteur, serves as an allegory for the transferral of the racial afterlife of the freed slave to a medium of communication.

The mutilation of Danby's painting generated much debate and controversy, with suspicion strongly tending towards political motive. This was to be expected, given the deliberate excising of the figure of the slave. Another theory advanced by Rooney is that the mutilation could have been prompted by an angered investor who felt tricked by the extended entrepreneurial efforts, bordering on racketeering, of the painting's owners. The public was invited to invest in the painting in the hope that they would be selected as its owners through a chance draw. Danby would undoubtedly have been surprised by the irony of the prospecting to which his work gave rise, especially given its uncompromising attitudes towards the mercenary institution of slavery. Among those who exploited the image was John Watkins Brett, art trader and self-styled inventor and speculator, who purchased the work in 1835. Brett fixated on profiteering from a vast art collection on either side of the Atlantic. Besides his efforts to sell works to the American Congress, he partook in altering the market in art by pursuing a pioneering strategy of the touring exhibition – which some referred to as Brett's art circus – and popularizing art through the sale of prints and mezzotint plates. A work of art advocating abolition became a mainstay in the speculative ambitions of profiteers seeking to benefit from the newfound spirit of the age.[19] But more strikingly, Danby's painting serves as a point at which the remainder of slavery is transferred to a new technological resource.

The compositional elements of the painting, including the figure of the emancipated slave, the kneeling slave (emblematic of the abolitionist movement), and the large-scale backdrop of the apocalyptic depiction of the sixth seal, point to the uncertainties of a future defined by the development of techniques of communication. Danby's apocalyptic sublime was a potent reminder of the uncertainties surrounding the meaning of freedom as technology threatened to displace the work of art in shaping a world picture. The restored painting, now with a noticeable stitch running through it, disturbed an episteme founded on the wealth of the slave system by redirecting our attention to a more menacing relation of the slave to the story of modernity. In the comparative history of art that narrates modernity, Danby's painting tests the meaning of freedom by conscripting our view on the end of slavery towards a point at which technological expansion becomes uncontrollable and irreversible. Its significance lay in the sense of futurity that the work entertains, especially when placed alongside similar discursive shifts in age and episteme.

50   Undoing Apartheid

What, for example, are we to make of Danby's painting when placed alongside Diego Velasquez's 1560 *Las Meninas*, which introduces Michel Foucault's genealogy of the epistemic shift from classical to modern orders? What manner of tension is discernible between Foucault's specular reading of the birth of the modern and Danby's apocalyptic sublime? Perhaps Danby predicted the uncanny return of the repressed elements of race in the plot from which modernity momentarily took flight in the nineteenth century. Coincidentally, the exhibition of Danby's *Opening* in New York in 1833 conveyed a waning belief in the spirit of freedom. By the time the exhibition of Danby's work closed in 1835, the narrative of modernity was exposed for its deception by a fanciful satire of the promise of progress and freedom made in the name of science, industrialization and liberalism. The effort to redirect the meaning assigned to freedom in the aesthetics of tragedy to the ends of scientific reason were put to the test in a series of newspaper articles directed at the subaltern classes of New York, who themselves were trapped between the spread of rumours about the end of slavery and a future built on the promise of science. They appeared trapped in a scene between heaven and earth, myth and reason, not unlike that depicted in Danby's *The Opening of the Sixth Seal*.

Communication and Satire

The implications of the entanglements of myth and reason emerging from Danby's apocalyptic sublime resembles a parody about the discovery of life on the moon published in the form of six articles by Richard Locke in *The New York Sun* in 1835. Locke later confessed to an act of deliberate deception, claiming that his was an attempt at exposing the extent to which religious belief had encroached on the spheres of scientific reason. The articles were aimed at depicting debates about plural worlds that had consumed scientific and religious communities of the day.[20] Inadvertently, the hoax catapulted the once paltry circulation of *The Sun* to about 20,000 copies and spread rumours about life on the moon to Britain, France, Germany and Italy. To give the story scientific credence, *The Sun* invoked the authority of John Herschel at the Cape, claiming he had discovered unicorns, bi-ped beavers and furry-winged humanoids resembling bats

Apartheid's Mythic Precursors   *51*

(*Vespertilio homo*) on the moon. The results, as it turned out, differed from what was intended, as the articles fed into a growing panic about the onset of slave emancipation in the USA.

Three global tremors framed the series on the apparent sighting of life on the moon: the abolition of slavery that had previously oriented the Cape towards the Atlantic world; the institution of the Aborigines Commission in Britain, which unsettled the civilizational myth of colonial conquest by transferring the health of the population to the health of the state; and an initial shift towards the standardization of time via a global agreement about the prime meridian that revolutionized navigational and commercial opportunities in the nineteenth century. The hoax parodied the promise of a world returned to nature at its most pristine and a plural society in which species lived in harmony. Reading from within the history of slavery in America, Kevin Young suggests that the Great Moon Hoax functioned as an allegory of race at the end of slavery.[21] The hoax resembled an anti-slavery text, in Young's view, that invoked the flourish of nascent pseudo-sciences in the 1830s. There, at the other end of Herschel's telescope, Young argues, 'wasn't just life but order, not just extinct craters but vibrant temples, not just sustenance but subordination, not just humanoids but hierarchies'. At one level, the articles of *The Sun* created an image of a world of racial hierarchy, but one of peace and harmony. At another, they conveyed the promise of liberalism in overcoming the turbulence wrought by the end of slavery.

When considered as an example of the genre of satire, however, the New York penny press articles suggest a pointed critique of the promise of liberal peace at the end of slavery. They scorn the professed belief in a reconciliation of human and nature, myth and reason. Besides deferring to Herschel's scientific authority, the Moon Hoax had a pie-in-the-sky quality that masked its sharp and pointed political critique. Claiming to have based its report on the *Edinburgh Journal of Science*, the advances in astronomy attributed to Herschel painted a picture diametrically opposed to the image of an anxious world overrun with technological drives and political uncertainty about the consequences of the abolition of slavery. The newspaper was effectively thinking ahead through flights of fancy, or, at the very least, mimicking the onset of a heightened phase in emerging modernity. All the elements of that specific phase of modernity

The Great Moon Hoax, *The New York Sun*, 1835.

are represented in a theatrical setting of the moon in which freedom, nature and interspecies existence co-convene in perfect harmony.

The Great Moon Hoax lampoons the political and intellectual promise of liberalism as the latter sought to wish

Apartheid's Mythic Precursors

away its complicity in the institution of slavery. Locke was a known proponent of strong abolitionist views, who held a class perspective that favoured the proletarian interests of his day. His musings about the discovery of life on the moon went to the heart of the mythological truce established between religion and science, but with one caveat indicated by his choice of medium: the battle for liberal hegemony had shifted from modes of production to the means of communication. A liberal sensibility presented a banal and conflict-free utopia blind to class contradictions. Abstracted from this fantasy, the farce in *The New York Sun* highlighted the force of the popularization of the newspaper as a means of communication. A mass appeal seemingly could elevate liberalism's ideals at the expense of the visceral experience of the ravages of unfettered accumulation.

We ought to read Locke's articles as signalling a fundamental reorientation of the world picture enabled by changes in the means of communication. The convergence of a farcical rendering of the speculations of scientific reason and the end of slavery perhaps cautions against the all-too-easy exits plotted in the name of the ideology of liberalism. To this end, the Great Moon Hoax inadvertently provoked popular reconceptualizations of race authorizing modern politics. Arguably, an exit from the reign of this popular sentiment could only be orchestrated by way of a bold and critical attitude towards technology.

Herschel's stargazing, which paved the way for a celestial constellation of the universe supported by the professionalization of science, was involuntarily drawn into a chapter in which race was being reconfigured by way of its intersections with empire. His *Preliminary Discourse* was also, along with Alexander von Humboldt's study, a worthy accomplice in the development of a theory of evolution that gained traction in bourgeois and settler colonial public spheres. Natural philosophy upheld an evolutionary system that both unleashed and set out to control speculation with greater confidence. The orientation of science towards a nascent public sphere was indirectly given a hypothetical and speculative value through a careful theoretical exposition of scientific method released from the rigidities of a slave order and freed from the strictures of time. In the wake of slave emancipation, race effectively became available as a signifier with no stable or immediate referent. This momentary unmooring from a slave order had significant implications for reordering and redistributing notions of race in a world placed on the modular path of progress.

We might say that race is that excess of slavery transferred to a technological milieu, where the latter operationalizes, distributes and controls its signification. In its latter guise, it mirrors aspects of Michel Foucault's studies of the birth of modern biopower and his forays into the dynamics of race war, where race presents itself as a basis for territorial securitization before it surfaces as a reference for institutionally policing an emergent discourse of abnormality.[22] Race in this territorial and institutional dispensation is a site for remodelling the exercise of power. Unfortunately, what Foucault misses is the way in which this technological milieu is infused with a mythic content in the colonial world. Unmoored from one of its inaugural formations in the history of slavery, the fiction formed around race was categorically extended across the nineteenth and twentieth centuries through the mystical instrumentalities of communicative infrastructure that undergirded the global spread of capital.

The telescope and the development of photographic or pictorial reproduction, alongside John Watkins Brett's telegraphic extensions connecting the continents recalled via a motif in Danby's painting, combined in the 1830s to supplement the surveyor's map and landscape painting with technological developments that sent shockwaves through colonial formations. Moreover, with the summation of the technological, we have a fuller picture of the implications of the end of slavery in a colonial setting such as the Cape Colony.

Two discernible effects are worth considering. Firstly, the end of slavery exacerbated the violence expressed in systems of colonial governmentality, as witnessed for example in the century-long war unleashed along the frontier zones of the Cape Colony. Secondly, the residues of race at the end of slavery were more readily available to be folded into a rapidly evolving orientation towards a yet to be determined future. In the case of the latter, the prevailing idea of race was reflected in changing attitudes towards technology, where it served to specify the convergence of race and labour in a general subordination of life to machinic functions. The telescope and nascent apparatus of photographic reproduction further opened up a space in which race could be projected as a speculative horizon of capitalist

Apartheid's Mythic Precursors

modernity in the colonial world. As if to cement the coincidence, John Herschel emerged as a crucial contributor to the science behind the invention of photography and mastery of the telescope.[23] The anticipatory potential of technology should not be underestimated. As Siegfried Kracauer noted over a century later:

> In a memorable statement published before the emergence of instantaneous photography, Sir John Herschel not only predicted the basic features of the film camera but assigned to it a task which it has never since disowned: 'the vivid and lifelike reproduction and handing down to the latest posterity of any transaction in life – a battle, a debate, a public solemnity, a pugilistic conflict'.[24]

For his part, Locke made apparent how technological drives enhanced the hegemony of the eye in an overarching circuit of projection and protension. The memory of race was not only projected from the past onto the present, but lay ahead as a standing reserve determined less by human consciousness or political and ideological will than by instruments that peered into the future. Increased speculation across the spectrum of political discourses resulted in greater uncertainty about the erratic effects of race, prompting a search for solutions to stabilize population and production in an increasing demand for efficient machines. If race was once a consequence of empire, the rise of an American century of prospecting gathered the racial remains of slavery into a process of the becoming technical of the human. In the Great Moon Hoax, we see how the dispersed ideas of race were mobilized towards an image of modernity in which myth eclipses reason. What then are we to make of the afterlife of slavery, of the marginalization of the figure of the slave in the changing orders of scientific knowledge across the centuries since?[25]

Star-eyed Despair

The scale of colonial prospecting enabled by speculative science and technological expansion showed signs of strain following the onset of war in Europe in the early 1900s. One South African intellectual in particular called attention to the consequences of surrendering the rising tide of racial feeling to a cosmological

56   Undoing Apartheid

horizon that, as Srinivas Aravamudan suggests, had been in vogue in Europe since the eighteenth century.[26]

Silas Modiri Molema, a South African medical student based in Scotland during World War I, contemplated the frightening revival of an idea of race at this time. Judging from his writing on the subject, he had become increasingly weary of the entanglement of freedom in the cosmological adventures of European thought in which 'speculations about extra-terrestrials increased anthropomorphic projections'. In *The Bantu: Past and Present* (1920), he turned to the poetry of Thomas Campbell with a hint of exasperation to express caution about the frightful fates awaiting modernity's belated subjects in light of the prominence given to astronomy:

> O Star-eyed Science
> hast thou wandered there
> To waft us home the message of despair?[27]

These few lines reflect a growing anxiety as unprecedented configurations of technology produced shifts in conceptions of race after World War I, not least in Molema's South Africa. His writing suggests a struggle to decipher this recent script of race in the world that seemed both familiar and recurrent, while normalized by a science tethered to progress.[28] Clearly, the hardening of attitudes that surrounded the mobilization of race as political signifier was cause for grave concern.

The political uncertainties that followed the abolition of slavery alongside the flourish of the industrial technologies created the conditions for a twentieth-century recasting of a discourse of race. A generation of intellectuals in the colonial world doubted liberal assurances that race would recede with the ascendancy of reason and access to education. Although unable to identify the problem precisely in these terms, Molema's writing nevertheless gestured towards a worrying shift in the discourse of race that had become palpable with the advent of World War I. As a medical scientist, he appeared to have detected a view about race that was not simply a consequence of a grand design of political rationality, but an incidental outcome of a scientific method of the physical and biological sciences inherited from the nineteenth century. That realization tallied with what had been exposed through a form of mechanistic thinking that 'rescued "new biology" from what were considered the doldrums of old-fashioned natural history, riddled with speculative and non-testable hypotheses'.[29]

In the search for a more confident posture that was encouraged by the fear of the loss of vitalism in his time, Molema worried that the promises made on the grounds of scientific method, like the era of slavery, elided its responsibility towards disqualifying race as a category for ordering life. The abdication of the critique of race by scientific reason proved important for its apparent reinvention, especially when traced in the normalization of race in everyday life.

World War I highlighted a pattern in the process of the reinvention of race. The 'technological nihilism' of the war, a platform upon which ideas of race once again came into vogue, echoed shifts that first became apparent in 1834. In both, race seemed destined to return as a banal and innocuous residue of a past violence.

Moral attitudes at the turn of the twentieth century amplified racial claims aided by the expansion and speed of technological objects of communication. For intellectuals of the Black Atlantic, the rising tide of racial sentiment appeared to be provoking a transnational reorientation and reinscription of an otherwise moribund nineteenth-century category for marking difference.[30] Molema himself belonged to a generation of scientists and intellectuals who were alert to the convergence of myth and reason that appeared to be distorting aspirations of freedom in the first quarter of the twentieth century. In the midst of a technoscientific convergence, some intellectuals of the Black Atlantic anxiously awaited the promise of freedom from the rule of race on which the hopes of an anti-colonial intelligentsia rested.

The anxiety is palpable in Molema's *The Bantu: Past and Present*, which, upon careful reading, calls out the true nature of the game being played in the name of race. The 398-page text might easily be mistaken for reaffirming the speculative horizon of race on which the burden of Europe at the southern tip of Africa rested. This explains why Molema puts science and philosophy into play as co-constitutive rationalities in the remaking of a modern concept of race. Ironically, by tracing this rationality, the text shows how the evolution of distinct disciplinary strands sustains the conclusion for separate development, as if to anticipate the threateningly dangerous idea of apartheid lying in wait. To underscore this sense of irony, Molema hazards speculation about the formalization of segregation on the principle of separate development set out by the Union of South Africa, but only 'if the white rulers were true to their word, on condition of absolute equality'.[31] Identifying an impossible resolution for what he called 'a dogmatism for which there is no historical precedent', he anticipated the fallout if 'the "native question" that exists for whites and the "foreign problem" that exists for blacks' was not resolved constitutionally: 'if fair allocation of land and resources was not guaranteed based on demography, and if a guarantee of complete national independence and absolute autonomy was not granted'.[32] Molema's writing drew attention to the dependence of what he called 'white society' on the 'African races', knowing full well that 'white' South Africans would have little to claim should separate development be dealt with justly by constitutional means. At the very least, we should read his account as an ironic reversal of the changing fortunes of domination exercised through the convergence of technoscientific and political forces.

Yet Molema's text was not only written to address South African concerns from the vantage point of exile. His was also an effort to reflect on the experience of race in Scotland, where, as a medical student, he felt compelled to respond to violent attacks on African, Asian, Chinese and Arab workers in 1919.[33] The attacks were sparked by competition for employment following postwar demobilization by a 'colour bar' enforced by prominent Glasgow labour leaders – and the subsequent retaliation sparked by these racial restrictions. Knowing that scientific method and rationality were failing to quell the flames of race hatred, Molema turned his attention to the sources of racial violence that had spread from Glasgow to the port towns of Britain as liberalism's political and economic promises of progress built on the foundations of scientific rationality dissipated. Throughout his text, there is an affirmation of the possibility of improvement in the arts of reason and the concomitant progress of Africans, notwithstanding liberalism's retreat into nationalism after World War I. In Molema's estimation, what was left in the wake of empire was endless speculation on the prospects of race that potentially threatened to inadvertently trap the colonial subject in a waiting room of modernity.

Apartheid's Mythic Precursors

With the deployment of education to the cause of liberal governmentality, trusteeship was being fine-tuned along the course charted by the Royal Commission of Aboriginal Peoples of 1835. Trusteeship was the humanitarian gift conferred by liberalism and empire to those belatedly due their share of the benefits of modernity. By the time *The Bantu: Past and Present* was published, Molema expressed growing concern about the prospects that many faced as hope in the accruals of trusteeship faded. He was not alone in seeing trusteeship as a deceptive promise of a future of racial distinction without violence. Reading the problematic of race through an expansive although sporadic treatment of the Western philosophical canon that included Kant, Nietzsche, Locke, Hobbes, Hume and Hegel, Molema arrived at a gloomy conclusion about the intellectual possibilities and impossibilities facing the colonized subject; even as writer, he struggled to reclaim a political standpoint for 'the African' from the intellectual resources of modernity.

It is erroneous to reduce Molema's concerns about the outcomes of the cosmological turn in science to a tendency that reaffirmed geographic or naturalized concepts of race. Rather, the text specifically narrates a history of race to escape its rationalization in the discourse of trusteeship that seemed to have modelled itself on the speculative tendencies of scientific reason. In harmony with the writing of W.E.B. Du Bois, whom Molema had corresponded with while studying in Scotland, *The Bantu* asks searchingly what it might mean to think about Africa on the stage of world history, even when that same world history made it increasingly impossible to be in and of the world defined by the project of Europe.

What Molema accomplishes is to unravel and identify the administrative mechanisms of race, where the idea of race functioned as a discourse of population control that thwarted politically committed concepts of humanism. His was an effort to link early critiques of race in anti-colonial nationalism in South Africa to traditions across the continent in order to present an autonomous intellectual and political subject, rather than merely the subject to be gambled upon by liberalism's uncertain future and capitalism's scattered and misleading speculations.

The Bantu: Past and Present pivots two global shifts in technological temporal objects: on the one side, the industrial revolution that was taking hold amid the abolition of slavery in

60 Undoing Apartheid

1834; and on the other, the shift in the discourse of race in the wake of the second industrial revolution in the first part of the twentieth century. As Molema notes,

> The slave, in constant subjection, with no independent existence, becomes a perfect machine.[34]

Within this emergent technological prognosis in South Africa, Molema identified an ominous sign in the accretion around race that he wished to embed as a caution in his token of appreciation to the people and country of Scotland for offering him 'a refuge during the world's titanic convulsions'. In its broadest ambition, his was a book directed at the European Enlightenment, and the educational promise that first took hold under its auspices in Scotland. Looking at South Africa from the perspective of exile, the text wavers in relation to biological, political and cultural scripts of race, but ultimately settles on parting ways with something hitherto unforeseen in its potentially virulent effect on the African continent after World War I.

Molema noticed that the tendency to render race superfluous had begun with the end of slavery. Yet, from the vantage of the early 1900s, it was being wielded to ever more deadly ends as a political instrument. In his reckoning, scientific intuition shielded itself from the public discord surrounding race by deferring to an economic rationality, and thus redirecting racial explication towards the political authority of liberalism. With this dispersal and redistribution of the meaning of race, its effects produced heightened feelings of dread among intellectuals such as Molema. The concern, however, was not restricted to a received idea of race, but included the threat its reconfiguration posed for the future of South Africa, especially as the category was increasingly refracted through the prism of a segregated public sphere. In an industrializing postwar setting in South Africa, the onset of job reservation and the application of a colour bar threatened mobility and similarly tended to limit the striving for freedom that the advent of cultural, educational and social qualifications held out. For Molema, the virulence of race lay in liberalism's exploitation of science in the reconstitution of the category in South Africa.

The study of medicine alerted him to questionable confidence in the abilities of scientific disciplines to shed the vestiges of error of irrational thought through a systematic method.[35] This methodological confidence simultaneously tended to elide the controversies surrounding the abolition of slavery, thus rendering scientific discourse vulnerable and open to abuse. While the virtues of subjectivity endowed with qualities of progress took centre stage in European Enlightenment thought, the figure of the slave was mostly obscured in the age of industrialization, notwithstanding the insistence on the part of a vocal intellectual tradition about the centrality of slavery in the Atlantic system.[36] The end of slavery certainly propelled an ascendant scientific worldview that in turn fuelled the ideals of humanitarianism, religious public morality and industrial expansion. All of this was achieved at the expense of the figure of the slave, who ultimately bore the brunt of the rupture and realignment of science and liberalism. The confidence in science to autocorrect those errors in the passage of technological progress permitted liberalism to claim the same for capitalist relations in the colonies, where the rationality of the market would depend on the service of scientific administrators.

For his part, Molema countered by exposing the scientific pretensions that obscured the accretions of race by noting how 'prejudice provoked prejudice'. Recalling Du Bois's *The Souls of Black Folk* (1903), he argued that 'facing so vast a prejudice could not but bring the inevitable self-questioning, self-disparagement, and lowering of ideals which ever accompany repression and breed in an atmosphere of contempt and hate'.[37] 'But race in South Africa', he averred, 'did not institute an ethical hatred, as being a revulsion of Morality from Immorality, of Good from Evil, of Moral Right from Moral Wrong.'[38] It amounted to race hatred, premised on the very constitutive difference to the 'haters' thoughts, words and actions'. And race hatred, he argued, 'was illegitimate, unethical and un-Christian'.[39]

By instituting a difference in the script of scientific rationality and liberal morality, and redirecting the problem of race through a rereading of the science of evolution of a diverse human species, Molema highlighted a disagreement that belonged to the scientific revolution of the nineteenth century. His was not merely a simple disavowal of liberal appropriation of science. Neither was the text merely a sign of its times. To better grasp the nuance of Molema's argument, consider the lecture on 'Possibilities and Impossibilities', delivered to the African

62 Undoing Apartheid

Races Association in Glasgow in 1919. For Molema, there is a necessary correlation between race feeling and race hatred, or prejudice, to use the term that Du Bois selected to use. This problem of race could not be overcome, in Molema's distinct view, merely by appealing to the rational precepts of scientific reason because liberalism had already appropriated science to its view. The problem was that liberalism presupposed a difference based on race to begin with.

'Science', Molema argues, 'had not proved any intellectual or moral inefficiency of the black races. Neither capacity nor incapacity has been shown conclusively to be characteristic of the backward races, or, more plainly, of the African race.'[40] Alongside this, one ought to read Molema's rather circumspect but generally favourable treatment of the offer of education to African subjects, first through missionary education and later, in 1854, with the arrival of Governor George Grey in South Africa, industrial schools. In all of these efforts, the emergence of education was limited to religious and industrial education, and to the care of books and tools, as Lovedale College in the Eastern Cape proclaimed in its mission statement in the nineteenth century.[41] The name given to this form of education was industrial arts and theology, through which race was carefully sutured to empire, nation and industrial capitalism.

We would be failing in our reading of Molema's text if we did not see it as eschewing political claims formed by recourse to scientific method. Of interest is the extent to which he opposes an industrialization of memory and instrumentalization of race with the democratizing ideal associated with the possibilities accruing in education. His is a discourse that shifts the attention given to race from the plane of politics to the promise of education, in which schooling assumes significantly greater prominence. How else are we to read the few choice words he reserved for the waning of a liberal promise in South Africa?

> In these things, we shall look, and look in vain, for the much vaunted 'Western liberalism'. In vain shall we search the actions for the so-called high political morality. We are reduced of necessity to the conclusion that politics has been dethroned and transferred from the region of speculative ethics to that of matter-of-fact realism, from the abstract law of altruism to the practical law of the strong – the survival of the fittest, down to the law which governs other animals, which governs the plants and even the destructive germs of disease.

Apartheid's Mythic Precursors

To this naturalism, which the same people think low, the civilised world has come down. Where then is morality?[42]

The argument proceeds along lines drawn from his reading of Nietzsche, claiming that such morality was merely 'a sign language, simply symptomatology'. If, as he put it, 'liberalism and morality are hollow, meaningless words and egregious tricks, then as well might a thirsty traveller expect to get water from a mirage as the Bantu [sic] hope to find emancipation by that morality and modern liberalism'. British liberalism, he argued, offered 'nothing to the Bantu of South Africa except such morbid creations and fancies as "the native problem"'.[43]

In arguing the case of social and economic prospects, he cites Nietzsche, claiming that 'morality in South Africa has long since been throttled and buried' and that 'slavery with all its sordid passions has been disinterred and revivified and re-established in all but name in South Africa'.[44]

> I say: as long as your morality hung over me I breathed like one asphyxiated. That is why I throttled this snake. I wished to live. Consequently it had to die.[45]

The suspicion emanates from the neglect of the differential aims of scientific philosophical education. Suggesting that a resurgent idea of race was a product of pure dogmatism, Molema offers a reading of capacity for change and education by delineating the limits of scientific progress, in order to recuperate something of its metaphysics that had been unnecessarily surrendered to a mythic claim with the rise of the European bourgeois public sphere. In his lecture to the African Races Association in 1919, he noted:

> It is a law of all scientific investigations to presume a uniformity and orderly sequence in the phenomena that are being observed, whether these be physical, chemical, or biological. It is a basic, a fundamental principle, an axiom and a law of philosophical history – in its inquiry into the social, moral, or intellectual evolution of man [sic] – to presuppose human progress and human perfectibility, throughout humanity, even though the visible progress may be haphazard, irregular, desultory, and zigzag; even though it may be full of failings and falterings. The underlying principle is – what one man can do, another can generally do also; what one nation can achieve, another nation can also achieve.[46]

64 Undoing Apartheid

Molema's reading of the world in 1920 was an effort to desta-
bilize this peculiarly confident standpoint about race in science,
both by burrowing beneath its rationality, and by introducing
an argument, however tentative, to question the hegemonic
pretensions of a particular version of reason. To put it even more
bluntly, Molema sought to outwit the rationality that seduced
so many intellectuals of his generation into believing that race
and reason were antithetical. Unfortunately, what he failed to
grasp was that the order of race that was being reinvented was
not merely a product of the failure of science to autocorrect;
but also a product of political mythologies unleashed by the
British abolition of slavery that persisted in the bourgeois public
sphere of Europe, well into the twentieth century, and in which
Afrikaner nationalism found a worthy justification for its origin
story.

The intellectuals of Molema's generation faced a future of race
with a sense of foreboding, based on nineteenth-century histories
of slavery and colonialism, and with the transfer of the measure
of race, both in terms of capacity and behaviour, by machines.
Looking towards the yet imperceptible but faint horizon of
apartheid, they may have seen a future of receding prospects of
freedom in the reinvention of race.

Cybernetic Loops and Circular Causalities

Better conceived in terms of a circular causality that threatens
uncanny returns, the surprise and shock that race produces have
often been the preoccupation of the work of art. To this end,
an aesthetic education raises the stakes for the global promise
of post-apartheid freedom that the struggle against apartheid
conferred as a gift to the world. It is after all racism's last word,
apartheid, that will serve as a watchword for difference in the
world that awaits. How are we to apprehend this version of race
specific to apartheid, to prepare for its uncanny returns while
finding ways to exit its circular causality? And how to face its
future when it has entered the realm of the co-evolution of the
human and technology?

Norbert Wiener's *The Human Use of Human Beings*,
published in 1950, two years following his ground-breaking text,
Cybernetics: Or Communication and Control in the Animal and

the Machine (1948), offers some hope in an otherwise despairing conclusion that there appears to be no end to this vast apocalyptic spiral.[47] Wiener's recapitulation of the manner in which sensory beings are ensnared in a circular causality with the onset of automated machines in an era of Cold War geopolitics was not merely a case of scientific and technological invention falling into the wrong hands. His concern about automated machines, which he himself helped to conceive, was an expression of anxiety at how the machine had been enveloped by the aura of the slave, emerging as a powerful metaphor after World War II. The premonitions were not unfounded, even as they proved to be somewhat partial. Devolving human and machine into a relationship akin to slavery also helped to explain a political concern about the subordination of human to machine. Yet it was not merely the hierarchical relation or capacity that altered the relation between human and machine. By Wiener's own reckoning, the image of the slave is the very source of linking race to machinic existence. His cautionary text that followed the work on cybernetics discloses how the co-evolution of the human and technology is skewed by the iterability of race.

Conjuring the threat of atomic warfare that engulfed the world in which he wrote in the 1950s, Wiener cites the New Testament story in which the demonic is transferred from a madman to a herd of swine, with ruinous consequences. As if to recall the scene in Danby's painting, Wiener hints at the failure of science to contain the excess of race when, resorting to metaphor to describe an impasse in scientific reason, he says, 'like so many Gadarene swine, we have taken unto us the devils of the age, and the compulsion of scientific warfare is driving us pell-mell, head over heels into the ocean of our own destruction'.[48] The reliance on a New Testament parable to describe the gloom of atomic warfare in the 1950s should not be missed here – not if we understand that science, insofar as it defines the historicity of our modernity, shunned an aesthetics of life while failing to forestall a politics of death from the very outset. For if indeed the demonic exorcism is transferred to the Gadarene swine, sending it hurtling over the cliff into the ocean, we are, according to Wiener, nevertheless summoned to witness the apprentice sorcerers who administer the new programme of science, often to our common detriment. In the return of myth, we should hear echoes of fascism akin to what Adorno and Horkheimer anticipated in the *Dialectic of Enlightenment* (1944). Modernity had encountered a specific limit in the mythic aura surrounding technology in which the human was increasingly ensnared.

The slave inaugurates and is constitutive of how we account for evolving relations between the human and the machine that have evolved with the contests over futurity in myth and reason. With the abolition of slavery in the Caribbean and the Cape Colony circa 1834, the image of the slave proved indispensable for the process of transfer and translation of communication technologies that laid the mythic foundation on which race feeds in its many returns. Several intellectuals in the early 1900s confronted the beginnings of this circular causality of race that would culminate in post-World War II technoscientific configurations of communication and control in human and machine.

Race is both adequate to and the excess upon which power thrives. In the guise of apartheid, it is both symptom and supplement in the co-evolution of the human and technology which sustains an apocalyptic world picture of modernity. Apartheid was perhaps a residue of a story of the ground that science ceded to myth in the hour of greatest promise of reason, when science failed to hold up the image of the slave as indispensable to mediating the relation between state, capital, and public sphere. To the extent that apartheid modernized the idea of race, it was tethered to myth, at times subordinated to it, where it periodically erupted in forms of violence that far exceeded the parameters of reason. As we will see, the birth of post-apartheid freedom is similarly tethered to a wager with the very devil from which it seeks to escape. What is certain, however, is that post-apartheid freedom, not unlike the fate awaiting the figure of the slave on the cusp of emancipation, will depend on how we select to relate to the mythic precursors of race that block desire. And so we return to Heaney's opening gambit as it plays out in theatrical works of fate and destiny, if only to gauge how recasting a version of the consilience inherited from the physical and biological sciences that altered conceptions of race in apartheid's modernity may offer yet another glimmer of hope for a concept of post-apartheid freedom.

Exeunt Herschel, Danby and Molema.

3
The Return of Faust
Rats, Hyenas and other Miscreants

Philoctetes:
I'll soon be tainted meat
For scavengers to pick at.
The shining eyes and claws
Of all the hunted creatures
Are sharpening for a kill:
Crows and wolves and vultures
And every animal
That was my victim ever.
I'm at their mercy now.
This is the last stand
And I haven't an arrow even.
All I've left is a wound.

Seamus Heaney, *The Cure at Troy*

Faustus on Safari

Tempting fate in a world precariously wedged between myth and reason, the eerie prospect of an incarnation of a Faustian wager created a heightened sense of anticipation about whether the end of apartheid would put paid to the vestiges of the orders of race in Africa. Would apartheid's end signal a concomitant finalization of colonial forms of objectification that proved

Faustus in Africa (III-23) – April 1995. Faustus confronts the Devil, played by Leslie Fong (right). Faustus is manipulated by Adrian Kohler (centre) assisted and voiced by Dawid Minnaar (left).
Photo © Ruphin Coudyzer FPPSA.

definitive of an order of race that took shape in the aftermath of slavery?

By endorsing a longstanding theatrical tradition of summoning mythic precursors in the act of laying to rest the ghosts of the past, William Kentridge and the Handspring Puppet Company's 1995 production of *Faustus in Africa* identified a fault line in the story of political transition, one conjured by the return of a relic from the European Enlightenment called Faust. Why, we might ask, reclaim a mythic figure such as a conflicted Faust – torn between the pursuits of knowledge and the temptations of modern life – to talk about the dreams of a post-apartheid future? Perhaps the answer lies in what John Noyes has identified as Goethe's conflicted relation to cosmopolitanism and colonialism, to which I would add Faust's availability to account for object life – of the human folded into machine – in the story of modernity.[1] Perhaps the circulation of the legend of Faust has something to do with an interest in object life, where life is threatened by a future faced with waning desire and an insatiable appetite to accumulate and consume, or simply self-preservation under conditions of techno-modernity. Faust is a proper noun

The Return of Faust 69

for a reciprocal vulnerability, where life is overwhelmed by the very mechanism through which it is lived. But what if we pit Goethe's Faust at the end of slavery against Kentridge's Faustus at the end of apartheid? What image of freedom from the burden of race does the Faustian legend lead to? What image of race are we left to contend with?

Against the backdrop of political transition in South Africa, *Faustus in Africa* is not limited to questions arising from political transition *per se*; it asks more probingly whether aesthetics might redirect our image of freedom by crafting a different perspective on a form of consilience to one that gnaws away at the very striving for freedom. After all, the production coincided with anticipations about the birth of a post-apartheid democratic future, and the anxiety about unfulfilled thoughts on freedom produced by cultural legacies of the Black Atlantic in the twentieth century that lay dispersed across a century of crippling warfare. At the level of its most idealistic articulations, the play marks the tacit belief in human overcoming where incommensurable drives linking desire and knowledge are momentarily reconciled to approximate the best that an aesthetic education offers. But Faustus also comes bearing a bad omen, a shadow of doubt born out of historical experience, and a caution about the dangers of conflating the flight from the past with an escape from the shadow it casts over the present.

With the rebirth of *Faustus in Africa*, we discover our avid learner dissatisfied with what he has achieved by way of clerical and intellectual investments in colonial service. To avert a descent into despair, he seeks to enlist the services of Mephistopheles, a devilish trickster who offers to guide him through the forbidden pleasures that modern life has to offer. We meet Faustus in an unhappy state while the idea of eternal progress is being professed. He is dissatisfied with his accomplishments in the study of philosophy, law, medicine and theology in a world where greater pleasures await. Accompanying Faustus is his servant Johnston, who suffers a barrage of insults, follows his master's self-destructive commands, and who will eventually resort to his own pact with the devil's aide, becoming emperor and overturning the colonial order.

An opening soliloquy offers the audience access to the inner turmoil plaguing Faustus. In Room 407, Hotel Polana in an East African port city, Faustus peruses a slideshow of a landscape

70   Undoing Apartheid

once criss-crossed in his intellectual pursuits, with flashbacks of a severed hand, a pool with rubble in it, and an occult pentagram.

> Here I am then. Philosophy
> Behind me. Law and Medicine too
> and – to my cost – Theology,
> all studied, grimly sweated through
> and here I sit, as big a fool
> as when I first attended school.
> True I surpass the dull incompetents –
> doctors, pastors and masters, and the rest,
> for whom there is no bliss by ignorance,
> but this pre-eminence I now detest.
> All my laborious studies only show
> that Nothing is the most we ever know.
> Scruples I've laid aside, doubts as well.
> I have no fear of Devil or Hell.
> This is what robs me of all delight –
> I cannot boast that what I know is right.
> I cannot boast my teaching will ever find
> A way to improve or convert Mankind.
> Two souls within me wrestle for possession
> and neither will surrender to his brother.
> One is of the senses, sensual,
> Slaking his appetites like an animal,
> The other strives for purity of mind
> To leave the world and its works behind.
> If there are spirits listening in the air
> Descend now from your golden stratosphere –
> carry me off to new life – anywhere.

The irresolution about worldly and intellectual pursuits refers us to the kind of entrapment of subjectivity imagined in colonial discourse, where the subject struggled against being persistently stripped of desire and rendered as mere instance of mechanical life. In this milieu the Faustian myth is helpful for reflecting on the dangers of a strand of German *Naturphilosophie* that presented itself as an alternative hermeneutics of nature as the saga of nineteenth-century colonial expansion unfolded. Contrasted with the mathematization of nature of British natural philosophy, the African setting of the Faustian pact reveals the failure to arrest the slide into mechanized forms of life with the onset of colonization and, later, the endpoints of

The Return of Faust 71

Naturphilosophie in German fascism. The effects thereof, we are reminded throughout the play, could be felt not only in Europe, but also in the concomitant violence that accompanied the demand for labour to extract raw materials and servitude in colonial Africa.

A farcical 'erotics of ascent' follows, resulting in an absolute saturation of the ego, as Gabriel Trop suggests, with the insatiable appetite of the colonial mindset emboldened by technological props likened to proliferating phallic symbols.[2] While Goethe emphasized the subjective conundrum occasioned by epochal change, in its African iteration, there is a noticeable shift towards exploring the non-human dimensions that mediate the onset of the new. What is rendered as farce is not merely the return of tragedy, but a tragedy mediated through a technical apparatus that appears to have entirely enveloped subjectivity. *Faustus in Africa* is set apart from its precursors by the attention granted to *techne*, as opposed to the tendency to see technology as purely invested in and by existing social relations. By foregrounding *techne*, *Faustus* explores how technology and alchemy (from the Arabic *al-Kimiya*) are folded into each other to form an aura of art and science in modernity. This very interplay of art and science that accompanied the rise of technological communication objects ultimately mediated the renewal of ideas of race in the early twentieth century. At the core of Kentridge's concern is the question about how race became modern, and how this transformation affected the image of labour in Africa by altering the relation between human and technology. Ultimately, we are left to ponder whether aesthetics, implicated as it is in the colonial project, may offer us recourse out of the unresolved problem of nature, the human and technology that became the fantasy enacted by Europe in Africa.

Faustus in Africa thus recapitulates the broad outlines of an aesthetic argument in Goethe's *Faust II* in order to flee the trappings of an unfettered colonial desire and the threat of the perpetual return of the same in the orders of race. Rather than simply mimicking Goethe, *Faustus in Africa* is also a work of aesthetic education. It brushes up against the limits of Goethe's search for a higher unity of the whole as he passes from medieval witchcraft to modern naturalism while grappling with those unresolved questions of morality in Europe that later became the burden of Africa.

72 Undoing Apartheid

Set against the backdrop of European colonial rule at the time of the defeat of Germany in World War I, the play explores the indecisions around questions of aesthetics from the vantage of Africa. The opening gambit presents us with a life instinct that is subordinated to disciplinary knowledge in the sciences of nature and the arts of life. The disciplinary matrix of art and science both sustained the project of modernity while decimating the African landscape. If knowledge and desire serve the incommensurable drives of Eros and Thanatos, of desire and death, the play records the consequences of the spectacularly macabre accomplishments of progress and modernity in an African colonial setting. We are in the midst of an aesthetics of incommensurability which tells a story about race and its uncanny returns – *here* as a story of human subjugation, *there* as one about ecological destruction, and *elsewhere*, as a story of the seductions and access to the technologies of communication.

At stake in Kentridge's undertaking is a search for intellectual pursuits that have been surrendered to mere expedience in modern life, with little consideration of its adverse consequences. The desire to acquire knowledge of the world is rapidly overtaken by an accelerated unconscious fantasy that combines unconstrained phallic drive and an insatiable appetite for accumulation and consumption. Part parable, part attitude of disappointment about failed pursuits of knowledge, Faustus goes on safari upon concluding a pact with the devil, indulging in elaborate feasts and buying sprees, attempting to consume all that Africa presents. His suspension of study exposes an archetypal greedy colonialist – laying to waste subjects and landscapes in an orgy of unremitting destruction. *Faustus in Africa* combines Christopher Marlowe's resort to magic and Goethe's conflicted relation to national allegory to reveal the impasse in the story of freedom in the wake of colonialism. Yielding no alternative resolution, the dramaturgical import of Kentridge's production commits the Faustian wager to account for exporting modernity's most enduring contradictions to the far reaches of empire. When the pillaging and destruction that colonialism wrought across the planet are accounted for, there remains the small matter of how Europe's internal contradictions were destined to be worked out in the colonies.

The expansion of technology that once promised to release labour from the drudgery of wage-slavery unexpectedly culminated

The Return of Faust   73

in a desperate search for sensory innervation. Kentridge takes us into the belly of the beast in Auerbach's tavern, this time in Dar es Salaam, where the human costs of relentless transcendental striving are laid bare amidst Marabi-style music from the gold mines of South Africa. Theatrically speaking, both iterations of the Faustian legend affirm a long-held view that the birth of tragedy is rooted in song. Against the backdrop of industrializing landscapes, Auerbach's tavern in Leipzig in the 1830s, and Dar es Salaam in the 1920s at the end of German colonialism in Africa, place us, in a moment of proletarian revelry, amidst the critical space of theatricality. The theatre mimics a form of labour that is seemingly dispensable yet expended to reveal a reserve of affective features of criticism, transcendence and freedom. It burrows through the psychic infrastructure to extract more productive meaning of immaterial labour away from the remit of capital.

Back to the Future

Teaming up with Lesego Rampolokeng and the Handspring Puppet Company, Kentridge styles a relational tale about object life and, by extension, race and technology, which lay repressed and unanticipated in the critiques of colonialism and apartheid, and their combined effects. *Faustus in Africa* is an admonitory tale in the dying days of political power that relayed ideas of race via instrumentalities of communication that included gramophone, camera and telegraph.

An opening scene set in Mephistopheles' bureaucratic clearinghouse in Lourenço Marques (present day Maputo) around the 1920s – a time that marked the end of German colonial ambitions in Africa – calls us to witness the hitherto unforeseen dangers that lie in wait in the apparently liberating urge to pass over from the old to the new with the onset of recent instruments of communication technologies. Mephistopheles' clerks frantically print and count banknotes, a sign of the value attached to colonial prospecting. As Mephistopheles takes a call from God, a voice filtered from the image of a megaphone is projected onto a screen alongside a clock and planetarium projector, so that subject and technical object combine to implicate the viewer in the drives of colonial modernity.

74 Undoing Apartheid

The audience is placed on the cusp of the great finalization of the scientific conquest of Africa and on the verge of the diminished promise of the second industrial revolution, as the ambitions of German colonialism are brought to a grinding halt in the wake of World War I. The controversy about the meaning of political transition is performed against the backdrop of emerging techno-political circuits of communication instruments. An elaborate stage setting offers a hint of the contradiction of colonial domination: colonialism would not materialize without the sheen of technology which Europe extended to conscript its colonial subjects into modernity. Inversely, the fate that awaited the subject of colonialism would haunt Europe as the very fate it failed to escape.

These very drives serve to rehabilitate corrupted souls that have fallen prey to the failed political and economic promise of renewal for over two centuries. Surrendered to expanding technological resources, Africa is inscribed into Europe's endlessly deferred promise – a symptom of the West's dismal, if not disappointing, shortcomings in averting a slide into a mechanical existence. Thankfully, the medium of theatricality has been ready to hand to direct us elsewhere, towards the appropriation of tragedy by the ill-fated subsumption of all life to the vagaries of capitalism and its intrusive instrumentalities. Katharina Keim's description of the opening scene of the Kentridge and the Handspring production emphasizes the primacy given to communication technologies over productive technologies. This, Keim notes, is an explicit feature of the stage set of *Faustus in Africa*, which hails Africa through the instruments of communication to the rule of capital:

> Mephistopheles acts as a clerk in a telegraphic office and as master of ceremony of the whole performance, thus taking over God's position in the 'theatrum mundi' metaphor. At the beginning, in a shortened 'Prologue in Heaven', he establishes contact via telephone with God, his master, who is presented only by a female voice and projection of a gramophone at the rear wall, imitating the disc label 'His Master's Voice'.[3]

To the extent that Kentridge brings a history of theatre into direct relationship with the effects of colonialism, he should perhaps be understood as registering two commensurate aesthetic arguments. The first relates to the way the theatre of the sixteenth

The Return of Faust 75

century, which gave rise to the Faust legend through Marlowe, converged with an era during which the Papacy encouraged celestial mapping, which in turn became a pivotal element of theatre design. The second asks that we consider how mnemonic machines were introduced to the theatre in an aesthetic form that sought to encapsulate all the world and all time.[4]

The elaborate stage set reminds us of Giulio Camillo's sixteenth-century *Theatrum Mundi*, or theatre of the world, built around mnemotechnic constellations that enabled the power of recall and the duration of memory.[5] Ruby Cohn suggests that the *topos* of *Theatrum Mundi* had retained its influence for twentieth-century theatre practitioners such as Samuel Beckett and Bertolt Brecht.[6] Theatre that had to contend with the tragic memory of violence deployed Camillo's method of engaging an extramundane audience to partake in complex judgement of the tragicomic business of the world stage. This development of Camillo's *Theatrum Mundi* relied on perspectives of a cosmo-logical order by way of deploying mnemotechnic constellations that, as noted earlier, place fate in relationship to instruments of memory designed to recall, record and communicate.

Goethe's *Faust*, which may be read as an allegory of the generalized psychic burden that slavery placed on the European imagination, is distinguished from its reprise in 1995 by an emphasis on the worldliness of technology that mediates colonialism. The quagmire of the Faustian wager is thus rearticu-lated, so that colonialism is less a regressive accompaniment of global capitalism than a prognosis of that specific future of capital built on drives in which divisions between human and machine are rendered indistinct. Unable to reconcile being with desire, the puppet caricature of Faustus sets off in search of a waning spirit, only to discover that spirit itself has fallen prey to the seductions of technology. Overwhelmed by his depleted spirit, Faustus is led to reflect upon an inconclusive aesthetic promise of Romanticism that once inspired his study of *Naturphilosophie*. To draw out the Faustian allegory of European colonization of Africa, Kentridge places the ecological and human costs of an intellectual formation alongside the pursuit of unfettered progress, enabled by the expansion of technological resources.

Faustus in Africa conjures feelings of revulsion resulting from the contradictions of being ensnared in the machinery of progress. Behind what is often too easily construed as the persona of a narcissistic hedonist, Faust(us) is perhaps better understood as a tragic figure in the quest for the sources of a spirit intrinsic to the arts of knowledge that have been rendered entirely functional: by capital, in the case of Goethe; and, in Kentridge, by a rapacious charge in the unfolding saga of colonial expansion and imperial conquest. As many before had noted, Goethe's *Faust* seeks redemption from a slide into the soul-destroying end signalled by the mechanization of life. This, he believed, was where the expansion of technology encouraged licentious behaviour that led to a decline of spirit, rather than making time for the civilizational pursuits associated with reflection as set out in the prevailing discourse of *Naturphilosophie*. The corrupting influence of capital sets Goethe's *Faust* on the path of fulfilment in demonic pleasures, only to be rescued from descent into an eternal hedonistic hell by way of an aesthetic reprieve. Approaching salvation, he meets the figure of Helen of Troy, in an encounter that expresses a yearning for the loss of a longed-for Hellenic ideal.

In Africa, however, there is no such redemption: Faustus remains on earth, playing cards with the devil, and scheming about the prospects that lie in wait in the future. Here the Faustian pact with the devil assumes an additional dimension in its African iteration: one that leads to a doubling of the stakes of the wager.

By linking human and machine to reflect on the return of race in the midst of a dying colonialism, the scene is set for a recuperation of a specifically psychoanalytic reading. The framing of the difference marked in the recurrency of race is undeniably Freudian. There is a definite fidelity to what Freud calls a model of 'repetition compulsion'. Like his predecessor Ernst Jentsch, Freud's forays into the uncanny held that such sensations were awakened when there was intellectual uncertainty about whether an object was alive or not, and when an inanimate object became too much like an animate one. In keeping with its earlier psychoanalytic elaboration, for Freud, the uncanny was not merely that which repeats, but that which is the cause of excitation. For the limited purposes of my argument, the uncanny compresses space so as to conflate elements of experience ordinarily distinguished by time. Unresolved aspects of the past thus have a tendency to present themselves with terrifying consequences in the contemporary

The Return of Faust 77

world of the subject. It is perhaps at the point of the uncanny that the unresolved aspects of slavery are transferred to the mechanistic reflexivity of machines.

The uncanny thus reappears by means of carefully reticulated spatio-temporal crossings of a continental map in which instruments of communication and travel accelerate the experience of time. A masochism of speed is plotted by means of intuition of a work of art. Thus Kentridge remarks that 'the principle behind all the work [of the play] whether on text, image, or puppet was to see if, in the process of working, of drawing, carving and rehearsing, a coherence and meaning could be made, rather than an established polemic be illustrated'.[7]

Differentiating between meaning-making and polemical illustration helps to identify how the work of art intervenes in anticipations of the end of apartheid in 1994. Highlighting this difference, the puppet accentuates the awakening of uncanny sensations through indecision, animating the journey of the spirit of an age towards materialization, and a despair inscribed in the object that awaits. How exactly to receive the object of the puppet in the performance reaches into a metaphysical core of a polemical crafting of political transition. One is never certain whether the puppet is animate because of its human and animal resemblance, or whether it is inanimate because of its status as a manipulated wooden object. The puppet is an uncanny prosthesis: one that conveys a sense of spirit, and that abides neither by received ideas of truth nor by premature declarations of reconciliation.

The arrival of the uncanny in the unending repetition of industrial time, marked from Faust (Goethe) to Faustus (Kentridge), is a task assigned to that most animate of tricksters: Handspring's cocked-legged, bandaged and androgynous Hyena, who gleefully makes it known that *they* are privy to a secret about modernity of which Faustus remains oblivious. Modelled on Bulgakov's cocked-legged cat, Behemoth, featured in Yuri Lyubimov's Faustian-inspired adaptation of Mikhail Bulgakov's *The Master and Margarita* (1966), the Hyena has two distinct functions in *Faustus in Africa*. Firstly, according to its creators, 'the hyena reverses the anthropomorphism in the classic sense, so that the fully animal puppet is given identifiably human values and strategies, rather than being the object onto which human behaviour is projected'.[8] Secondly, the Hyena's

78 Undoing Apartheid

mastery of the game of trickery spurs the gullible human towards Mephistopheles' temptations, thereby endowing the object with spirit and vitalism reminiscent of the philosophy of life that emerged around the 1920s in Weimar Germany, the time in which the play is set.[9]

Hidden behind the puppet's crafty wooden smile, a lucrative secret makes for a valuable bargaining chip in associations with those patently compromised by colonial complicity. In keeping with its reputation as a gravedigger, the Hyena unearths a repressed element in the critique of capitalism and colonialism. When the unruly cohort of Mephistopheles draws the servant, Johnston, into an accord, a particular impasse in the interpretation of the Faustian wager is unlocked. Psychic scavenger that he is, the Hyena extracts from Johnston the confession that he wants out of the 'twisting and turning of self-hate', to escape being the servant and shadow to Faustus, and 'to be at the helm of this empire'. Johnston ends up pledging his freedom to the Hyena – if the latter delivers on their promise. The stakes of the Faustian wager are thus doubled by a surrender to a puppet imposter. When Johnston does become emperor, through no direct intervention of the Hyena (who nevertheless takes credit), the empire has been ravaged by war and the earth abandoned by God.

The endpoints of theatre in prophecy and redemption, however, also adjudicate theoretical disagreements about the alteration of subject–object relations instigated by technologically induced shifts in temporality. The theatre allows for theory in motion. The potential for theorizing is further activated by the way theatre allows for the artifice of prosthetic objects to stimulate and provoke audience responses. What distinguishes *Faustus in Africa* is the use of theatrical devices to solicit a response of sense-perception that mimics the haphazard co-evolution of human and technology. Theatre, in this instance, mimics life lived in relation to the external stimuli of objects; and by way of the idea of history calling twice, both as tragedy and farce, activating that which lies repressed in what is ordinarily rendered immaterial. The theatre delays the circuits by which knowledge is routed in the service of capital, making provision for a brief window in which it works to animate the world. What is crucial here is not that theatre feeds some innate need for criticism, often claimed as indispensable for humanistic enquiry, but that the theatre postpones the folding of *techne* into technology by making available the spirit of an age. It is perhaps this yearning or striving for spirit that makes the Faustian legend into a play about the false starts of modernity – from which followed the mayhem of colonialism and the orders of race in an age of capitalist expansion. Inasmuch as the theatre that rehearsed the predicament of modernity recapitulates the function of tragedy as a site of criticism, it admits to a repetition in which a wound is re-inflicted in order that it *might* be healed.

How are we to approach the distinction that Kentridge establishes in relation to Goethe's version of the play, especially the indecision that results from entanglement in the competing impulses of progress and preservation? Goethe's efforts rested on an attempt to find in tragedy the redemptive resources of German Romanticism. Through Kentridge's production, we are better able to grasp the extent to which European Romanticism interpellated Africa, or more precisely, how Europe preserved what remains of Romanticism through its projection of controversies of *Naturphilosophie* onto Africa. What comes to the fore is the difficulty of identifying the devil in the detail, or, as it turns out in a study such as this, the detail in the devil. If trickery and magic are tropes through which an aesthetics opens colonization to more intense scrutiny, we would do well to travel with a figure of European ambivalence, Faust, to the far reaches of the colonial world, where, as Kentridge's Faustus soon discovers, his search for *pure jouissance*, or mindless pleasure, encounters a limit in a specially prepared script of the becoming technical of the human – the very thing he is determined to escape.

Doubling the Wager

When migrated to Africa, Faust is a character torn between colonial speculation and the disappointments of anti-colonial nationalism. A noteworthy example of the translation of the Faustian myth in Africa is Djibril Diop Mambety's *Hyena* (1992), about a wealthy elderly woman, Linguere Ramatou, who bribes and solicits the loyalty of a village in exchange for an agreement to kill Dramaan, a man who denies fathering her child. Here, as elsewhere, the Faustian pact is a means to access the psychopathology of the postcolonial condition torn between

80   Undoing Apartheid

personal survival and loyalty to authoritarian personalities, each
emboldened by the aftermath of colonial rule. The Faustian myth
in this instance is the source of a non-dogmatic reckoning with
the remains of colonial domination and its anti-colonial nationalist shortcomings.

Similarly, when W.E.B. Du Bois viewed a performance of
Goethe's *Faust* in Berlin in the 1890s, he drew from it both
the soul-preserving lesson and a sense of overcoming limits
through striving that together formed the enduring concept of
double consciousness in his *Souls of Black Folk*. For Du Bois,
commerce had fissured the traditional civilizational concept
of race, laying bare an intense struggle against its usage as a
marker of cultivation through the pursuit of knowledge and
a newfound desire to overcome its entrapments. Du Bois's
'double consciousness' referenced the discourses of psychology
of his time while building a link between German Romanticism
and American Transcendentalism.[10] The legend of Faust had
become available to intellectuals who wished to reckon with
the psychic dilemma of race that resulted from the technological
shifts internal to capitalism. Du Bois discovered in the emerging
discourse of race the unresolved paradox of slavery, where long
after its dissolution it continued to exact a toll in the American
South, where the promise of racial integration appeared to have
been failing from the very outset.

Faust's reappearance, especially in the early 1900s in Africa,
coincided with what Donna Jones identifies as the rise of 'life
philosophy' in the aftermath of World War I. Life philosophy
recognized a strand of metaphysical critique of technology
emerging from these ruins in the work of subsequent generations of intellectuals associated with the Negritude movement,
including Aimé Césaire and Léopold Senghor.[11] The promise
of the industrial and scientific revolution upon which liberalism's nineteenth-century speculations of a global modernity
rested lay in tatters after the war. The premonition of a life-
affirming co-evolution of the human and technology that was
the promise of the industrial revolution and abolition of slavery
was rapidly transformed into an all-consuming struggle over
the meaning of a liveable life. Jones's study of 'life philosophy'
describes conditions that produced a shift in attitudes towards
technology and, by extension, colonialism in the first part of
the twentieth century. Césaire, we learn from Jones, 'would

The Return of Faust   *81*

famously and disturbingly proclaim that the putative African failure in technology revealed the existence of an alternative, superior epistemology unforgotten in the course of colonial slavery'. This, Jones tells us, Senghor qualified by pointing out how 'such technological nihilism was itself a product of the rationalization of slaughter in the Great War'.[12] A generation of intellectuals schooled in the arts of reason specific to the faltering promises of scientific reason, not least those in the colonial world, were asked to hedge their bets on a future of freedom. As with S.M. Molema, a distinct tone of gloom can be detected in writing from this period by intellectuals of the Black Atlantic, deepened by the frightening convergence of a discourse of race and an expansion in technological resources, supported by an expanded science that appeared to be overwhelming the human sensorium.

Enter the Devil

The invitation extended by the devil to Faust sets the latter on a journey to rediscover a will to knowledge founded in Romanticism, only this time in Africa. The seemingly inescapable contradictions of modernity set against the backdrop of colonial expansion are presented through a theatrical production about a disillusioned colonial intellectual who foregoes the securities of his study by surrendering to the temptation of earthly pleasures. Unfortunately, he soon finds himself distracted from establishing meaningful human relationships by a demonic trickster.

The plot, we might say, thickens with time. While the Faustian legend, with its forays into the inner individuated psychic contest against external temptations, has retained a degree of consistency over a period of four centuries, the interpretive force of the paradoxes it lays bare has often been mobilized unevenly but productively against the spirit of the age in which it has been performed. It was Goethe's reworking of the Marlowe legend over a period of sixty years that altogether altered the political stakes of its reception.

Sara Munson Deats's historiographic account of the legend points to a concern about the steady trivialization of Marlowe's original rendering of the theatrical work since the late 1500s, when it was first performed.[13] For Deats, this trivialization arises from the way in which Marlowe's version arrived in the nineteenth century, in the form of farcical English and German puppet plays that a young Goethe is said to have encountered. Ultimately, Goethe salvaged the legend of Faust from infantilization through a long process of rescripting that addressed shifting concerns in the transition from the European Middle Ages to the modern. He is widely credited with rescuing the legend from the ridicule that had enveloped the tragic, gullible figure of Faust, who surrenders his fate to the dead ends of necromancy and trickery. Given its prolonged gestation, Goethe's adaptation, like those that followed, appears fragmentary and disjointed to audiences. How could it be otherwise, especially in a theatrical work that offers views about such disparate and contested themes as fate, destiny, ethics and spirit? The Goethean remake confirmed the late-nineteenth-century claim that the legend of Faust had the quality of the Homeric plays, where the unity of the piece only became apparent when looked at from a distance.[14]

This is precisely where it encounters a limit that will be projected onto Europe's colonial ambitions. Goethe's Faust flees the dour pursuit of knowledge which, he presumes, had blocked access to the titillations of leisure that accompanied revolutions in instruments of industrialization. Rather than being rewarded with redemption, the intervening figure of Mephistopheles leads him to an unprecedented and unanticipated discovery of the spirit of the age against which he rails. This hidden kernel amounted to exposing the limits and consequences of German Romanticism's attempts to forestall the drift towards more mechanized forms of life.

In addition to appeals to an emerging proletariat to question a freedom acquired through bonds of blood, Goethe's *Faust* further emphasizes a form of striving by relying on the countervailing sources of Greek tragedy. It is well known that in its early version, German Romanticism inadvertently contested nationalist sentiment by reaching into the aesthetic resources of *Sturm und Drang* (storm and stress). For Goethe, German Romanticism was unfortunately held back by an overriding fidelity to metaphysical foundations in myth. In an attempt to create a union of Romanticism and Greco-Roman classic tradition, Goethe leaned towards a unity of modern and classical conceptions of life.

The Return of Faust   *83*

The impetus to strive beyond the limits of national spirit is presented in a detour that Faust takes via Auerbach's tavern, where the fate awaiting Faust's proletarian lover, Gretchen, is preordained by mourning the loss of the tragic spirit. Gretchen's failure to achieve salvation through piety points to the role of Mephistopheles in prescribing a proletarian fate. The debauched scene into which Faust stumbles when crashing the drinking party brings Goethe's audience face-to-face with circumstances that lead to a thinning of the lifeblood of Germany. Gretchen's demise in Goethe's *Faust* is an allegorical reckoning with the fate of the proletariat consumed by the corrosive consequences of capital. That end courted a dangerous metaphysical gamble that dominated Goethe's late attitude towards German Romanticism and its attendant yearning for a foothold in tragic drama.

To go beyond such diminished subjective conditioning Goethe turns to a Hellenic spirit to augment the erring of German Protestant efforts in an age of the technological displacements of labour. He summons the Trojans through the figure of Helen of Troy to animate German attitudes towards the idea of striving with a sense of the wholeness of nature. Faust's infatuation with Helen of Troy creates room for greater attention to the value of immaterial labour, to reach beyond the storm and stress of blood ties that bind German culture. In a profound sense, the guiding influence of Helen of Troy on Faust ensures that 'he no longer gazes at the stars while his feet are in the mire'.[15] It is not merely an aesthetic teaching to which Helen directs Faust, but an ethical one, iterated through the mutually reinforcing discourses of German Romanticism and Greek tragedy.

German Romanticism encouraged a penchant for the cosmic in *Naturphilosophie* beyond simply grounding itself in the pursuits of aesthetic education. For our purposes, Goethe's *Faust II* repeats themes of myth and technology found in Danby's *Opening of the Sixth Seal* and the satiric Great Moon Hoax (discussed in the previous chapter), by contrasting the mechanistic physics of British natural philosophy and the speculative tendencies of *Naturphilosophie*. We should not be surprised by the coincidence, given that the abolition of the trans-Atlantic slave trade ushered in an era of speculation that paralleled the massive strides taken in the science of astronomy.[16] A paradigm shift was clearly underway in natural philosophy, one that reoriented perspectives about not only nature and the human, but also the human and technology.

Faust II, by all accounts, proved more difficult to complete, possibly because Goethe, like so many of his day, was embattled by the intellectual uncertainty of the early nineteenth century. It is therefore not surprising that Goethe should have turned to the heavens in search of some respite from making sense of the world he inhabited. As Carl Hammer confirms for us, Goethe's interests in astronomy were influenced in large measure by the work of William Herschel (father of John Herschel) and the speculative frontier opened by the astronomical sciences.[17]

The fate that awaited *Faust* as he contemplated and eventually consummated the cosmological endpoints of *Naturphilosophie* is 'an erotics of ascent', to recall Trop's suggestive phrasing.[18] Rather than functioning merely as a discourse or codification of knowledge, Trop invites us to consider *Naturphilosophie* as a grid of knowledge that encourages heterogeneity in the orders of the sensible.[19] Such heterogeneity is in keeping with an undercurrent in *Naturphilosophie* about human striving in an encounter with the finitude of forces of attraction and repulsion. What is thus achieved is the postponement of a redemptive narrative, one that opens the way for a reiteration of the Faustian myth, and knits together the long and often unassuming epistemic inheritance of *Naturphilosophie* from which, subsequently, the discourses of race frequently drew sustenance.

Perhaps the focus on the animation of nature in Faustus also works to stress how Africa was hailed as a site for cosmological and natural adventures. In Goethe's *Faust II*, the 'high mountain gorges of heaven' serve as the backdrop against which the final scene of the play unfolds. Goethe accordingly places his protagonist Faust in the folds of a sublime yet uncertain setting that would also be reinterpreted by Kentridge as the scene of colonial landscape in his version of the play.

If Goethe thought that the Hellenic route was a way of escaping a prevailing European predicament, *Naturphilosophie*'s promise was kept alive in an image of abundant opportunity in a colonized Africa. In signposting a futural and prospective image, Goethe animates his concerns about the demise of the ideal of ennobled labour conveyed in the sad fate of a cellar rat in Auerbach's tavern in Leipzig. In a song about a poisoned rat, Faust is confronted with the frightful epiphany of the 'fall

The Return of Faust   85

of Man' if ever he were to surrender his fate and destiny to Mephistopheles' temptations. It is here, where Goethe saw the threat to German culture as it withdrew into parochial pleasures of a mechanical idea of work, that Marx descended into the depths of a nascent capitalism – into a cellar, that is – to glimpse a future that ought to be steered towards a different end to avoid the hell of an eroded life. It was Marx's reading of a line in Goethe in which we glean the making of a modern concept of race, inflated with later expectations of the vitalism of life philosophy, yet beholden to an image of immaterial labour – a labour of non-material resources of informatics and affect that is for all intents and purposes immeasurable, that seduces as it impoverishes. African regimes of work instituted by colonial force rehearsed these scripts of immaterial labour, which was tantamount to the price paid for an investment in modernity while being denied access to the fruits of that very labour.

A Rat in the Kitchen

In the act of laying out a plan to study the changing conditions of manual labour in an age of expanding industrial technology, Marx appears to have committed to memory a line from Goethe's Faustian drama about the story of a cellar rat in Auerbach's tavern in Leipzig. Preparing notes for his study of capital (later published under the title *Grundrisse*), in a brief entry titled 'Fragment on Machines', he gestures to a chronicle of a death foretold by repeating a pithy line about a cellar rat from Goethe: 'the appropriation of labour by capital confronts the worker in a coarsely sensuous form; capital absorbs labour into itself – "as though its body is by love possessed"'.[20] Marx's preference for this enigmatic phrase as place-keeper for an expanded critique of capital's intrusion into the leisure of the worker can be heard while eavesdropping on a drinking party in Auerbach's tavern. There one of the revellers, Brander, bursts into a song about an ill-fated cellar rat who has grown fat on lard and butter, like Martin Luther, the source of the work ethic that fuelled nineteenth-century Protestantism and capitalism. As the refrain that Marx quotes goes, the rat, upon being poisoned by the cook, becomes sick and convulses with cramps, 'as if love's tortures twinged him'.[21]

86 Undoing Apartheid

Much ink has been spilt in an effort to decipher the full implications of the enigmatic fate of the cellar rat in the nineteenth-century writings of Marx, mostly directed at making sense of the shift from concrete to immaterial labour in the making of late capitalism. An initial condensation in the notes on 'Fragment on Machines', whence the scene of the cellar rat is drawn, provided the critical impulse for tackling speculative shifts of capitalism towards immaterial labour and the incipient communism of the machine in the late twentieth century. As Michael Hardt and Antonio Negri put it, immaterial labour refers to the production of immaterial goods such as a service, a cultural product, knowledge or communication.[22] Between Marx's reflections on machines and contemporary commentators on immaterial labour, a space has opened for considering the changing forms of labour brought about by the expansion of technological resources. However, with the exception of George Caffentzis, few have granted the differential precarities introduced by a capitalism resting on forms of immaterial labour. Likewise, what matters for a reading of Kentridge's rendition of the Faustian wager is the coincidence of Africa's insertion into a European modernity by means of instrumentalities of communication and the dependence of capital on immaterial labour that lays out the consequences of such differential precarities.

From the extract in the *Grundrisse*, and for purposes of the argument here, Marx is especially concerned with the possibility that labour would be deprived of sensuous human activity with the displacements wrought by a greater reliance on industrial technologies. In responding to the sensuous deprivation entailed in folding the worker as subject into the means of production, later critics of capitalism advocated for a category of immaterial labour as a productive site for the reinscription of labour, in anticipation of the conjunctural crisis of postindustrial capitalism. Released from the obligations of physical labour, the worker could be allowed to expend time on intellectual pursuits that benefited humanity as a whole, not unlike the aesthetic pursuits prescribed for Faust.

One crucial interpretation is often downplayed in this ongoing debate about the fleeting but prescient reference from Goethe's play in 'Fragment on Machines'. It relates to the altered conditions of labour that shaped a hermeneutics of suspicion specific

The Return of Faust 87

to the critique of capital on the one hand, and a parallel rise of speculative scientific reasoning that capital absorbed into its own lifecycle on the other.[23] Marx bitterly bemoaned the fact that science was being turned into a business, particularly through the ascendancy of the physical and chemical sciences. The contest was over whether the prosthesis of the machine belonged to the future of the worker or to the future of capital – or perhaps neither. An expansive interpretive space opened by this otherwise pithy phrase from a reveller's repertoire focused attention on the precise consequences for a theory of labour as it transitioned from concrete to increasingly immaterial forms. The cellar of Auerbach's basement tavern was the scene of a crime for which an emergent hermeneutics of suspicion proved indispensable in laying bare the riddle of capital and its relation to colonialism.[24] In fact, the fate of the cellar rat would inadvertently support the critic of capital to hold together a theory of labour and a spirit of criticism that laid bare the fate and destiny of the human in ever-more intense processes of the mechanization of life. This was effectively a script that was being prepared for the colonial world.

Two somewhat counterintuitive ideas of the human and technology present themselves when one rereads 'Fragment on Machines', especially the point at which Marx reflects on the question of unalienated labour. Both themes are identifiable in the image of the poisoned rat culled from Goethe's Faustian pact. The first bears directly upon the fate of the cellar rat, where the dialectical endpoints in the struggle of the human against nature call for a reconfiguration of what can be expected from that which remained of the category of the human. The second relates to immaterial labour, where relations between humans and machines enable what Marx calls 'idle time or time for higher activity': a time not bound by the strictures governing alienated labour relations.

In the first, capital's intrusion into the far reaches of the globe, through the twin processes of colonization and imperialism, can be traced back to a working out of the spirit of capitalism. It is often extended to the process of colonization entailed in Europe's efforts at crafting a world in its own image by taming the forces of nature. In the second, which offers a prognosis of immaterial labour, the expansion of technological temporal objects, particularly in the area of communication machines, leads to a form

88 Undoing Apartheid

of unalienated labour, beyond necessity and approximating a further frontier, in the pursuits of an endlessly deferred desire.

Marx's decision to follow the lead into the cellar depicted in Brander's song about the rat in the Leipzig tavern has been read by David McNally as an allegory for leaving the 'noisy surface of circulation' to enter the 'hidden abode of production'.[25] Given that the fate that awaited the cellar rat follows the scene in which Mephistopheles signs a blood contract with Faust, Mcnally opts to read the former as a sign of capital's appropriation of the labouring body to the point where it possesses (and poisons) that body, resulting in physical convulsions produced by an unseen power. The pact with the devil provides a counter-movement to Plato's ascent from the cave, in which the descent into the basement cellar is likened to an effort on the part of Marx to journey 'from the sphere of form – the value form of labour – to the domain of bodies and of their labours'.[26] What McNally misses, however, is the flicker of the pharmakon in the story of the cellar rat, so that Marx's venture into the cellar implicitly indicates an instantaneous search for an exit from the macabre scene. Lest we forget, the poison is always also, in reverse, the medicine. And at this point, where capital is both the source of the symptom and the antidote, Marx parts company with Goethe because the latter risks being beholden to the sad fate of the cellar rat:

> Once in a cellar lived a rat,
> He feasted there on butter,
> Until his paunch became as fat
> As that of Doctor Luther,
> The cook laid poison for the guest,
> Then was his heart with pangs oppress'd,
> As if his frame love wasted.

Marx's recapitulation of the line from the Brander song in Goethe's version of *Faust* is a circuitous route into the devouring spirit of capitalism founded on the principle of expending effort in order to become expendable. This coincidence can be found in Thomas Kemple's *Reading Marx Writing*, which offers important hints about the aftermath of the rat's death in an enticing analysis of the detour taken by Marx into the cellar, where he discovers a reason to shift direction and change emphasis in the study of capital.[27] In a chapter titled 'Science, Technology and the Cellar

Rat', Kemple assigns Goethe's statement about the sad fate of the rat to a crucial element of Marx's rendering of the problem of capital in relation to the rise of machines of production. Absorbing science and chemistry to its own ends, capital, on this reading, expresses itself as possessed in demonic and crazy ways. The machinery of capital acts out a development that, as Kemple puts it, runs contrary to the direction of the historical road it has been taking.[28] Brander's song, in this account, chimes with the ambience of Marx's writing as he penned his suspicions about the role of science.[29] In a beautifully crafted exposition of how song resonated with notes on the relationship between science and technology, Kemple places Marx among the revellers, where the chorus to Brander's verse is echoed. Listening in to the call and response between Brander and Marx, Kemple shows how the latter would be led to worry about the machinic displacements of capital that threatened to render the worker indistinguishable from the slave: indistinct from 'the artificial, vegetative state' to which the slave had been reduced. Beyond the difference marked by the slave in Marx's notes, the allusion to Goethe invites us to gauge how Marx was tuned into the harmonies and dissonances of his time: into the incommensurability between Faust's dread of the future and Mephistopheles' tempting offers of mindless pleasure when at play in distant fields.

While the first part of 'Fragment on Machines' deals with the subsumption of the worker and the reign of machines, the second, by way of the song of the cellar rat, is distinguished by virtue of a foreboding prognosis that Marx discovers in Auerbach's basement tavern. Kemple amplifies the musical repertoire here, not merely to read Marx writing, but to *hear* Marx reading. Not only does this signal the death knell of labour as we know it, but Marx speculates that the worker is destined for a future of immaterial labour, one for which the speculative horizons of knowledge have prepared the terrain of capital.

Much has been said about how 'Fragment on Machines' operates as a predictive text of that which is to come. That conclusion can indeed be drawn from the tragic structure of the Faustian play from which the allegory of the cellar rat is extracted. What is more crucial is that the shift from living to dead labour, and then to speculations about the rising realms of immaterial labour, produces the conditions for a game of trickery with the ascendancy of machines of communication, especially

90 Undoing Apartheid

those that coincided with the onset of a colonial modernity. It is to this trickery that the figure of Faustus is mobilized in his African sojourn, and which proves to be the recurring nightmare of Auerbach's tavern that accompanies Marx as he plots another future for the worker being enticed into a life of recurrent slavery. Beyond the psychopathology of the raucous revellers and the sad fate of the rat, Marx, as Kemple tells us, is not advocating a life 'of loafing and laziness, of substituting leisure for labour, or an aesthetics of play for an ethic of work'.[30] Marx's project, it turns out, is in favour of a new science and a new technology for human beings to achieve freedom. This will require not an aura of infinite play, but 'the most damned seriousness [and] the most intense exertion'.[31]

More than a sign of the times in which he is writing, Marx undertakes a reading of the battle between the cellar master and the rat that offers a different inflection of Goethe's concern about the revelry at Auerbach's tavern. What Goethe presented as a scene of debauchery, Marx saw as a transformation of idle resources into potential value that would become part of capital's career. To grasp fully his interest in the meaning to be assigned to the poison, Marx would have us know that the proletarian classes were being surrendered to the manufacturers, merchants and bankers who would go on to devour all they could. 'Then', Marx suggests in reference to the European proletariat who would be spared the immediate experience of immateriality (and, as if retracing the sensibility conveyed by Francis Danby's *Opening of the Sixth Seal*), 'the thunder bursts forth, the earth shakes and opens, Historic Destiny arises ...'.[32] The question of immaterial labour raised by the antics in Auerbach's tavern is however left suspended; the racial remains of slavery folded into machines would give rise to a precarious script of immaterial labour that depended on colonial speculation for its outlet.

A Goethean reading of the fate of the cellar rat takes us directly to attitudes towards wasteful idleness and senseless leisure. To redirect this idle resource of wasted energy, Goethe resurrects the Hellenic ideal in which human form and cosmos converge in a poetics of its time. This was a script later perfected under colonialism, in which notions of idleness were folded into a speculative economic activity and distributed across science, religion and metaphysics in the form of immaterial labour. For Marx, by contrast, the scene of the cellar rat's demise in the

The Return of Faust

91

tavern is tantamount to a deceptive plot that awaited both the European proletariat and the colonial subject. Historic destiny was not to be sourced from the throes of the past, but from that which lay ahead, away from Goethe's search for the heroic or redemptive outcome of Hellenism.

Marx insisted that the modern revolution would seek inspiration from its own content. In fact, it would have to define the very content upon which the revolution might come to rest. Writing at the same time he composed his 1851–2 essay 'The Eighteenth Brumaire', before setting out his plans for the study of capital, he demanded a different attitude towards the dead, when he suggests that:

> The social revolution of the nineteenth century cannot draw its poetry from the past, but only from the future. It cannot begin with itself before it has stripped off all superstition in regard to the past. Earlier revolutions required recollections of past world history in order to drug themselves concerning their own content. In order to arrive at its own content the revolution of the nineteenth century must let the dead bury the dead. There the phrase went beyond the content; here the content goes beyond the phrase.[33]

Evidently, Marx rightly predicted the limitations of Goethe's cosmopolitanism, especially, as John Noyes points out, when considered alongside the latter's conflicted aesthetic attitudes towards European colonialism.[34] This, despite the fact that the Faustian wager bears the traces of colonialism through extensions of the debate about labour and value. The story of the death of Gretchen, for example, like that of the cellar rat who dies 'as if a body by love possessed', while expressing Goethe's disdain for the habits of idleness among the German underclasses, could easily be transferred to the distant reaches of the colonial world to signal the death-knell of idleness.[35] The far-reaching implications of repurposing this idleness are spelt out in Goethe's fourth act, in which Faust receives imperial sanction to redeem broad tracts of land for settlement. By seeking a reconciliation between a concept of nature that idealizes the real and realizes the ideal, we come closer to the fulfilment played out as the model of colonialism. If Goethe sought to transform idleness into cultivation – in both senses of the word – Marx saw in idleness an opportunity to remake the world of work and to reclaim the desire for intellectual pursuits.

92 Undoing Apartheid

The critique of colonial domination was wedged in an indecision that bedevilled the critical traditions of nineteenth-century Europe – especially as instruments of communication provided an opportunity for remaking the self and the world in the image of freedom while simultaneously working to extend colonial domination. Far from lagging behind Europe, from the intoxicated vantage-point of Auerbach's tavern, the colonial world was where Europe could replay the failure of its imagination and the destructive path it had set itself in its headlong rush down the route of industrialization. Kentridge shrewdly stages Goethe's idealism in its encounter with the uncanny: Africa appears as the psychic hatch through which Europe seeks to escape the catastrophe it confronts in its struggle to reconnect the human to nature. Stated differently, Africa is the stage onto which Europe projects its fantasy of an aesthetic existence and its elusive desire to escape a slide into mechanized forms of life by a dependence on the immaterial labour of a racialized other.

Resituating Goethe's idealism in what Kentridge calls the 'earthy materialism of colonialism in Africa' substantially revises the implications of the wager with the devil, which is tantamount to letting the cat – or in the case of *Faustus in Africa*, the Hyena – out of the proverbial bag. What Kentridge stumbles upon in his reworking of Goethe is how *techne* has become indispensable for modern subjectivity – a subjectivity that has become entangled in a heightened struggle between the competing claims of nature and technology. More pertinently, he discovers a story that tendentiously reorients our understanding of the idea of race underpinning colonialism and apartheid by locating its intensification in the midst of the competing drives of technology.

Thus alerted to what is pending with the introduction of Handspring's Hyena into the Faustian fray, we are left contemplating the implications of the magical aura that surrounds the spectre of a technological shift in capitalist production as it becomes specifically palpable in the postcolony. This, after all, is where the fantasy of modern capitalism comes to settle. And perhaps it is in the spectre of the elsewhere of Goethe's play, where schemes for some of capital's most audacious tricks are performed, that the image of Africa as what lies ahead aids an uneven spread of a capitalist mode of production. Trop's study of the link between the theatrical production of Faust and *Naturphilosophie* provides a helpful translation of this

The Return of Faust 93

complex shift. Goethe's *Faust I* and *II* endeavour to ground and exceed the emergence of the modern subject through shifts from a sublime experience of tragedy to a reconciliation between human and nature in *Naturphilosophie*.[36] Calling attention to the differentiations underway in a total aesthetic system, Trop reads the normative (the ethical pursuits of knowledge) and extra-normative (the demonic) as they produce a field of attraction and repulsion that redefined the terrain of the mythic. This elaboration of the fractured, yet totalizing, schema assigned to the liberal subject represented by Goethe's *Faust* – one that is both totalizing and self-aggrandizing – helps to explain the mode of striving implicit in justifications of European colonialism.

The fate of the cellar rat is the underbelly of this colonial ambition. With the example of the cellar rat, Marx identifies what would become the conundrum of colonialism: to understand whether it was a discourse of nature or a discourse of technological futurity. Perhaps a nascent aesthetic theory might beg the question of whether something other than the domination of nature structured and defined the intractable drive of colonialism in Africa. What if the commonplace image of capital's global inequality based on consumption and overconsumption masks a Faustian pact that traps the colonial subject in a perpetual cycle of self-referentiality – a myth of a dark continent in exchange for yet another myth of a dark continent? If Africa is the destination towards which the Faustian wager is directed, then the signifier 'Africa' serves as a site where the irresolvable tensions involving the human, nature and technology are deposited.

Transposing *Naturphilosophie* into a colonial setting provides an important interpretive frame for apprehending the significance of Kentridge's *Faustus in Africa*. As a recuperation of the humanistic elements of *Naturphilosophie*, the play struggles to keep the heterogeneous subjects of its enactment grounded in colonialism's 'earthy materiality'. This, as suggested earlier, has much to do with the speculative dynamics etched into the intellectual history of Goethe's time, something often overlooked in critiques of colonialism, even as a tendency towards speculation potentially revises understandings of colonialism in Africa. Adjacent to the Fanonian and Senghorian meditations on colonialism as a psychic event, we may also need to explore how the discourse of *Naturphilosophie* circumscribed the drive towards isolating and disarming foundational racial fictions by means of an aesthetic

94 Undoing Apartheid

intervention. The colonial world, however, was not only where labour was racialized, but also and precisely where racialized labour was immaterialized.

Setting Goethe's *Faust* loose in the far reaches of colonial expansion, exploration and displacement tells us something about the irrepressible epistemic stakes of Europe's African fantasy. Inadvertently, what the most recent instalment of the Faustian myth reveals is not merely 'the earthy materiality of colonialism', but also the form of Europe's speculative view of Africa that was the residue of Romanticism's infusion of *Naturphilosophie*. Beyond the violence of colonial power to divide, separate and exploit Africa and its resources, a more enduring colonial fantasy was being concocted between the lines of Goethe's *Faust*. That fantasy proceeded from a belief that the conquest of nature had been largely accomplished in the Americas and the winding down of Europe's dependence on the institution of slavery.[37] European colonization proceeded from an image of Africa not simply as backward, as commonly assumed, but as a site where infinite experimentation on nature, culture and reason could be undertaken.

Uncanny Returns

Faustus in Africa uncovered the perplexing if unconscious intrusion of myth in political transition, reminding us that overcoming apartheid depended on coming to terms with its monstrous oppression well beyond its requiem. Such imagery punctuated a prolonged process that careered through slavery and colonialism, culminating in the rise of a rapacious and ecologically destructive globalization. To the extent that Kentridge's reworking provides an alternative relay of sense and perception to that prescribed by a European aesthetic debate, the plane of race places aesthetics in direct relation to political rationality. What we discover in Kentridge's focus on *techne* in the modernization of race is the way in which the experience of colonialism was supplemented by forms of immaterial labour. It was the foundation on which the project of petty apartheid later rested. Unravelling this level of the operation of race in relation to the scripts of modernity requires an understanding of the overlapping epistemic, technological and aesthetic folds by

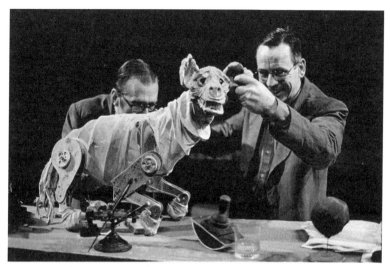

Faustus in Africa (III-8), April 1995. Puppeteers Basil Jones and Adrian Kohler manipulate the Hyena (voiced by Basil Jones). Photo © Ruphin Coudyzer FPPSA.

which the subject became ensnared in an apparatus that emerged in the aftermath of World War II.

To surpass the limits of colonialism and capitalist modernity at the point where apartheid appears as a symptom and supplement, Kentridge introduces the feral Hyena, who literally crashes onto stage when shot at by Faustus. The corrupting presence of the Hyena betrays the ease with which race is deployed as a marker of civilizational cultivation or bourgeois taste. It is significant that in the iteration of the play performed on the eve of the birth of a post-apartheid South Africa, the Hyena is culled from Goethe's avatar of the wild dog – a black poodle that reveals a demonic essence – and transformed into a consort endowed with cunning, and powers of seduction and connivance.

The Hyena appears as the supreme corrupter that feeds off weak intellectual temperaments. When passed through the story of the experience of colonial rule, such a twisted demeanour is put in the service of a technologically driven machine of global capitalism. The Hyena harnesses the corruption of the cast of characters in Goethe's original play, exploiting the unresolved desire conveyed in the unstable convergence of Romanticism and *Naturphilosophie* that underwrote modern capitalism's colonial enterprise. But in Africa it assumed a further dimension of the transfer of the effects of race from slave to machine, in which race is tantamount to being a product of the excitation of the senses by machines – trains, gramophones, cameras – that altered the experience of time and space in the everyday.

In the ensuing chaos, the Hyena beckons us to hyper-sexualized drives, further heightened by the speed of technology that catapults Africa into a future that Europe once feared in its own encounter with unfettered technological progress. In a montage of Faustus and Helen, her body is replaced by the Hyena, in shadow, holding her head on a stick. The Hyena is then pursued by a hyper-masculinist image of a penis on wheels before being violently conjoined to Helen. The Hellenic is thus thoroughly debased by the Hyena's antics.

Effectively, the Hyena condenses an intuition that accompanied the advent of capitalism in which the pain of finitude, as Joseph Lawrence puts it, becomes 'little more than a necessary waystation in the emergence of the Absolute'.[38] For Europe, spirit's reach (*Geist* in German) is thus released from the trepidations and obstacles encountered along the journey. Distinguished from the empiricist tendencies of Newtonianism with which English Romanticism contended, *Naturphilosophie* functioned as an alibi for a later fascination with animism. The reason perhaps resides in how *Naturphilosophie*, according to Susanna Lindberg, allows the philosopher of nature to see the *becoming* of things: not the causal processes that move them externally, but their own internal becoming.[39] Lindberg similarly suggests that the Romantic strand of *Naturphilosophie* welcomed the element of surprise that enabled it to respond by considering the whole of the situation in which such novelty happens.[40] In light of this conceptual inheritance, *Faustus in Africa* engages another tenuous link between *Naturphilosophie* and a later development of *Gestalt* theory in the early twentieth century, implicitly when the ideal of holism brushed up against the psychosocial fragmentation resulting from war and the shocks administered by the discipline of experimental psychology in its study of nerve mechanics.

The Hyena touches a raw nerve in this confluence of the emergent disciplines of the mind and a second wave of mechanization after the war. Placed alongside debates about *Gestaltism* that defined a significant intellectual preoccupation amidst the

The Return of Faust   97

sensory evisceration of World War I, Kentridge productively maps the remnants of *Naturphilosophie* onto the discourse of vitalism and the African experience of the war in the early 1900s. He exploits the fissure running through this inheritance in the encounter with the object of art, much like the Dadaist art movement in the period, to expose the instabilities that belie the idea of race.

Often recognized by the pithy formulation 'the whole is more than the sum of its parts', *Gestalt* theory emerged at the University of Berlin in the first decade of the twentieth century in opposition to the experimental psychology and structuralism of an earlier form of *Gestaltism* forged in Leipzig towards the end of the nineteenth century. The Berlin school, Karen Koehler notes, emphasized the learned aspects of perception, in which 'sensations (which are external) are turned into perceptions (which define the juncture of living being and world, subject and object)'.[41] If this thinking took hold of the holism prevalent in vitalist thinking of the time, what later became known as apartheid could be thought of as derivative of a hopelessly inadequate reading and in fact a fatal misreading of *Gestaltism*. Cryptically put, if apartheid aspired to *Gestalt*, to an image of a whole, petty apartheid was where the triumph over chaos would be secured. In the domain of petty apartheid the neglected parts would be surrendered to the determinations of machinic existence. This appropriation of Wundt's experimental and structuralist consilience of physics and psychology to political ends, much like what had happened when Felix Krueger took over the running of the Leipzig laboratory after 1920, had consequences for both the idea of race and the everyday. The concern of course was that *Gestaltism*, despite its affinity for perceptual wholes, underestimated the sensory innervation in the play of parts. The difficulty was embedded in the experimental apparatus established around the study of perception.

Since apartheid might be thought of as a bad copy of experimental psychology developed in Leipzig, it likewise denied any aspirational element in the relationships between behaviour and learning. In other words, a minor strand of *Gestaltism*, against which a major synthesis was constructed, aided the reconstitution of race that was built on isolating elements of sensations and feelings in consciousness, tautologically expressed through parts that constituted the supposedly lesser realms of

98   Undoing Apartheid

experience. Effectively, it transformed a modern concept of race
into an everyday concept of race. For this branch of *Gestaltism*,
machinic qualities increasingly distinguished human essence.
Anne Harrington argues that the dialectic between a cosmology
of holistic life and mind science on the one hand, and mechanization on the other, seeped into the racialized thinking of
Nazism during the 1930s. Harrington notes that the method
of the Leipzig *Gestaltists* laid the foundations of a metaphoric
transformation of the sources of life among those defined as
Aryan, alongside the castigation of those who were reducible to
mere mechanization. For Nazism, Harrington concludes, the Jew
was the epitome of mechanized existence, a view that tallies with
the racial thinking that undergirded the subject of race which I
discuss in the following chapter. Ultimately, it was a metaphoric
transformation of *Gestalt* theory that gave meaning to the
coincidence of holism and Nazism.[42] Such metaphoric transformation was not only one that produced racialized Others; it
distinguished between those endowed with a capacity of pure
Gestalt for expressing the holism of life, and those racially or
physically marked so as to threaten such coherence because of a
supposedly inherent mechanistic outlook. If, therefore, 'the Jew
and seriously disabled people' were considered 'machine people',
then their existence was clearly not in the service of life.[43]

Trapped between the deductive reasoning of Darwinism and
the inductive method that transformed *Gestalt* cosmology of
holistic and mind science, those marked by a wretched script
of race were left with diminished access to the realms of what
counted as thought and perception. As renowned literary theorist
Abiola Irele would later point out, African renderings of the
question in an era defined by colonial and industrial expansion
contested this pseudo-scientific orthodoxy.[44] For Irele, this shift
in the effort to realign sense and perception was achieved in
movements like Negritude, for example; through a poetic form
that denaturalized race, disrupted the tendencies that treated
it merely as a product of projection, and redirected its critique
towards a fold running through sense and perception.

Kentridge attends to this fold by combining artistic techniques
that include object theatre, puppetry arts, sound installation and
video art that enlarge the frame of aesthetic elements at work
in the aftermath of war. Tantamount to an aesthetic education,
the play reaches towards another life philosophy, one in which

The Return of Faust 99

the *techne* associated with enchantment of objects functions as an unexpected re-enchantment of the story. In this surreptitious rearrangement of techno-aesthetic resources, configurations of tragedy in earlier iterations of the Faustian legacy (Goethe's in particular, where the aesthetic is treated as a necessary supplement to a spiritual striving) are overturned in the interests of mimicking the overconfident aesthetic attitude towards technology in modernity. Since the distinction is so important for what follows, it will help to mark the differences between Kentridge's Faustus and Goethe's *Faust II* more precisely. That difference hinges on the redemptive prospects of the aesthetic: where, in Goethe, freedom resides in a choice between an either/or, in Kentridge, it resides in a neither/nor. Stated differently, for Goethe, freedom lies in striving for an aesthetic fulfilment of an ideal, whereas in Kentridge, aesthetics is itself a striving for a freedom that eludes fulfilment.

In both, the wager that is conveyed through the medium of theatre implicates aesthetics in the tragedy of colonialism, and the contrasting positions taken up in respect of that unfolding tragedy. This is a premise for exploring the choices between knowledge and desire that come with human striving, which knows no bounds. Rummaging like a hyena through the remains of European Enlightenment, German Romanticism, *Naturphilosophie* and *Gestaltism*, Kentridge seems to eschew a polemic about colonialism in order to explore whether the work of art might highlight the thin line separating aesthetic complicity in colonialism and aesthetic indispensability in overcoming coloniality. To this end, he mines a familiar and perhaps overworked thematic of domination and freedom for a cautionary tale about the trappings of colonial excess activated by epistemic and aesthetic desire. The image of burrowing through the traditions of theatrical aesthetics is not dissimilar from the decimation of landscapes through the activity of gold mining that is the iconic motif that runs through Kentridge's works of art.

In Kentridge's hands, the production veers towards the aesthetic in an attempt to retool the senses and to hone perceptions formed around an emerging world picture – both of which are reconstructed from the ruins of race. Faustus permits a glimpse of the threshold between the supposedly old order of, and the presumably emerging attitude to, race, a distinction which had been central to both colonialism and apartheid but

100 Undoing Apartheid

generally overlooked as an inheritance of racialized global modernity. Thus Kentridge's reframing of Goethe's cosmopolitanism, an encounter with the hegemony of science under which aesthetic theory labours, is a source of struggle internal to the work of art.

The Wound

When the Hyena is shot and lands whimpering on the stage, Johnston bandages the wound, announcing, 'There's no bandage/ there's no suture/for the wound of a slashed future'. These ominous remarks continue to haunt the play and its unfinished double wagers. In the end, as the Hyena is about to drag Faustus to hell, Emperor Johnston intervenes to declare a general amnesty, as 'Every villain is part of the resolution'. To those masters of a former empire, he says:

> You, Mephisto, we pardon all your crimes –
> we need your temper for these times.
> Faustus, my one-time master,
> I need you here to plaster
> over the cracks in my new empire.

We are confronted with an ambiguous conclusion, as well as the prospect of a wound that may be covered, but never entirely healed. The despairing endpoints of the Faustian pact with the devil tempt us to journey along the fateful if uncertain endpoints of an aesthetic rendering of the problem of overcoming apartheid. Fighting and defeating apartheid is one thing. Tackling what it dismantled in the dynamic of sense-perception and revitalizing the senses through renewed attention to the object would turn out to be quite another. At the dismal end of the play, the devil remains, and the devil's work remains. *Faustus in Africa* appears to be asking what the options might be when faced with the awakening of uncanny feelings. To grasp the force of its African iteration, we are called to follow the trail of the uncanny in a world ravaged by the plunder of colonial rule. Ultimately, the uncanny resides in the way a memory of race had shifted from subject to machine as classicism was punctuated by the birth of Romanticism and the latter's preoccupation with the slide into mechanized forms of life.

The substitution of sense-making in Kentridge's process of the attempt to eschew polemic deserves to be taken seriously. What we hear in Emperor Johnston's injunction, 'Nobody leaves the room', recalls that which potentially eludes the mastery and excessive and absurd performance of the rituals infatuated with exercising authority at all costs. Much as it wishes to ground colonial excess in the complicities of knowledge and the instruments of scientific discovery and revolution, or in the earthy materiality of colonialism, the assemblage of aesthetic resources tells much about Goethe's failed cosmopolitanism to avert the slide into mechanized life. Like Faust's ascent from his study, and the inner turmoil that defines Faustian striving (*das Streben*), the legend of Faust nevertheless brings us to a conclusion that the work of art may yet point to what is necessary to shape and achieve freedom.

For all intents and purposes, Kentridge's reworking of the script of the Faustian wager suggests that the repurposing of aesthetics to serve science in its hour of greatest need foreclosed possibilities for a viable concept of freedom to be assembled from the resources of immaterial labour.[45] Rather, in its colonial setting, we are witness to a hardening discourse of race which was the product of a process that unfolded with the end of slavery; when Goethe failed in his attempts to summon the Trojans to rescue German Romanticism from the adverse effects of capital's emergence on the national subject. At the core of the Faustian wager, in the lacunae of the end of slavery and the rise of industrial society, the play conveys a subtle warning: dealing with the devil is not merely a game of bluff, but a calling forth of a *techne* that places a heavy burden on the desire for and meaning of freedom embedded in the core of the theatrical rendering of the suffering subject. The proverbial devil remains in our midst. The devil's work is never done. And the excess of race in this devilish inheritance continues to be caught up in the Faustian wager on the path of many returns.

Exit Faustus.

4

Woyzeck and the Secret Life of Apartheid's Things

Philoctetes:
Odysseus, you have taken everything I ever had and was.
The best years of my life, my means of self-defence,
my freedom, the use of my two hands.
Everything that made me my own self,
you've stripped away.
And now you're going to take my second self.
Seamus Heaney, The Cure at Troy

Apartheid's Subjects

In critiques of apartheid, the migrant labour system is seen as metonymic of violence that results from a bifurcated apparatus delineating citizen from subject, while forcing the rural and urban into an uneven relation of forms of governmentality prevalent in late coloniality. Apartheid, by this reckoning, is reminiscent of a model of power derived from forms of indirect rule elsewhere in Africa. Often overlooked in this modular rendering is how a concept of race that had taken hold in the disciplines of the mind around the 1920s functioned to call into being the subject of apartheid. The conundrum of subjectivity found in this disciplinary milieu, beyond the critique of apartheid's grand ambitions and repressive hypothesis, arises starkly

Woyzeck and the Secret Life of Apartheid's Things   *103*

in William Kentridge and the Handspring Puppet Company's staging of *Woyzeck on the Highveld*, a play about a migrant worker and his nemeses: a stripe-suited, pipe-smoking military captain, and a bloated, cocksure medical doctor.

As if to anticipate how apartheid altered the meaning of race, the captain and the migrant worker deliver soliloquies about their different experiences of the monotony and pointless nature of modern life in the mining city of Johannesburg. Both bemoan the seemingly unending and meaningless repertoire of life, albeit to distinctly different ends. The captain, doubting that anything will ever be different, settles on asking God to grant him life's supposedly simple pleasures – figs, melons, good bodies and beautiful voices. We are 'made up of identical parts', the captain muses, wallowing in a self-assured sense of privilege, 'so that everything happens twice'. Woyzeck, the migrant worker, by contrast, asks for the sun to be blown out, so everything can roll around in lust, on and on. 'A sin so fat and wide', he frets, 'stinks enough to send the stars from heaven, on and on and on.'

Woyzeck's sensibilities are clearly coming apart, his command over the tools of his trade further betrayed by a world in which work is increasingly stripped of meaning. He is emblematic of the psychic breach effected by petty apartheid in which the subject is not merely incidental but contrived by disciplinary and bureaucratic means. As he fulfils the tasks of his servitude in slow, rote-learned, repetitive gestures, he responds to the captain's mocking chastisement, rebutting the charge of a lack of virtue, questionable morality and stupidity. The desperation heard in Woyzeck's verbal response is exacerbated by his erratic and confused gestures. Presented with the task of setting the table, he falters, stumbling into a confused choreography as he arranges and rearranges the cutlery and crockery several times without being able to manage the correct settings. Beyond the veneer of morality, virtue and the protocols of bourgeois habit lies a subjectivity whose sensory world has all but collapsed as a result of a sheer mechanization of life that strips individuals of desire, striving and futurity.

Woyzeck on the Highveld challenges the viewer to de-constitute apartheid subjectivity at the point at which the sensorium facilitates a relation to power – better known as the scene of interpellation in Marxist philosophy from the 1960s. The play invites us to ask how we account for Woyzeck's subjectivity,

104   Undoing Apartheid

whose recourse to being a victim of the vagaries of capital
is called into doubt by his complicity in an act of femicide.
It narrates an experience from the perspective of a migrant
worker in the 1950s (a period often historically defined as high
apartheid), who has succumbed to the numbing effects of a
labour system through which his subjectivity is constituted.

The play invites us to look beyond what we already know
about how race functions deterministically to ensure the reproduction of capital. Woyzeck's placement in the circumstances of
apartheid helps to emphasize the concatenation of apartheid and
capital, while raising serious doubt about where to locate the
effects of race in the formation of subjectivity. The play turns
its attention to the mental state of Woyzeck, here stripped by
class and race inequities to make way for the competing claims
of *techne* and technology on the subject. There is something
murderously mundane yet dangerously effective about reading
apartheid at this discreet level of technology because, other than
prefiguring a racial subject, it allows for apprehending race as it
appears to us in mnemotechnic constellations – in this instance,
objects of image-making used for linking memory and mining
– that have a direct bearing on the subject. Rather than engage
in the protocols of a familiar critique of race and class, the play
thereby calls into question the limited horizon of humanism and
historicism in undoing apartheid. To the extent that *Woyzeck
on the Highveld* places before us the implications of the sensory
manipulation of the subject in the everyday, it demands that we
rewrite the scripts of how individuals become subjects under the
aegis of an emergent science of population control. The varying
possibilities for reading the play as a work of criticism notwithstanding, I wish to ask if there is indeed a way to approach
Kentridge's iteration of the nineteenth-century play against
the backdrop of South Africa as telling us something specific
about apartheid's racial subjection. How, for example, do we
hold together conflicting and elliptical tendencies in the scene
of interpellation to apprehend the constitution of the subject of
apartheid?

There appears to be a correspondence between an invisible
element of interpellation in *Woyzeck on the Highveld* and the
search for elusive sources of race in the formation of apartheid.
This has often resulted in competing claims about the meaning of
apartheid. This is a point alluded to, although seldom qualified,

Woyzeck and the Secret Life of Apartheid's Things   *105*

in several historiographical debates. Hermann Giliomee, for example, contends that the latter was not an expression of ideological coherence; nor was its justification derived from German National Socialism, as is often assumed.[1] He argues instead that the justification was mostly derived from the failure of integration in the American South, and the need for an alternative model of decolonization as the winds of change swept through Africa.[2] For Giliomee, ideologues of apartheid were more prone to reference the negative repercussions of the British abolition of slavery at the Cape in 1834 than German National Socialism in order to rationalize segregationist policies. By contrast, Christoph Marx argues that for a leading ideologue such as Verwoerd, ideas of biological notions of race difference may have been rejected on sociological grounds; but they did not preclude drawing inspiration from a mentor at the Leipzig School of Psychology, Adolf Ehrhardt, who focused his studies in the 1930s on typologies and racial stereotyping by applying character types to population collectives.[3]

Ultimately driven by the determination to jettison the notion that apartheid was a product of biological racism, or that racism was reducible to immutable cultural differences, the effort to simply name the problem of apartheid as ideological construct proves to be similarly inadequate to account for the lived experience of race.[4] Where then to locate the force of race in the making of apartheid subjectivity?

Kentridge and the Handspring Puppet Company alert us to a persistent and perverse affective and institutional experience of manipulated life. Through the kinetic prosthesis of the puppet, we are drawn into an encounter with what often remains obscure and unavailable in this experience, beyond references to ideological precedents cultivated through the rise of German fascism, Afrikaner nationalism, or the aftermaths of segregation in the American South. The play asks us to attend to the apartheid of the *senses*, in which race is constellated by means of disciplinary entrapment in the emerging sciences of the mind. There the subject is destined for a near-inescapable and predetermined fate.

If the puppet provides an involuntary response, it is to the extent that it functions both as a signifier for a state of being and an exemplary device through which to observe an anecdotal, everyday enactment of the experience of race. Given

106 Undoing Apartheid

its otherwise uneventful everyday object status, where it moves only when called upon and made to do so, we are drawn to witness, again, how the performative aspect of the scene of inter-pellation approximates the rituals of life under petty apartheid. This is a scene where petty bureaucrats and minor ideological purveyors of technoscientific disciplines summon, command, humiliate and affirm what remains of a subject once state and capital have exacted a pound of flesh. Like the unfairly tainted figure of the puppet in popular politics, a carved and manipu-lated Woyzeck is both subject of and subject to the taunts and mockery of everyday life.

On stage, the puppet amplifies a voice that comes from elsewhere, endowed with a fictive capacity to communicate an unenviable predicament of inner subjective torment. Rather than entrapping the avatar of the subject in the circular causality of interpellation by way of an ideological state apparatus and a disciplinary apparatus respectively, the puppet allows us to access something specific about the relationship of race to the experience of apartheid. It conveys the duality of subjectivity described by Wilhelm Wundt, a founding figurehead of modern psychology, between a subject imposed upon and one equipped with performing psychic causality. The aim is to gauge how the grand and petty articulations of apartheid tracked and predicted the movement and behaviour of the subject by depleting the psychic resources of causality.

Staging a play about a South African migrant worker in the 1950s by referencing a theatrical script conceived in 1836 and 1837 works to defamiliarize understandings of race specific to a local context. According to this reading, the production lends itself to an exploration of the distinct manner in which objects are endowed with a capacity to commandeer the agency of the subject through an infiltration of the sensory apparatus. As an allegorical theatrical inscription, *Woyzeck* is both the name of a symptom of a modern psychic condition and the name of a play inspired by the story of Johann Christian Woyzeck. The latter was an unemployed wigmaker, barber and former soldier in Leipzig, Germany, who confessed to killing his mistress in 1821. On the South African highveld, Woyzeck is transformed into a migrant worker in the mining city of Johannesburg, who reawakens from the nightmare of Franz Woyzeck in Georg Büchner's theatrical work.

Theatres of Subjection

To begin a reflection on what *Woyzeck on the Highveld* tells us about the work of petty apartheid in the constitution of the subject of race, I turn to Judith Butler's example of the workings of power and subjection. Like Butler, drawing on Althusser's model for describing how individuals become subjects, I too wish to ask what is obscured in our understanding of apartheid. Inaugurated by a hail, the scene of interpellation proceeds when a policeman summons a pedestrian with the shout 'Hey! You! Over there.' When the latter responds by turning towards the source from whence the pedestrian is being beckoned, an instance of reflexive recognition establishes a relationship that results in the one being hailed caught in the web of power: transformed from individual to the position of a subject.

Butler reads Althusser's *Ideology and Ideological State Apparatuses* (1970) against a later confessional text, *The Future Lasts Forever* (1993), to reopen reflection on a well-rehearsed scene of hailing. In *The Psychic Life of Power*, she asks, in contrast to Althusser's theorization of the formation of the subject in the act of hailing, how we are to make sense of the instinctive, perhaps automatic, confession to killing his wife, Hélène Rytmann-Legotien, in an act of femicide. Butler recalls specifically 'how [Althusser] rushed into the street calling for the police in order to deliver himself up to the law'.[5] In placing two examples of interpellation alongside each other, she asks under what condition the theological fantasy of the law operates. How, in other words, are we to anticipate the hail as if the prior condition of the law does not exhaustively explain the scene in which a pre-constituted subject recognizes the force of law?

The very condition of interpellation depends on an assumed automatism by which the process of subjectification unfolds – a process best described in terms of a subject who willingly surrenders to the hail by virtue of an automatic reflex activated by a guilty conscience. For Butler, the religious references to the process of hailing in the scene of interpellation produce 'a contestable syntactic conceit' of formulating phrases 'without an immediately assignable subject'.[6] She anticipates the problem of the source of the hail as presupposing a reflexive, automatic response in the subject thus hailed. Against the concession to

108   Undoing Apartheid

the power of law, Butler sets to work on a desire that might offer 'an agency that outruns and counters the conditions of the emergence of the subject in law';[7] or, in Althusser's case, the disciplinary formation of medical science and psychiatry that adjudicated his case. The function of automatic response within which Butler relocates the force of the hail is central to my exploration of apartheid subjectivity, to which I return later.

In an extended discussion of Butler's revision, Étienne Balibar, an indispensable contemporary voice in the critique of neo-racism, finds that the productivity of Althusser's study of ideology lies in 'the dramaturgic model of the political function and political transformation of ideology'.[8] Althusser identified a shift in models of classical and epic theatre towards a theatrical machine in his 1962 essay 'The "Piccolo Teatro": Bertolazzi and Brecht. Notes on a Materialist Theatre'. To lay out what is at stake in the departure proposed by Butler, we should consider three aspects of Balibar's assessment of the revised focus on the performative dynamic of interpellation, which will prove important for how we anticipate the place of *Woyzeck on the Highveld* in constellating apartheid.[9] First, the theatrical machine, according to Balibar, makes 'visible' or 'perceptible' the invisible – ideology's grip on the consciousness of its subjects. Second, it allows for a reflection on inner conflict by virtue of its spatial conversion of the structures of time and the shifting positions it assigns to its heterogeneous subjects – the actors and the spectators – that make it possible to materialize the impossible. Finally, the theatrical machine paves the way for a double installation, whereby, Balibar notes, the spectator is brought into the scene in order for that very scene to intrude into consciousness.

The theatrical apparatus recalls the model of theatrocracy but directs its mnemotechnic tools towards the altered conditions of late capitalism in the aftermath of World War II. In the Althusserian model of interpellation, the voice of authority does not originate from the policeman, but from a source concealed by a 'veiling effect that produces an effect of transcendence'. Balibar notes that 'the concealment of the origin of the voice becomes part of a generic machine, the *Machine*, as it were, that ... set[s] the pattern that everyday interpellations reiterate'.[10] This patterning of everyday life that is the product of a machine – or a technological temporal object – perhaps correlates with the way race is reproduced in the milieu of petty apartheid.

In its Fanonian paraphrasing, where the subject of race is of similar concern, it is a child who says, 'Mother, look, a Black man': a voice that Pierre Macherey suggests cannot conceivably be constituted entirely by way of the consciousness of the child.[11] While we should not permit the singular anecdotal scene to account for the full extent of the experience of race, there is something telling about the scene. Fanon, and later Stuart Hall, each reference the indeterminate quality of the hail in the making of racial subjectivity.[12] Althusser's insistence, according to Hall, on grasping interpellation as a system left something elusive in its wake: a resource that could be either surrendered to domination or acted upon as a transcendent release from tutelage. That this veiled voice of racial hailing is not accompanied by a recognizable or definitive source is not, however, merely an indication of dispersal of authority. Rather, the invisibility of the source of the hail means that the very scene of interpellation has become increasingly difficult to intercept completely, for reasons related to the expansion of technological temporal objects by which power and subjection feed off each other.

Enter *Woyzeck on the Highveld*, this time with an unchanging pained and perplexed expression etched into wood. Harry Woyzeck's highveld experience confronts us with a world that is both familiar and unfamiliar, and over which we are called upon as spectators to exercise ethical and educated judgement. We are on the cusp of the very remaking of modernity's subject. The return, in the dying days of apartheid rule in the early 1990s, to a story made famous by Georg Büchner's *Woyzeck* typifies Balibar's meditation on the work that theatrical machines perform to describe the scene of interpellation – with one noticeable difference. Neither tools of craft nor tools of the senses provide any guarantee that the subject might escape the grip of banalized power. To this extent, the mnemotechnic constellations of theatre potentially lay claim to the role of aesthetics in directing our attention to the technique of apartheid's strategies of subjection.

A parody about the subject in the guise of a puppet and caught in the grip of a bureaucratic and disciplinary apparatus clarifies the shift marked by race when we place Woyzeck alongside Jean-Luc Nancy's reappraisal of the Marxist theorization of commodity fetishism.[13] The puppet draws us closer to understanding the subjective uncertainties on the eve of the industrial revolution, not unlike that at the dawn of post-apartheid

110   Undoing Apartheid

freedom, faced with a slide from alienation to immateriality. This sense of immateriality borne by a subject that is divested of meaning and de-individuated by the subtle enchantments of object life is accentuated when the mysteries of commodity fetishism are manipulated by bureaucratic and disciplinary instruments.

Allow a brief recap of Nancy's 'The Two Secrets of the Fetish' to nudge us to reconsider the conundrum faced by a Woyzeck-like subjectivity. What interests me in the attempts to decipher Woyzeck's de-individuation is the humiliation suffered as object life. At a metacritical level, the decision to recast Woyzeck as a migrant who is subsumed and psychically consumed by the logic of the system of accumulation conveys a familiar experience of alienation. But it is the level at which the play also engages the question of the indistinction between subject and object that is of particular interest here. This level recalls Étienne Balibar's reminder that the subject of ideology in Marx migrates to a discourse about the object of commodity fetishism in *Capital I*.[14]

Incidentally, Nancy also returns to the figure of the puppet to aid his description of the concept of commodity fetishism while registering a shift in the scene of interpellation. He takes us to a well-known place and familiar street scene in Renaissance Italy. There, he stumbles on the spectacle of a preacher who is being ignored by the crowds because everyone is trying to see the marionettes at a nearby puppet show.[15] The preacher, we are told, waves his crucifix as he shouts, '*Ecco il vero Pulcinella!*' The scene that Nancy recounts is meant to relay a theatrical manoeuvre in which the representation of the subject shifts from production to the enchantment of an unrelated and mystical symbol. This is a level of mystification that is not easily available for the kind of scrutiny associated with critical projects of demystifying capital. In fact, it is the enigmatic core lying behind commodity fetishism that confers communicative enchantment, not unlike the technological objects in which memory, consciousness and communication combine to give contemporary capitalism its magical aura. To better grasp the turn to a theatrical work from the 1830s to talk about the subject of race in the 1950s in South Africa, we must return to veiled sources of the hail in a script of the original play written in a Europe haunted by the spectre of the slave.

Büchner's Woyzeck

Georg Büchner, an ailing medical student, dramatist and young revolutionary, turned his attention to a beleaguered subject, one Johann Christian Woyzeck on trial for femicide in 1821. The intrigue of the play related to the determinations assigned to the work of fate in a verdict that ended with execution. Following the playwright's untimely death at the age of twenty-three, the fragments of his *Woyzeck* script, recast as a story of the soldier Franz Woyzeck, resurfaced and were reassembled and published by Karl Emil Franzos. He arranged the text in such a way that the grotesque and tragic aspects of Woyzeck's story received equal treatment – both the act of femicide, and the tragedy of a soldier's desperate life circumstances. This marked the beginning of the script's legendary status, stemming partly from its depictions of the effects of capitalism, the concomitant strides in scientific research, and their combined effects on the psychic life of a proletarian subject.

Büchner shines a light on the forces that brought Woyzeck to commit such a heinous act of violence. Woyzeck's diminished capacities and dehumanization turn his guilt over the murder of his lover, Marie, into an equally painful disclosure, as Sander Gilman puts it, of the power structures that deformed and destroyed his life. Central to this secondary layer of Woyzeck's fate, Gilman adds, was the institution of new scientific medicine.[16] Apparently Büchner modelled the character of Dr Johann Christian August Clarus, an anatomist and surgeon appointed by the courts to determine Woyzeck's mental state, on one of his Griesen teachers, whom he disliked intensely.[17]

Dr Clarus's insistent and humiliating examination of Woyzeck requires careful reappraisal for what it tells us about Büchner's conflicted views of Woyzeck. In retrospect, the text that resulted from Büchner's fragmentary archive not only discloses the productive relation that gives rise to a sense of alienation but also another more repressed level, for which the instrumentality of medical science is summoned as a last-ditch effort to dig up the symptoms of a decaying psyche. The aim therefore is to discover an element of social weakness expressed as uninhibited desire, to see if it might be restored to avail itself of a more stable process of interpellation. Here it is worth recalling the

112 Undoing Apartheid

scene in Büchner where Woyzeck is chastised for 'pissing' in public.

> WOYZECK: What's the matter Doctor?
> DOCTOR: I saw you, Woyzeck. You were pissing in the street, pissing like a dog down the wall – and I'm giving you two groschen a day, and board! It's bad, Woyzeck, bad. The whole world's going completely to the bad; completely.

It is not surprising, then, that a medical doctor trained in anatomy was called upon not only to probe the symptom, but to dig into the unconscious to retrieve a buried psychic causality that activated the course of events. As indicated by the medical doctor in *Woyzeck*, the gesture to a second level of subjection obeys neither the command of the hail nor the surrender to the confession. It has a more sinister constitution, one that takes us back to the illusory subject that Büchner struggles to discover as a point of identification and scorn for what has supposedly gone wrong in its resistance to power's subterfuge.

Sixty years after Büchner's death, a friend of his recalled 'a questionable revolutionary fervour of someone whose political judgements were mercenary of his class position and educational standing':

> Frankly we didn't care for this Georg Büchner. He wore a tall hat, always pushed far back onto his neck, constantly had a distasteful expression like a cat in a thunderstorm, held himself completely apart, had dealings only with a ragged genius fallen on evil days, August Becker (generally referred to as 'red August'). His aloofness was considered arrogance, and he was evidently involved in political agitation and had once or twice let fall revolutionary remarks. It often happened that on our way home from a tavern, we would stop silently in front of his lodgings and give him an ironic cheer: 'Long live Georg Büchner, preserver of the balance of power in Europe and the man who abolished the slave trade.' ... he pretended not to hear the yowling?[18]

Setting aside the small matter of the veracity of an anecdote, this is not a figure one presumes to be cut from the same cloth as a schooled political theorist. Are we to assume that Büchner's ambivalence concerning the great social causes of the day – slave or proletarian – and the diminished figure of Woyzeck obscure

Woyzeck and the Secret Life of Apartheid's Things   *113*

a deeper struggle with identification across hardening social boundaries of class, race and gender? We can never know for sure. However, the taunt in the anecdotal account by Büchner's friend shows a conflicted critic, one torn between an internally divided Europe and a struggle to come to terms with the morally reprehensible legacy of the afterlife of slavery in the world. Perhaps the play should be read as a Dionysian pursuit of a sense of self poised between reason and mental illness, explaining the prolongation of an incomplete drama from the nineteenth century. Against this backdrop, we are better placed to ask what configuration of the object converged to bring about Marie's demise?

Büchner remained suspicious of the verdict of 'maniacal melancholia' – known more commonly today as bipolar disorder – that resulted from Clarus's diagnosis of Woyzeck. He was certainly steadfast in his view that Woyzeck's afflictions were caused by poverty, which had increased exponentially with the sweeping social changes brought about by the industrial revolution. The case was a source of great consternation, especially as it mirrored Büchner's personal state of ill-health, alienation and feelings of betrayal. The unscrupulous, uncaring and destructive Dr Clarus, intent on experimenting on the poor, emerged as a proxy for Büchner's self-diagnosis. The complex identification with Woyzeck warrants consideration.

Ultimately, the playwright discredits a prevailing theory that a lack of protein in the diet of the working classes was a source of widespread depression.[19] Büchner believed that Woyzeck suffered from the social and political disease of poverty rather than simple mental illness. It is not surprising, therefore, that Dr Clarus should be portrayed as a villainous 'scientific buccaneer' living off the rewards and authority of the scientific revolution of his day.

Displacements of Animate Objects

The themes of alienation and technological displacement, much like those found in Goethe's *Faust II*, are pronounced themes in *Woyzeck*. The combined threat of the expansion of technological resources and advances in science that Marx later identified as leading to divesting labour of meaning rooted in *techne*, where

114   Undoing Apartheid

labour is emptied of sensuousness, is a discernible weave in an otherwise disjointed play. Unlike Faust, Woyzeck however has no recourse to God, or the Hellenic, to resolve this conundrum or seek redemption, and therefore no possibility either of escape from his predicament. He is for all intents and purposes a prisoner entirely not by his own choosing.

Beyond individual failings, we are treated to a despair about the national spirit through which the bourgeoisie claimed to have revolutionized the world, only to sacrifice human sentiment on the altar of a disciplinary society. Büchner seemed patently aware that disciplinary instruments of knowledge were proving indispensable and complicit in producing a revised script for the subject of power. This concern must be read against the general tenor of a view that Marx espoused, in which 'the machine does not free the worker from the work, but rather deprives the work itself of content'.[20] An added anxiety about participation in the fledgling public sphere where a newfound spirit of the use of reason differentiated access to a nascent public sphere and its cultural resources was another consideration on the part of Büchner in pouring the final years of his life into the case of Woyzeck.

It is here, under conditions of the immiseration of the worker and a society that allowed the evisceration of the senses of the underclasses, that the spectre of the slave could be found wandering the alleyways of critical thought, into cellars and basements of the taverns frequented by the working poor. If the overall characterization of Woyzeck is reduced to what Marx later referred to as a condition of the worker in 'a degraded and vegetative state', the analogous subjectivity of the worker was becoming equally, yet unpredictably, explicit. The worker, in other words, was threatened with a descent into the degraded status of the slave. Stephen Dowden, for example, notes that Woyzeck's disenfranchisement was hardly less than that of a slave, so that it might be possible to think of the worker similarly as a 'spiritual cousin' to that most radically disenfranchised group – African slaves.[21] Such sweeping statements tend to overstate political claims on the basis of verisimilitude; that is, a conflation of the form of the theatre with history. Perhaps, another way to view this coincidence between slave and proletarian in theatrical works of the time is along the grain of the scene of interpellation.

Woyzeck and the Secret Life of Apartheid's Things   *115*

The idea was not simply a matter of invoking slavery as a metaphor for the condition of the working class, even as a notion of wage-slavery to denote the circumstances of the nineteenth-century proletarian proliferated. The distinction between wage-slavery, that is industrial workers, and slavery was critical for a theory that held onto the worker as signifier for the entrenchment of relations of production centred on the commodity form. Productive relations were critical to a process in which appearances and metaphors mixed, where the worker resembled a slave for purposes of adjectivally describing the ravages of capitalist expansion. The work that the slave performs here is heuristic – a veil for capitalism's emergence and its processes of extraction of surplus value, the proper analysis of which a mere substitution of terms will prove to be inadequate. Thus, Marx suggests that slavery has little to do with race as such, but with the productive forces that relate slavery to newer conceptions of race.

> 'What is a Negro [*sic*] slave? A man of the Black race?' The one explanation is worthy of the other. A Negro is a Negro. Only under certain conditions does he become a slave. A cotton-spinning machine is a machine for spinning cotton. Only under certain conditions does it become capital. Torn away from these conditions, it is as little capital as gold is itself money, or sugar is the price of sugar.[22]

What strikes one immediately is the misstep in this excerpt between the signifiers slave and race that leads Marx's concept of the objectification of labour along the passage to capital. We need to find in this misstep the critical space opened up – by Du Bois, Stuart Hall, Kwame Anthony Appiah for example – where race might be understood as a free-floating slippery signifier in a discursive field whose effects remain to be undone. Such missteps in Marx may have been the result of haste to dispense with that which had passed in the institution of slavery in his day. As Fredric Jameson has shown, by the time Marx enters the 'most astonishing' figural development in the emergence of capital, namely the rise of the commodity form, he has shed the Hegelian master–slave dialectic. In other words, the slave is no longer symbolic of a regime of labour, but of displacement. The 'recognition scene' in which the slave aspires to the condition of the master is replaced with new transformations of inert things into

Undoing Apartheid

commodities – where things come alive. Notwithstanding Marx's hasty departure from the question of slavery, Jameson usefully holds onto the image of the slave in this transformation in a manner that helps us to see what transferences between subject and object are underway in the rise of the commodity form. The evocative example from Marx that Jameson rephrases is worth recalling in full, because it dispenses with the contingency in the struggle for recognition entailed in the master–slave dialectic. Jameson permits a figurative relocation of the central struggle for recognition to the domain of objects expressed as relations:

> [B]ut rather that in which – as in the magical toy-shop – the inert things, now commodities, come alive, the table changing 'into a thing which transcends sensuousness ... it not only stands with its feet on the ground, but, in relation to all other commodities, it stands on its head, and evolves out of its wooden brain grotesque ideas, far more wonderful than if it were to begin dancing of its own free will.' It does not yet dance however ...; rather, now that human *Träger* have been removed and their human properties transferred to the hitherto inert commodities themselves, these last begin to examine each other, to exchange looks, and to develop precisely those human relationships to which they now have a right and which their human accomplices have now forfeited.[23]

The intrigue relates to the discussion of the displacement and transference of human traits into the enigmatic core of the commodity. Of specific interest is how the redefinition of value elaborated in the metaphor of the table foregrounds what had shifted in disciplinary attitudes towards subjectivity, especially in the emergent disciplines of the mind. Most notably, the latter attempted to redirect an aspect of the thingness out of which objects are related to consciousness by way of a study of apperception. Apperception, we recall, related to the study of consciousness devised by Wundt in the late 1800s and early 1900s whereby the intensity of a sensation was correlated to clarity of perception. In contrast to a structure of perception, which ran along the lines of stages of development of culture, and which Wundt outlined in the ten volumes of *Elements of Folk Psychology* published in 1920, the study of apperception depended on recording the effects of elementary stimuli to the senses – shock, empathy, anxiety – to produce a measure of psychological resilience and vulnerability. Both elements of the

Woyzeck and the Secret Life of Apartheid's Things   *117*

study of consciousness appeared to have left an impression on a young Hendrik Verwoerd's understanding of the predicament of race in South Africa as he retreated to Wundt's laboratory in the 1920s – a point to which I shall return later.

Known for 'an anticipatory system of the grand scale', Wundt's expansive psychological studies are too detailed to comprehensively summarize here.[24] For the purposes of this argument, what is crucial is that his work allows us to ascertain what was later going on in the space of petty apartheid, particularly how sensation was taken up discursively to mediate between physical and psychic worlds, and how the instinctive and disorderly character of sensations was brought into the ambit of communication and control. Wundt's interests in the mechanics of the nervous system, insofar as its traces can be found in the exercise of petty apartheid, provide us with a subject that is less biological than it is one configured as live-wire circuitry.

For now, the turn to the object as a stimulus of an apperceptive schema, as Bill Brown suggests, tends to be the trivial things of everyday life, stripped of use and exchange value.[25] If an example of such triviality is sought closer to home, consider the pencil test, conducted to determine racial belonging, prescribed by the 1950 Population Registration Act.[26] Based on whether a pencil dropped out of someone's hair or remained attached, it attempted to trivialize the experience of racial feeling, while serving as a humiliating aspect of a bureaucratic procedure to establish racial designation. Setting aside the absurdity of the procedures of apartheid, such emptied and revitalized objects – those that fail the classic definition given to a commodity but nevertheless retain an ability to communicate and stir emotional responses – raise questions about the meaning we give to this lesser condition of subjection, particularly for how it reorganizes our views about race. What, in other words, are we to make of the use of a pencil to reveal an emotional and tyrannical quotient in the determination of racial subjectivity in South Africa? Might this, for example, explain the misstep that Marx makes between the signifiers 'slave' and 'race'? With Jameson's rereading of Marx's theory of the commodity, we can roughly tabulate a difference between the signifiers 'slave' and 'race' that will prove necessary for unlocking a key distinction in our understanding of apartheid. Jameson identifies how the *absent-present* figure of the slave is revealed in the fetish of the commodity form. This

118 Undoing Apartheid

is a form of objectification that has been absorbed as a sign of value intrinsic to the commodity. In the process of the iteration entailed in such objectification, however, the racial excess of the slave is irreducible to commodification, but retains a capacity to bind subject and object on a distinctly different plane. This is a form of objectification premised on the idea of race not lodged in the commodity *per se*, but in the association that builds between a de-individuated subject and the trivial things in everyday life.

If petty apartheid is the working out of this bifurcated legacy between de-individuated subjects and trivial things, Woyzeck the puppet is a site where this distinction is fully revealed: first through relating the slave to the quality of objectification associated with the commodity; and second, by finding in race a point for the excitation of the nervous system through trivial things endowed with the capacity to communicate and humiliate – where objects lay claim to the subject.

Neither Saint nor Sinner

Büchner seems to have gathered that something in the conception of the object had shifted with the alteration in the conditions of the subject. This was borne out by the interchangeability of the experiences of Woyzeck and Büchner's own circumstances as student, writer and revolutionary thinker. Woyzeck, as theatrical subject, provides a narrative frame for an impasse that pits psychic causality against a disciplinary mechanism, where aesthetics is invoked to plot an escape from an irreducible and preordained fate. In the guise of a puppet in its more recent staging, we meet a subaltern subject who falters as the psychic gaps of vulnerable subjectivity are exposed, and is subsequently sustained through the manipulation by an apparatus of power. The puppet recalls not only the recognition of power, but a doubling that is acted out as a desire for the disavowed object. Everything, as the captain says, 'happens twice', to which Woyzeck replies, 'on and on and on'. Herein, we might find an elaboration of an earlier proposition that apartheid happens twice: as both grand and petty apartheid, with the second instituting a circular causality mediated by mnemotechnic instrumentalities. As we gather from the play, these are the very instrumentalities used to prop up the subject of race in the midst of psychic despair.

1 Nelson Mandela delivers his first public speech in twenty-seven years, on the day of his release. City Hall, Grand Parade, Cape Town, 11 February 1990. Photo by Chris Ledochowski.

2 Ubu (Dawid Minnaar) confers with his 'Dogs of War' prior to a night outing. (Puppeteer, Mongi Nthombeni at right).
Photo by Murdo Macleod.

3 Francis Danby, *The Opening of the Sixth Seal*, 1828.
Courtesy of the National Gallery of Ireland.

4 The Great Moon Hoax, *The New York Sun*, 1835.
Courtesy of the Library of Congress, Washington, DC.

8 *Woyzeck on the Highveld* (17) – February 2008. Woyzeck (manipulated and voiced by Louis Seboko) speaks to Maria (manipulated and voiced by Busisiwe Zokufa).
Photo © Ruphin Coudyzer FPPSA.

9 *Woyzeck on the Highveld* (35) – February 2008. Woyzeck (manipulated Adrian Kohler, assisted and voiced by Louis Seboko) speaks about his Child (head at lower right of image) with Maria looking on (manipulated and voiced by Busisiwe Zokufa).
Photo © Ruphin Coudyzer FPPSA.

10 *Woyzeck on the Highveld*, February 2008. The Doctor (manipulated by Adrian Kohler) peers into Woyzeck's brain (manipulated by Louis Seboko). Photo by John Hodgkiss, courtesy of Adrian Kholer.

11 Ranschburg memory apparatus.
Courtesy of the University of Toronto.

12 *Woyzeck on the Highveld*, 1992 (35) – February 2008. Woyzeck (manipulated by Adrian Kohler) gazes at the night sky (animation by William Kentridge). Photo © Ruphin Coudyzer FPPSA.

13 *Ubu and the Truth Commission*, Edinburgh Festival, 2014. Testimony at the Truth Commission. Puppets manipulated by Mongi Nthombeni at left and Mandiseli Maseti at right.
Photo by Murdo Mcleo.

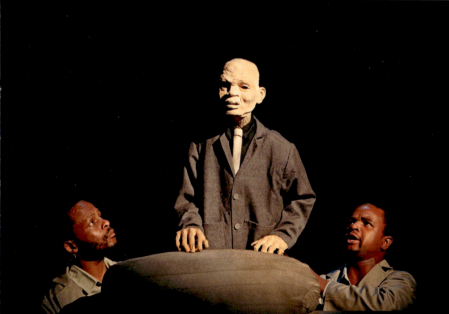

16 Ubu with the spiral, Edinburgh Festival, 2014.
Photo by Murdo MacLeod.

18 Trojan Horse Memorial, Thornton Road, Athlone, Cape Town.
Photo by Paul Grendon, courtesy of Tina Smith.

19 Juliette Franciscus (glancing over her shoulder), Karen Britten, Sean Stockenstroom: Belgravia High Students on the corner of Thornton and Kromboom Roads, 1985. Photo by David Hartman.

20 Willie Bester's *Trojan Horse III*.
Courtesy of Bowman Sculpture.

21 Sculpture in memory of Coline Williams and Robert Waterwitch, Athlone.
Photo by Paul Grendon, courtesy of Tina Smith.

Woyzeck and the Secret Life of Apartheid's Things   *119*

It is not only the law that prescribes the subject's fate. In the case of the theatrical figure of Woyzeck, the apparatus of the discipline of medicine envelops a confessional subject in a manner that discloses the ultimate authority towards which guilt is directed. At the other end, judgement over the confession to Marie's femicide is spread across a spectrum of meanings assigned to the apparatus of power that historically mediates the crime. Büchner's query is whether it is possible to contemplate psychic agency when the subject is so completely stripped of any semblance of individuation. Yet Woyzeck remains trapped between the law and the disciplinary formations of knowledge, as both vie to exercise a hold over his subjectivity. In the final analysis, the event from which the theatrical script was drawn ends with indecision. Adaptations of the play end either with Woyzeck's suicide (attributed to his 'losing his head') or with the state exercising its monopoly over violence by executing him.[27] Refusing the role of arbiter, tragedy sets out to reaffirm the psychic self of a subject in the throes of de-individuation to contest the claims made by medical science and law to script the fate of Woyzeck in his absence.

James Crighton argues perceptively that Woyzeck is a subject scarred both by the technological revolution of the nineteenth century, and also a new disciplinary science invented to sufficiently maintain the psychic well-being for the ends of alienated labour.[28] Beyond that inevitable outcome, under the scrutiny of medical science, Woyzeck emerges as irredeemable by the standards set out in the redemptive ideals of tragedy to which the likes of Goethe appealed. Büchner was well-placed as a medical student to recognize the enclosures forming around the subject under conditions of enveloping technologies and disciplinary formations with which he himself had grown disillusioned. But as a revolutionary thinker committed to a notion of subjective freedom, he turned his attention to the sad fate lodged in the tragic consequences of psychic causality that were entirely not of his own making. In the end, he appears to be entertaining a depiction of Woyzeck's confession of guilt that directly implicates the disciplinary apparatus feasting on his wretched condition. How, if at all, is an eviscerated subject recognized as having a psychic life capable of the egregious act of femicide? The struggle here is one that prolongs the agony, if only so that we might grasp the investments of power in the psychic life of a

120 Undoing Apartheid

degraded subject such as Woyzeck. By this account, Woyzeck is neither saint nor sinner, but a subject who is the incarnation of the mystification that abounds when animate objects wielded by disciplinary and bureaucratic instrumentalities lay claim to the subject.

A framework of conflicting interpellations (cf. Mowitt) opens up the difficulty that Büchner would have experienced in preparing his Woyzeck script. Much like the slave experience of violence across the Middle Passage, Büchner has to reckon with the undisclosed trauma of the passage in the scene of interpellation, from 'Hey you!' to 'Over there'. It is important to mark the interstitial space between the two utterances, a space where we might apprehend petty apartheid in its functioning, and where the mediations necessary for interpellating the subject prevail. If for Büchner, this is a space mediated by discipline and bureaucracy, for Kentridge it is mediated by technological displacements of labour for which the puppet serves as an exemplary prosthetic device. In both, we discover a biopolitics that is less biological than machinic, where the subject acts as a live-wire and where the frequencies linking and delinking sense and perception can be interrupted and redirected. Through the medium of the puppet and the transformation of Woyzeck into a degraded subject in the role of a migrant worker, the interest in the automatic reflex (cf. Butler) and live-wire technology (cf. Massumi) is sufficient reason to suspect that apartheid was more than a mere replica of a colonial modality of power. We might deduce that *Woyzeck on the Highveld* falls upon a scene where race is the product of the shuttling between subject and object, hailed to and from by an apparatus of communication and control to produce a feeling of utter bewilderment.

As in Büchner's *Woyzeck*, the arrival of a migrant worker in *Woyzeck on the Highveld*, mired in a world of diminishing subjective choices and proliferating commodities, conjures a subject in the throes of psychic exhaustion and sensory depletion. Yet it would be tragic to waste as powerful and enduring a figure as Woyzeck as a mere reminder that capitalism can be a draining experience. Rather, the figure of Woyzeck leads us to the trappings of speculative wandering in a networked system of capitalism in search of ways to keep the subject barely ticking over. Perhaps the casting of Woyzeck in the nineteenth century, like the slave whom he will replace in the orders of downtrodden

Woyzeck and the Secret Life of Apartheid's Things   *121*

and diminished subjectivities, is constituted as subject and object simultaneously in a model specific to industrial capitalism. The problem is not entirely new when considered in relation to the longstanding traditions of critical theory that accompanied the birth of modern capitalism. Yet it bears repeating, especially in the light of how race in the twenty-first century is proving to be the exacting condition that connects immaterial labour to networked capitalism.

The rapid expansion of the means of communication has firmly established the division between the technological and the cultural in the ambit of critical theory. The puppet in *Woyzeck on the Highveld* pegs the worker to the effects of industrialization, only to forestall the latter's descent into the uncanny valley of indistinction with machinic existence. It achieves this by restoring a gesture otherwise obscured by new technologies and endowing the puppet with the illusion of breath. This, as Ute Holl says, is the point at which sense organs touch technology.[29] As a bearer of sentience, the puppet reconfigures the meaning of interpellation in an age of vastly expanded resources of communication. As Woyzeck performs the role of an increasingly desensitized subject at the mercy of capitalism, and his pathways to personal redemption for the violence that ensues are closed, the puppet invites us to breathe life into an otherwise lifeless object. It effectively prolongs the fate awaiting instrumentalized life.

More crucially, the puppet animates the meeting of seemingly discordant figurations of the object and subject in the process of interpellation. The first relates to the manner in which the scene of interpellation is the result of the subject's drift towards the authority invested in an object. The second relates to the longstanding scientific principle dating back to John Herschel's *Preliminary Discourse*, which stressed the force exerted by an inanimate object as integral to the understanding of causality, much like the function of a coiled spring.[30] Both would have consequences for contests over naming the political subject of modernity in terms of its responsiveness and responsibility towards technological objects, and for our purposes, to make sense of the chaotic character of the operation of apartheid in the everyday.

Taking our cue from Büchner, we might find a different rendering of the political stakes involved in undoing apartheid. It

122 Undoing Apartheid

certainly revises the growing concern about the depoliticization of the play that David Richards has identified in the controversy surrounding Büchner as playwright. Accused by some of betraying his conviction of the need to change the conditions of the common people by opting to flee political persecution, later iterations of the work sought to repoliticize Büchner's attitude to the working classes, emphasizing his disdain for the intellectual and cruel representatives of the bourgeois ruling class who had distanced themselves from life and humanity.[31] Unfortunately, the calculations of Büchner's political commitments ceded the figure of Woyzeck to the needs of an elementary tragedy that engulfs the subject under fascism. Under Nazism, Woyzeck emerged as a representative figure of cosmic suffering, akin to what Richards calls a 'naturalistic tragedy'. He is claimed as the vulnerable subject in whom we discover a 'loss of security of inner life'.[32] How then to receive Woyzeck the migrant labourer on the highveld at the height of apartheid, without surrendering his subjectivity to the dictates of apartheid?

Woyzeck in South Africa

The incarnation of Woyzeck as a migrant worker on the Johannesburg goldfields discloses the dilemma of understanding apartheid's appropriation of the signifier of race that accords with Büchner's earlier interventions about proletarian life. In its South African iteration, the elementary aspects of oppression and exploitation are folded into a performative contradiction. We are faced with a subject ostensibly stripped of meaning, and who is given a lease on life via the animated kinetic instrumentality of a puppet. In short, we are in the presence of the uncanny return of a form of subjectivity that is not merely a product of capital, but also object life. In the space opened by Büchner for permitting varied and contradictory appearances of such a humiliated being, Kentridge and Handspring reconsider the meaning of the object under apartheid through the performativity of the puppet: which reopens the critique of apartheid, beyond the prescriptions of nationalist historiography.[33]

The theatrical deployment of the puppet to provoke sensory responses tells another story about how consciousness was regulated by mnemotechnic technologies that recall, communicate

Woyzeck and the Secret Life of Apartheid's Things   *123*

and record. The puppet complicates our understanding of the making of apartheid subjectivity. It reminds us that the commensurate effects of trivial objects from everyday life tend to be underestimated when the subject of apartheid is believed to be a product of a preordained ideological script only. In the act of its manipulation, the puppet discloses how race functions as a slippery signifier. We are invited to encounter debates about the crafting of apartheid subjectivity by way of the technologies at its disposal.[34] If apartheid leaves us with the impression that it is the result of a series of false starts, *Woyzeck on the Highveld* highlights the extent to which its operation relates to the faltering disciplinary formations of experimental psychology inaugurated by Wilhelm Wundt in Germany in the 1900s (and first discussed in Chapters 1 and 2).

As an intellectual formation spawned by a second wave of industrial capitalism, experimental psychology turned its attention to a distinct level of the fetish object – the secret core that generally eluded processes of disciplinary demystification. It was this core that experimental psychology attempted to capture in the late nineteenth and early twentieth centuries, mainly through the laboratory in Leipzig established by Wundt, and replicated at the University of Stellenbosch in 1917, where one of the later leading proponents of the idea of apartheid, Hendrik Verwoerd, was schooled.[35] By gaining access to transactions between sense and perception, or in developments of ethno-psychology and techno-psychology, the strand of apartheid thinking most closely linked to 'native administration' infiltrated a communicative aspect of the fetish object. Cryptically put, apartheid was more than a product of the dialectic of epidermal-ization or lactification in the sense that Fanon outlines when he opposes the reductionism evident in post-World War II critiques of race.

Apartheid's modality for constituting subjects is perhaps best thought of as an early precursor to the neoliberal strategy of a post-World War II racial order. It represented a cobbled-together form of practical reasoning aimed at reconstituting a society of control through combining a pre-war rise of experimental psychology, the remains of a shattered liberal pluralism, and a labour regime that infiltrated the sensory networks – what Jean-Luc Nancy calls the second level of the secret of the fetish object. In short, the interpellation of apartheid's subject ought to

124 Undoing Apartheid

focus on the role of petty apartheid. In analyses of apartheid, the experience of petty apartheid is often subordinated to the infrastructural ideological state apparatus that presumably became its most recognizable point of mystification. I believe this to be a fundamental error of political judgement, one that upon realization foregrounds the need for an education of the senses in the wake of apartheid's intrusive psychic consequences. Petty apartheid, with its Immorality Acts, restrictions on leisure, and curtailments of mobility were efforts aimed at wearing out the subject. It amounted to a massively intrusive mode of governmentality that reached into the connective tissue of subjective desire; it continues to undermine efforts to escape the stranglehold of race.

Woyzeck's depleted subjectivity is symptomatic of the experience of labour under the migrant labour system that became integral to various sectors of the Southern African economy, especially in the late-nineteenth-century mineral revolution; and particularly with the political ascendancy of Verwoerd, who became Minister of Native Affairs in 1952, four years after apartheid's formation as a state project. The fact that South Africa's Woyzeck is cast against the backdrop of the highveld in the 1950s makes this connection particularly noteworthy. Demystifying race at the level of political economy, while analytically critical in the fight against state power and racism, has tended to downplay debates about the psychic consequences of processes of objectification underway in political projects sustained through a racial division of labour. *Woyzeck on the Highveld* confronts this oversight in light of the prospects for post-apartheid subjectivity.

Apartheid presents a bigger problem than is often assumed because it infiltrates the very indeterminacy of the essence of the object in which a displaced desire resides. *Woyzeck on the Highveld* asks that we search elsewhere for the source of the lingering problem of race in the experience of apartheid; that is, in the effort of its disciplinary apparatus to infiltrate the secret core of the fetish object that was initially disavowed in the critical work of demystifying the ideological basis of capital.

To this extent, apartheid subjectivity is not merely alienated labour, but a form of racial capture of desire that has the subject *hanging-by-a-thread*.[36] Apartheid strips desire, not only by mobilizing race to its ends, but by endlessly identifying the secret kernel of the object as a way to garner expressions of race. By interiorizing subjection, and externally controlling and manipulating the sources of stimulation, a residual consciousness retreats in search of an elusive inner core. In this way, the subject reveals its innermost desire upon which power in turn acts. Apartheid mobilized a trick of subjection by design while making the subject responsible for its own redemption. What it hoped to achieve was to make race a matter of an endless pursuit: a self-perpetuating mythology that repeated with every movement the desire it communicated.

'One thing after another', laments Woyzeck after his spirit is depleted at the hands of nemeses who together empty his sense of self by constantly probing his mental state. He cannot sleep. Everything is turning, and he is plagued by a voice from the ground. As Woyzeck spirals out of control, the sources of his symptoms are there for all to see. Woyzeck reaches this conclusion fleetingly by failing to resist the elliptical modality of power and control to which he is subjected. To comprehend apartheid along these lines, we should approach its rationality in the tricks it performs on the apparatus of sense-perception. The tendency to suspect apartheid of trickery should not be passed over as merely a sign of its myth-making. Apartheid attacked the very desire of the subject while tricking the senses into believing in an aspect of self-representation. Ironically, despite all its Calvinist and technocratic verbiage, its potency rests with the game it plays as a devil's advocate.

Between buffoonery and its consequences, the politics of ridicule aimed at the doctor and the captain fails to adequately account for the evisceration of desire on the part of Woyzeck. This problem also applies to anti-apartheid representations of Verwoerd. Stanley Uys, for example, in the pages of *South African Outlook* in 1959 depicts Verwoerd as someone who is part buffoon and part vindictive bureaucrat, like the composite image of the doctor and the captain in the Kentridge and Handspring production. Uys paints a picture of a man of excess, so that when one writes about him, 'one is afflicted with his verbosity'.[37] His political programme, according to Uys, is best summed up in a poem by Anthony Delius:

But words, like alcohol with other men,
Are his compulsion, theories, words, and schemes,
Poured in dull rivers from his tongue and pen

126 Undoing Apartheid

To sail his paper argosies of dreams . . .
Statistics, numbers, races fill his vision,
Ransacked from Europe, Africa and Asia
And patched together with a schooled precision
To form a bold, methodical fantasia,
His Hundred Year Design,
His Master Plan,
To keep the Neths the masters – and their clan.

Anthony Delius, 'Judgment Day'

Verwoerd's incoherence attests to the mindless repetition endured by Woyzeck at the hands of his overseers. Apartheid, like Verwoerd, could only be experienced as interminable. This, however, is not mere coincidence. It goes to the very heart of what we understand, and what we seemingly do not understand, about apartheid.

In contrast to the politics of ridicule, there have been several scholarly attempts to connect Verwoerd the scholar and Verwoerd the Minister of Native Affairs, and later Prime Minister, responsible for the shaping of apartheid power (as alluded to in Chapter 1). Roberta Balstad Miller, for example, questions the emphasis on consistency between the academic and administrative aspects of Verwoerd's life, while suggesting that insufficient attention is paid to his early career in critical assessments of the rise of apartheid.[38] As Miller suggests, the relationship between scholar and administrator, while tenuous, should not be underestimated. She too notes Verwoerd's training in a laboratory at Stellenbosch University modelled on the experimental psychology laboratory established by Wilhelm Wundt at Leipzig University. Later, in 1926, as a postdoctoral fellow in Leipzig, he honed his writing and experimental skills when given the opportunity to work on Piorkowski's 'Attention- and Fatigue-meter'. On his return to South Africa, he took up an academic position as Professor of Applied Psychology and Psychotechnics at Stellenbosch University. According to Miller, the term psychotechnics was used at the time to describe applied individual psychology topics such as vocational and industrial psychology, and child guidance and juvenile delin-quency.[39] On the other hand, there was also the Verwoerd of incessant speeches, consisting of curious parables, with which he addressed vast *indabas* (meetings of ethnic authorities), so displaying exaggerated claims to expertise.

The convergences of intellectual and administrator should also not be underestimated in the individuated and infrastructural consequences of processes that reshaped ideas of race. The birth of the discipline of psychology in the first half of the twentieth century implicitly records such reshaping in the attention given to shifting relationships of individual to community collective that derived from changing regimes of work and the expansion of communication technologies.

This certainly applied to Verwoerd as laboratory technician. Miller notes that Verwoerd's intellectual formation was drawn from myriad sources. Training in Leipzig was supplemented by his enthusiastic response to developments in American social sciences, not least in the social sciences forged in the aftermath of the Great Depression. His thinking merged with what became commonly referred to in the US as the age of 'social engineering', a phrase he encountered on a visit to the US, and which resonated with his own views about how to address the so-called poor-white problem in South Africa. Miller suggests that this perspective was aided by forays into sociology while Verwoed was at Stellenbosch University; although she also notes that he was not entirely convinced by the discipline, and only partly applied some of the terms derived from the American example in this respect.[40] Verwoerd, we are told, was not an advocate of biological racism, leaving further room to ponder the strands that made up his attitude to race. Finally, we learn that Verwoerd's disavowal of race as biological was often at odds with the ideologically charged views about race held by his peers in the Afrikaner political establishment at the time of his political ascendancy.

Much of Verwoerd's early preoccupations with the poor-white problem in his roles as psychologist, sociologist and social worker were themes explored in his doctoral dissertation, *Die Afstomping van Gemoedsaandoeninge* (The Blunting of the Emotions) (1924). More crucially, an insistence on scientific social work tended towards identifying the detrimental psychological effects of poverty on the senses and emotions at the level of the individual. As a student of Raymond W. Wilcocks, founder of the experimental psychology laboratory at Stellenbosch University, and later as a postdoctoral fellow in Leipzig, Verwoerd was educated in the interconnecting paradigms of ethno-psychology and techno-psychology – or *Völkerpsychologie* and experimental psychology. His intellectual formation, and his political

128 Undoing Apartheid

philosophy, bear traces of the ambiguous inheritance of Wundt himself and the field of experimental psychology. Yet, as Kurt Danziger (the South African historian of psychology), and later Christoph Marx, suggest respectively, apartheid was not a simple derivation of the *Gestalt* psychology developed in Leipzig.[41]

Verwoerd's training nevertheless yields a crucial imagistic trace of apartheid when refracted through the debates on *Gestalt* psychology at the Leipzig Institute. A contest over emphasis involving purveyors of a complexity principle and proponents of an atomistic natural science framed the work of the Leipzig laboratory in ways that offer a grid for comprehending the contradictory impulses seen in the idea of apartheid that Verwoerd would later champion. This complexity paralleled the disciplinary direction charted by Felix Krueger, Wundt's successor as director of the Institute, who railed against the empiricism of natural science that relied on the developmentally alien mechanics of Western Europe at the expense of an individual spiritual process. This was a view that clearly attracted Verwoerd as he grappled with possible resolutions to the poor-white question in South Africa. Krueger's holistic psychology, in contrast to the *Gestaltism* of his Berlin contemporaries, infused approaches to the mental world of individual subjects by endowing the enquiry into economic, historical and social sensibilities with spiritual agency. The study of subjective experiences was thus expanded to include rational and irrational drives, as well as public and private configurations of the individual in its social existence.

For someone like Verwoerd, who was preoccupied with the South African poor-white question, Krueger's 'affirming activation' of the *Volk* provided a creative synthesis of a social impasse. Whether Krueger's lectures influenced the young Verwoerd to alter the initial premise of his doctoral research (which advocated the isolation and study of emotions towards embracing psychology's potential to activate a larger cultural history) is unclear. Perhaps Verwoerd gained from this encounter an inkling that the 'poor white', more than a problem, were the subject of a complex socially determined process of individuation, and that salvation lay in the collective promise of cultural awakening.

The impact of Krueger's theoretical interests on the young Verwoerd is debatable. However, the opportunity to engage in

Woyzeck and the Secret Life of Apartheid's Things   *129*

the experimental aspects of applied psychology, which attended to the atomic level of emotions, persisted as a feature of the Leipzig Institute, and evidently enthused Verwoerd. It is this atomic level of emotion, no longer merely the object of empiricist recording, but instigation, activation and development, that would become foundational to petty apartheid. Petty apartheid, as a commensurate reckoning with emotions at an atomic level, corresponded with the shifts that defined *Gestalt* psychology and the search for new sources of vitalism in the early twentieth century.

The study of emotions marked a minor but consequential adjustment of earlier attempts to establish the life sciences by turning to commensurate methods developed in the physical sciences.[42] At Stellenbosch University, where Verwoerd conducted his doctoral research, machinic thinking about the universe resulted in an emphasis on models that could be broken down into individual parts, in which the higher-level entities are described as combinations of lower-level entities. Transposed into the early twentieth century, the foundations of apartheid echo Wundt's insistence that 'magical motive is in harmony with mechanical effect'.[43] In Leipzig, the record of this emotional quotient was used for activation towards a higher ideal, or, as apartheid bears out, to the ends of population control. Herein lies the nub of the idea of petty apartheid that Verwoerd contributed to the political discourse of Afrikaner nationalism, which set to work on realigning sense and perception, magic and science, poor white and native, educator and administrator, subject and object: all establishing a futural orientation whereby recurring memories of race were subjected to the measure of technical instruments and in turn modified.

Tracking aspects of apartheid via a laboratory in early-twentieth-century Leipzig helps us to see how it emerged from studies into measured psychic variations in accordance with categories of *Völkerpsychologie*, experimental psychology and applied psychology. Somewhat innocuously, Verwoerd measured sensory variations caused by external stimuli through the instruments of memory machines. A machine that fascinated him in Leipzig, and about which he wrote in the *American Journal of Psychology*, was the Ranschburg memory apparatus. What this machine demonstrated was that sense and perception could be folded into an instrumentality that measured, commanded,

130 Undoing Apartheid

calculated and ultimately managed emotional responses according to varying sources of psychic energy. An abstract from the *American Journal of Psychology* in July 1926 on 'A Method for the Experimental Production of Emotions' places the novelty of this discovery in perspective.

Verwoerd's research involved the use of the Ranschburg memory apparatus to induce introspective reports by flashing discs of colour over periods of five seconds or less. The introspection was called forth after the investigating subject declared a correct reaction, fell into a trap, or incurred punishment (in the form of shocks of varying intensities). The entire experiment was given to provoking emotions so that these might fall under the sway of the rational. The idea that scientific method, and a memory apparatus, could be deployed to measure emotional response time to stimuli was *ipso facto* also a precedent for recalling the authority of science in controlling nature.[44] Much like the setting of the laboratory, control was to be exercised through minute orchestrations aimed at provoking responses at the level of sense and perception, in a manner that conformed with and confirmed the racial attributions of industrial capacity.

Ross Truscott and Michelle Smith identify the political implications of the psychotechnic experiments underway in South Africa; their account deserves some elaboration:

> For Verwoerd, in his 1926 experiment, the 'Ranschburg memory-apparatus' functions, despite its name, as a forgetting-machine, designed to activate working memory but suspend all else except the task at hand, intensified by the anticipation of inevitable shock. For Verwoerd, there is an immediacy to the reception of shock, a direct emotional effect that can be read off the instant reaction of an experimental subject. The only delay is that of 'blunting', which follows the initial production of an emotion; around this emotional reaction, a callus of consciousness, hardened to shock, forms. According to the conventions of early twentieth century experimental psychology – a rigorous thoughtlessness that persists in the discipline – the only concern is under what conditions this response can be reliably reproduced. It is possible, however, that the shocks of Verwoerd's experiments would only arrive decades later, once he left his academic post at Stellenbosch to take up a career in politics. Indeed, if we take Verwoerd seriously when he states that his test items 'show fundamental similarity to situations of every-day life', that they are simplified versions of those found in

Woyzeck and the Secret Life of Apartheid's Things 131

the workplace and, one might say, in the shocks of 'every-day life', then we can understand the predicaments of the post-apartheid as a series of aftershocks both yet to cease and yet to arrive, lived in anticipation.[45]

What ought to be added to this precise assessment is consideration of the discursive frames of *Völkerpsychologie* that permeated the milieu of psychology in the first part of the twentieth century, especially as experimental psychology took hold in deeply racialized societies such as the US and South Africa. Both were marked by histories of slavery and colonization. For the purposes of this argument, the arrival of experimental psychology in the US, particularly with former Leipzig scholar Hugo Münsterberg, to whose ideas Verwoerd was attracted, did not result in a complete abandonment of *Völkerpsychologie*. Rather, Münsterberg traded the cultural logic of *Völkerpsychologie* for a racial logic of industrial capacity in his adaptation of the method of applied psychology. While much of the repudiation of Wundt's earlier structuralism is narrated by referencing the American appropriation of psychology to commercial ends, by making psychology available to industrial application in areas of management, vocational decisions, advertising and employee motivation, little attention has been given to the political implications of the entrenchment of this applied version of the discipline. Applied psychology served commerce and racial subjection equally well as it gained confidence in its ability to study the human sensorium, more importantly, to commandeer the senses.

Not enough attention has been paid to the receding interests in *Völkerpsychologie* as it was mapped onto racialized social formations, both in the US and South Africa. For a generation of graduates of the Leipzig Institute, *Völkerpsychologie* appeared to lack the necessary capacity for dealing with the alteration in industrial technologies in the early twentieth century, which had already acted directly upon and fissured the relation between sense and perception. This explains Münsterberg's study of cinema titled *The Photoplay: A Psychological Study* (1916) to understand the effects of this new industrial technology through the film/mind analogy, in which film retreats from the physical world to the mental world. It is also not surprising that in the early 1900s, he convened the St Louis Conferences on Arts and

132   Undoing Apartheid

Sciences to feature social psychology in anticipation of the new American century of industry and commerce.

Verwoerd was enthused by Münsterberg's idiographic and nomothetic approaches to studying the subject, especially the implications of the latter's search for behaviour controls achieved through the 'scientific administration of rewards and punishments'.[46] His most glaring provocations as state official – questioning, for example, the need for mathematics education for black youth – repeated views from Münsterberg's *Psychology and Industrial Efficiency* (1913), which argued that 'hiring workers who had personalities and mental abilities best suited to certain types of work was the best way to increase motivation, performance and retention'. To the extent that petty apartheid was an effect of the shift from Wundtian *Völkerpsychologie* and experimental psychology to Münsterberg's applied psychology, it parodied a concomitant disciplinary drift from culture as a product of sense-perception to race as an industrial capacity in which the mind could be trained to abide by the rhythms of production and consumption.

Like his mentors, Verwoerd's training in experimental psychology resonates with both the structural precepts of Wundt and experimental techniques, which allowed for deductions about the differences in perception across culturally designated collectivities. An orientation towards industrial capacity assumed prominence through an applied psychology refracted through American industrialization and racialization. Stated differently, new technological resources in the twentieth century complemented cultural scripts of nationalism to pave the way for a newer, mechanized concept of race. Culture is received, whereas race, on this score, is conceived, and therefore available for renewal. In short, race is now available to pass judgement on cultural precepts related to the human sensorium. This epistemic shift in which race displaces culture as a dominant signifier had similar precedents in South Africa. As Dunbar Moodie argues, Verwoerd insisted that race trumped culture in response to attempts to incorporate a 'Coloured' population group in Afrikanerdom based on shared language. It is this hyper-rationalism which would be fed into the machinery of communication and control, resulting in the intensification of the Manichaeism of a racial state. Moreover, this ascendancy and confidence in scientific claims of psychology partitioned the senses through

Woyzeck and the Secret Life of Apartheid's Things   *133*

responses generated by images, while transferring such images to the technological instrumentalities of measurement, communication and control.

Wundt's thinking was that the 'primitive' perception of tools is assigned to nature, while the heroic is assigned to forms of theatricality where myth could be secularized, and higher orders of individuation achieved. A *Gestalt* formation in Leipzig emphasized parts over wholes, as well as a countervailing tendency of holistic thinking that factored in community collectives – to explain differences at the level of perception. An excerpt from Wundt's *Elements of Folk Psychology* may help to describe how cultural stimulation was mapped onto the secularization of myth. In an excerpt worthy of extended exposition for its echoes of Balibar's reflections on interpellation discussed earlier, Wundt writes:

> Common to the responses of the congregation and the chorus of the dramatic play, is the fact of an active participation in that which is transpiring. Though this participation is inner and subjective, in the one case, and objective, in the other, the response of the congregation to the priest in the liturgy is nevertheless preparatory to the chorus of the drama. It is inevitable, however, that this change should gradually lead to a break with liturgy. The portrayal of the sacred action is transferred from the church to the street; the clergy are supplanted by secular players from among the people. Even within the sacred walls folk-humour had inserted burlesque episodes – such, for example, as the mimic portrayal of Peter's violence to the servant Malchus, or the running of the Apostles to the grave of Christ. These now gained the upper hand, and finally formed independent mimetic comedies. The serious plays, on their part, also drew material, even at this time, from sources other than sacred history. The newly awakened dramatic impulse received further stimulus from various directions. The old travelling comedy, wandering from market to market with its exhibitions, now of gruesomely serious, now of keenly humorous action, was a factor in the creation of the modern drama, no less than were the amusing performances of the accompanying puppet-show.[47]

This comes from a comparative analysis of a branch of Wundtian *Völkerpsychologie* that studied higher mental processes across the world, and related ethnology to the study of the stages pertaining to mental development. This branch of psychology was distinguished from but not inconsequential to physiological

134   Undoing Apartheid

psychology, which studied the mechanics of the nervous system. The latter was where human physiology apparently obeyed the laws of thermodynamics. The ongoing work of connecting the central nervous system to popular technologies of telegraphy and electricity in physiological psychology and transversal cultural connections established through *Völkerpsychologie* is present in later discourses on race, albeit not derivatively. There is a short step between this view and Verwoerd's attempts to distinguish culture from race, where cultural difference denoted the stages of development and race reflected nerve mechanics. However, Verwoerd's differential responses towards the 'poor-white' and 'native' questions in South Africa are more likely explained by the interest he developed in Wundt's physiological psychology of nerve mechanics.[48] We can manage only a truncated view of the connections between Wundt's psychology and Verwoerd's borrowings. A welfarism formed around the sociology of the 'poor-white question' ultimately transpired in a differentiation of industrial capacity, sustained by a disciplinary formation that measured thresholds of stimulus response, and resulting in the control exercised in the name of a racialized 'native question'. Apartheid, in the extended metaphor provided by Wundt's comparison of Indian and Greek drama, emerged from building the chorus of the church only to end with a puppet-show in the marketplace. It drew inspiration from the stimulation of the senses and perception that Wundt proposed by bringing 'the test subject and the measuring instrument into more proximate forms of communication'.[49] Henning Schmidgen tells us that in this schema, 'nerves became "conductors"; nerve impulses, "signals", or messages; and their propagation throughout the nervous system, "transmissions"'.[50] With Wundt, we learn that psychologists joined astronomers to explain their epistemic objects in telegraphic terms of the nervous system.

Petty apartheid may be that instance of interpellation of the subject in anticipation of a future in which race is gradually dislodged from culture by way of technological remediation. An orientation of race towards the machinic envelops the subject so that a desire presumed to be a product of 'free will' is rewired to respond to external stimuli of the senses. Stated differently, race plotted the time across stages of cultural development. If this sounds like a familiar description of what we have come to call neoliberalism, with all the caveats that Stuart Hall issued

Woyzeck and the Secret Life of Apartheid's Things   *135*

about the capacious use of this term, it is because apartheid was formed around a false problem, identified by Henri Bergson, of a version of *Gestalt* psychology that, in seeking out the elements of perception of objects, ends up privileging the causality of parts over wholes.[51]

The image of the migrant labourer in 1950s Verwoerdian apartheid drained of the resources of life by being availed to endless experimentation is presented in *Woyzeck on the Highveld* against the backdrop of commodities patterned in cosmic constellations, in a scene shot through with falling stars. Between Herschel's speculative cosmology and Wundt's psychologies of sense-perception, the floating signifier of race appears trapped in a cybernetic loop of communication and control from which there is no easy exit.

Confirmed by an emergent experimental psychology that contributed to a refigured attitude to race in the twentieth century, apartheid's purported ideological coherence obscures the process by which the subject is confounded by the lure of the crucifix, the *Pulcinella* and other trivial things. Each provides access to a process in which race is looped between human and machine through communication and control. Lydia Liu notes that 'the dynamic of human and machine has been constitutive of psychoanalysis all along'.[52] Turning to Masahiro Mori's uncanny valley hypothesis of 1970, which expresses the worry that robotics will lead to a frightful resemblance between human and humanoid, Liu invites us to maintain vigilance and radical openness towards the future. For readers of Mori, the openness that Liu calls for might be found in the use of the Bunraku puppet – like the tradition adapted by Handspring Puppet Company – as an antidote to a slide into the uncanny valley, a point that is also the interest of this study. As a prescription for education, such an orientation is indispensable to counteract the narcissistic attachment to the self-image of the human, and the danger of dropping into the abyss of the uncanny valley. A failure to account for technology, she tells us, will mean that 'the unconscious will remain hidden in plain sight'.[53] By the same token, for the purposes of my argument, there is a need to reinterpret apartheid as a mechanism that oriented race towards technology.

While Dr Clarus decided the medical fate of Büchner's Woyzeck in the wake of slavery, Dr Verwoerd went to work on

136 Undoing Apartheid

a psychotechnical experiment that delved into the emotions. The year 1834 produced conditions for the extension of the category of race to account for the depleted autonomy of the labouring subject; 1948 provided the conditions for the return of race in an endless cycle of communication and control. It is here that apartheid's violence is found to be indistinguishable from the interplay of desire and object, thus making possible the breach of a psychic structure. As complex as this transition appears at first, apartheid ideologues proposed a simple formula to demarcate psychic preparedness for modernity by way of a taxonomic order of racial qualification. The answer that the bureaucrats of apartheid sought had already been prepared when race became the target of predicting and acting upon the behavioural dynamics of the parts of sense and perception that placed the subject on the path of inevitable collision with technological objects.

Exit Woyzeck.

5

Post-Apartheid Slapstick

Philoctetes:
My whole life has been
Just one long cruel parody.

Seamus Heaney, *The Cure at Troy*

In a twist of fate, the experience of apartheid in South Africa was confronted by a frightful regularity of depictions of slapstick in the passing of the twentieth century. The national subject of the anti-apartheid struggle, once beholden to the image of love and revolution to survive apartheid's absurdity, begrudgingly found its desire calibrated in a post-apartheid idiom of truth and reconciliation. At the expense of substituting a desire for naming freedom in terms of history repeating itself first as tragedy, then as farce, the end of apartheid brought home the unfortunate experience of apartheid as one formed by a series of mistimings. Beyond the spoils of love that found their nesting place in truth and reconciliation, no other image of a post-apartheid future adequately supported an emergent concept of freedom, coming, as apartheid did, after European fascism.[1] Fantasies of revolution forged at the height of the Cold War were equally misplaced alongside the collisions orchestrated by petty apartheid in everyday life.

The disappointment in anticipations of the end of apartheid was that the awakening from the nightmare was unaccompanied

138 Undoing Apartheid

by a vista of spring.[2] At best, apartheid's end left in its wake a notion of race that conformed to a mere mechanical existence, undifferentiated from a world which seemed to have caught up with its racial logic. What if a new attitude towards a knowledge of technology combined with a notion of aesthetic education was brought to bear on, and charged with, the desire for post-apartheid freedom? How does the collision between human and technology in the construction of the terrifying pursuit of a perfect machine of apartheid redirect an education towards learning the virtues of stumbling in slapstick?

Absurdism

Around 1896, a theatrical work titled *Ubu Roi* (King Ubu) was performed on the stage of Théâtre de l'Œuvre in Paris. The play drew widespread condemnation, not least because the author, Alfred Jarry, had purposefully set out to offend the bourgeois sensibilities of Parisian theatre audiences. By all accounts, Jarry's intention to offend the dominant public sentiments of his time proved so successful that the play was shut down after its first performance.

One hundred years later, at the Market Theatre in Johannesburg, Jarry's central character, the oafish, grotesque and ridiculous figure of Ubu, was reincarnated in a theatrical production written by Jane Taylor, directed by William Kentridge, and performed by the Handspring Puppet Company. *Ubu and the Truth Commission* was an effort to trouble an otherwise complacent audience about the fate of reconciliation at the end of apartheid, mocking gullible spectators who might otherwise believe that the tragedy of history would be masked behind a titillating tale of love. It drew attention to a corruption of the idea of love as it was mobilized to surpass the experience of violence. More than a critique of the TRC, the play locates theatrical politics at the very heart of a national narrative built on the presumed symmetry of truth and reconciliation. To what ends of tragedy, then, might such theatrical resources of comedy be deployed effectively before affect is overwhelmed by the tragic? What latent political meaning is availed through comedic theatre for countering the burden of past violence?

Post-Apartheid Slapstick   *139*

Ubu and the Truth Commission is indebted to two sources: a century-old theatrical form widely acknowledged for having kept alive the dream of freedom under conditions of the twentieth century's devastating world wars; and a cinematic form commonly referred to as slapstick. Both provided a resource for popular politics, artistic practice and critical theory through mimicking, parodying and colliding with the sensory excesses of moribund forms of modern state power. Slapstick's potential resides in the absurdity entailed in the indecision about whether decrepit forms of power ought to be represented in the idiom of tragedy or comedy.

Confounded by the troubling uncertainty of not knowing whether to laugh or to cry, the two productions by Jarry and Taylor, on either side of the twentieth century, mobilize a mode of theatre that Martin Esslin labelled 'Theatre of the Absurd' to grapple with the conflicted sensory experience of modern power.[3] Absurdism provides a disposition to face a world in which nothing seems to make sense, and embracing the fact that our lives can be both terrifying and ridiculous.

In keeping with the genre of the theatre of the absurd, both plays engage nationalism's political unconscious. As a model of theatrical politics, absurdism complicates the task of remaking freedom. Beyond the obvious repetition of the figure of Ubu, the staging of *Ubu and the Truth Commission* makes use of absurdism to parody the excesses of power in postcolonial Africa. However, in *Ubu and the Truth Commission,* absurdism is less about ridiculing power than laying bare the mythic aura of violence under apartheid.

The plot intrudes on the private lives of Ma Ubu (Busi Zokufa) and Pa Ubu (Dawid Minnaar), who in their interracial union reveal the collisions spawned by past attitudes to racial policies. Behind the hideous spectacle of a lovers' quarrel, Pa Ubu's association with conniving beastly puppets, Niles the Crocodile and the Dogs of War, implicates him as he attempts to hide his complicity in secret acts of state violence. Pa Ubu's effort to hide this past amounts to an act of self-preservation rather than a sincere disavowal of his atrocities. Sited in the crosshairs of tragedy and comedy, the play sets out how a fantasy of an interracial love affair proves to be inadequate as a foundational fiction for forging an imagined political future in the wake of apartheid. *Ubu and the Truth Commission* stages a

140 Undoing Apartheid

conflict of forms: between the tragedy of the testimony delivered to the TRC and the comedy of slapstick, between the kinesis of the puppet and cinematic memory, and between confession and testimony – each distinguished by a scramble to hold onto the shards of a broken world. Beneath the veneer of a fantasy to make the world whole again, the play's investments in the repressed aspects of the national political unconscious are laid out in two related scenes.

Ma Ubu takes Niles the Crocodile aside to determine the reason for his bulging belly. Shoving her hand down his gullet, she digs out a scrap of paper from the bag that doubles as the belly of the beast, thinking that she has finally uncovered evidence of Pa Ubu's sexual indiscretions. What she finds instead is infinitely more damning. The unravelling of the scrap of paper depicts an apparatus of torture at work, set against the backdrop of the metallic mangling of human and machine. Interspersed with images of bodies falling through space and subjects contorting with pain in their encounters with instruments of torture, Kentridge shows the relays of a 'truth' that upholds violence as it passes through a labyrinth of loudhailers and telephones. The crumpled script that Ma Ubu retrieves describes a technique of torture called tubing, in which a rubber tube was used to suffocate the detainee, with a small slit from which the tongue was allowed to protrude. The idea, Pa Ubu later discloses, was to extract the truth. The longer the tongue, the closer the detainee was to telling the truth – or to dying. If the detainee wet his or her pants, the torturer would know that the detainee was before the Pearly Gates. And if 'truth' could not be extracted after all, the detainee was to be beaten to death with iron pipes.

Ma Ubu is visibly disturbed by the discovery of her husband's dark secret, which reveals his involvement in the so-called dirty tricks of apartheid security forces. Pa Ubu's plans to dispense with his guilt by discarding the evidence of his complicity in acts of violence are fortunately intercepted by Ma Ubu. Appearing as a larger-than-life apparition on a screen, she confronts a cowering Pa Ubu. She taunts him, threatening to sell his secrets as an investment towards her retirement, while he, skimpily clad in underpants, trots around the stage, dodging the larger-than-life projections of Ma Ubu and her revelations of torture. In the end, he threatens Ma Ubu with the consequences of her betrayal,

Ubu and the Truth Commission (V-26) – March 1997. Ubu (Dawid Minnaar, right) feeds secret documents to Niles the Crocodile (manipulated and voiced by Adrian Kohler).
Photo © Ruphin Coudyzer FPPSA.

stating that her disclosure of official secrets will be as much to her detriment as to his.

To the extent that *Ubu and the Truth Commission* aligns aesthetics and politics, it matters for my argument that it achieves this by referencing Jarry's theatre of the absurd. The duplication of a signature spiral emblazoned on the torso of the burlesque figure of Ubu in both the 1896 play by Jarry and the 1997 Taylor–Kentridge–Handspring production attests to the shared commitment to rethink the political through aesthetics. To this end, the turn to slapstick serves to awaken the senses under conditions where violence cannot be entirely remanded to the securities of reason.[4]

However, Taylor's Ubu, in contrast to Jarry's, is offered no leeway for escape from the consequences of his complicity in apartheid violence. In fact, complicity is precisely where an aesthetic exploration is worked out, renewed and reclaimed for an ethics of post-apartheid freedom. Beyond toying with Pa Ubu's desperate measures to hide incriminating documents that reveal official secrets about state violence, the play also raises questions about how art accounts for apartheid.

Taylor references a subversive genealogy of theatrical politics by casting a sinister and farcical petty agent of apartheid in a format first made available by Jarry. She establishes a specific limit on the absurd as she sets about reincarnating the character of Ubu. Her Ubu is thus brought face-to-face with the consequences of violence anticipated in an earlier iteration of the theatre of the absurd. Pa Ubu's orientation to the world is both incredulous and absurd, resulting in a bipolar dissonance between a need for love and an insatiable appetite for violence. In the unfolding of the drama, he is made to confront the moral, political and ethical limits of his actions, which also lie beyond his control. As we see Pa Ubu threatening to spiral out of control, surrounded by screen apparitions, enigmatic puppets, and cinematic recalls of the instruments and techniques of torture, Taylor invites us to grapple with the violence buried beneath the expressions of love. She places us at the other extreme of Jarry's spiral, in the very future that he refuses to contemplate. Taylor thus approaches Jarry with the benefit of hindsight, beckoning us to reflect on the violence of the twentieth century. This invitation is issued in the

Michael Meschke as King Ubu (with spiral).
Image by Beata Bergström, 1964, courtesy of Daniel Bergström.

interests of returning notions of truth, memory, narrative and image that had been claimed as the monopoly of the legal frameworks of the TRC to the aesthetic. Shorn of the humanitarian impulse on which the TRC rested, Taylor reinstates the activating concepts of the Commission to draw out the trials and tribulations of a love that rings hollow in the face of violence. Rather than as a work representing violence, the play should be read as a dramatization of the encounter between aesthetic theory and critical theory in the wake of twentieth-century fascism, and in the wake of apartheid.

The recollection of aesthetic and critical theories counteracts a defensiveness of the discourse of the TRC that tended to locate affect at a remove from the procedures of law. By shielding the law from an otherwise deeply affective process, the TRC unfortunately rendered the shock of violence illegible and generally unavailable to the process of reimagining post-apartheid freedom and subjectivity. Had the TRC adopted a less defensive attitude, the element of shock, as Siegfried Kracauer suggests in the context of critiques of fascism, might have demanded a more productive unfolding of experience, memory and interaction after catastrophe – not dissimilar to the ambition set forth in *Ubu and the Truth Commission*.[5] A reckoning with the experience of shock would have potentially enabled a concept of freedom drawn from somewhat anarchic transactions between people and things in everyday life; transactions that exceeded the tragic mode of judicial commissions to which the experience of violence was consigned by law. To the extent that *Ubu and the Truth Commission* combines aesthetic education and critical theory in an age of rapid expansion of technological resources of mass communication, Taylor returns to the experience of apartheid by recalling the indecision of an earlier critique of fascism in Europe, particularly among scholars associated with the Frankfurt School of social theory in Germany, about how to interpret the genre of slapstick.

Slapstick in Critical Theory

Without substituting a desire for naming freedom in terms of the proverbial return of history as farce, *Ubu and the Truth Commission* presents us with an education about how the birth

144   Undoing Apartheid

of the post-apartheid was a product of collision and mistiming involving a nascent national subject and the instruments of mythic violence. The TRC accordingly failed to establish itself as a site for adequately theorizing the predicament of the post-apartheid by the frameworks imposed on it by the discourse of transitional justice. It neglected to stake a claim amidst an *aporia* that Miriam Bratu Hansen identified as a 'paradigm of slapstick', in which the national subject is left unclear about what the future holds in light of the experience of violence. Given apartheid's instrumental reason, the TRC seemed surprisingly oblivious of the functions of technology and mass culture in its reckoning with violence.[6]

Ubu and the Truth Commission returns us to this missed opportunity, one resembling Hansen's attempts to make sense of the disagreement about slapstick between Benjamin and Adorno, proponents of the Frankfurt School. For Hansen, slapstick is precisely where critique sets to work on anticipating the convergence between the absurdity of the sources of violence and the experience of violence. While laying out the stakes of the disagreement between Benjamin and Adorno on the relationship between humour and catastrophe, she implicitly asks whether the flip side of slapstick might affirm a new attitude to technology rather than one bound up in the rituals of fascism. Rearticulating Benjamin and Adorno's effort to make sense of Mickey Mousing (the technique of synchronizing music and movement on screen), Hansen relocates a reading of the potential of slapstick amidst the rise of fascism in Germany. If caricature is permitted for such a complex and nuanced debate, we should at least consider Adorno's caution about the macabre element of slapstick as precisely that which prompted Benjamin to salvage something of its effect. Benjamin's effort can be construed as a tactic to counter the deadening of the human sensorium that accompanied the rise of post-World War I mechanization of industrial capitalism.[7] If Mickey Mouse encapsulated the German popular spirit of the 1930s, Benjamin sought to anticipate how it was not only the site of a possible break in the timing of the formal principle of the assembly line in industrial capitalism, but also a reckoning with the shock that could potentially awaken the senses. The motif that Benjamin mobilizes in this depleted sensory script, Hansen informs us, is the way Mickey Mouse and Charlie Chaplin open space for play, even as they register the experience of unprecedented human alienation.[8] According to this reading, it is clear that Hansen's forays through Benjamin's commentary on slapstick shed light on the conditions for retrieving a concept of freedom from the accretion of memories of violence. The tactic is to be found in the mechanization of industrial capitalism and the rise of fascism that a new technological emergence buoyed in the first half of the twentieth century.

The debate on slapstick as a way to respond to fascism nudges us to reflect differently upon forms of mythic violence, which Benjamin described as a form of 'law-preserving' violence. Hansen draws our attention to kinaesthetic learning, through which we might, by extension, resist the temptation to approach the TRC merely as an archive that recalls the tragic consequences of the violence of apartheid. Kinaesthetic learning asks that we grasp the manner in which the TRC unfolded an action that may best be understood as recoiling from violence. Crucial here is how survivor testimonies disclosed the ways in which subjects collided with the instruments of grand and petty apartheid. The element of shock in the exercise of apartheid's violence was surrendered to a therapeutic mechanism in everyday life, rather than being revealed as a question of technology's overt relation to violence. Recoiling from the horror of scenes of mutilation, murder and massacre, the TRC foreclosed a Benjaminian attitude towards slapstick that inadvertently affirmed *affect* as necessary for recrafting freedom. It short-circuited the relationship between the affective and legal constructions of post-apartheid subjectivity by refusing to linger over the layers of meaning produced by the experience of shock.

In Hansen's reading of Benjamin, catastrophe is prolonged by locating violence in the spiral that exemplifies the spatio-temporal coordinates of modernity. While technology for some appears like an 'accelerating spiral of decline', for Hansen 'the spiral of shock, anaesthetics and aesthetics could work to diffuse the deadly violence unleashed by capitalist technology'.[9]

Similarly, Taylor appears to locate apartheid's violence on the spiral of modernity – a perspective which she develops in relation to Kentridge's Ubu series, animated by the kinaesthetic prosthetics of the Handspring Puppet Company. This form of theatre links moving objects made up of springs and spirals that prolong the memory of violence, if only to wrench meaning from the unfortunate collisions of everyday life. One hundred

146   Undoing Apartheid

years after the debut of *Ubu Roi*, Taylor's play reappeared as a foreboding sign of a Nietzschean eternal return, and a cautionary tale about the end of apartheid in a reinscription of Jarry's prognosis of what modernity had in store for the twentieth century. Through the motif of the spiral, Jarry's jarring parody of the sensibilities of European bourgeois modernity resonates with Taylor's rendering of apartheid as an unaccounted-for consequence of that very aesthetic critique of modernity that theatre instigates. In both productions, the spiral fixes attention on what is at stake in the eternal return.

Jarry's presentation of the character of Père Ubu personified the amoral aspects of the human condition. In keeping with the theatrical shift, several reiterations of Ubu, as in Wole Soyinka's *King Baabu*,[10] for example, enabled what Alastair Brotchie calls the birth of black comedy in the modern sense of the term.[11] Jarry's Ubu is not simply reducible to the symbolic equivalent of the tyrant in history. We are called upon instead to contemplate the subject through the pre-semantic symbolism of the spiral, which functions as a pataphysical phenomenon (the term is unpacked below) *par excellence* – a subject that is free-falling with no ground on which to stand. Citing Deleuze and Guattari, Steve McCaffery confirms the diffuseness of the spiral as 'a figure in which all points of space are simultaneously occupied according to the laws of frequency or accumulation and distribution'.[12] Effectively, the theatre of the absurd that Jarry initiates works to simulate the turbulence of modernity. As a motif to describe the experience of modernity, the spiral questions the seemingly absurd euphoria surrounding the idea of unfettered progress.

In two recent studies, by Nico Israel and Erman Kaplama respectively, the question of the meaning of the spiral for modernity provides helpful insights into how the twentieth century appears as a geometric formation to the twenty-first. Nico Israel's wonderfully perceptive *Spirals* suggests that Kentridge's *Ubu* is co-constitutive of the physiognomy of the spiral through which the nineteenth century is discernible to the twentieth century.[13] Israel notes that for Kentridge, 'the centres and edges of spirals express the inaccessible limits of reconciliation and truth'.[14] To this we might add that while Kentridge's subject matter is specifically drawn from the South African experience, his form is reminiscent of the spiral that began

Post-Apartheid Slapstick

with the early nineteenth-century machine drawings of Gaspard Monge, passed through Alfred Jarry's 1896 *Ubu Roi*, and culminated in the irresolution of the critique of violence in the theatre of the absurd.

This may be one way to read *Ubu and the Truth Commission*: as a version of theatrical politics in which ideas of truth and reconciliation orbit in the spiral of imaginary solutions. Kentridge has long been fascinated with machines that never materialize – much like the failed experiments of Jarry's Paris on the cusp of the twentieth century. Similarly, Jarry's endearingly invented science of imaginary solutions – pataphysics – did not merely name the theatre of the absurd, but was the very enactment of the absurd, and of that which lay latent in the work of conception and invention. As a wordplay on its precursor – metaphysics – pataphysics was also always the play on the absurd in the midst of the *aporia* of tragedy and farce.

In a second example of the centrality of the spiral in the image of modernity, Kaplama's study of the Nietzschean Dionysian views the spiral as a process of extending forward (protension) in an overabundant cycle of eternal recurrence.[15] If extending forward is understood as the zeal to create, the spiral's circular movement, he argues, should be understood as zeal to know and understand. In *Ubu and the Truth Commission*, the zeal to know and understand appears at first to overtake the need to create. But through the medium of the puppet and the cinematic, the spiral distinguishes the spheres of *techne – poiesis*, or bringing forth – and technology to reconfigure the nexus of humans and machines. The mediation of humans and machines unfolds in all the complex ways in which modernity relies on technological mythologies that perpetuate violence. The performative, by contrast, might be said to result in negotiating an uneasy choice between the theme of eternal recurrence and the will to power, without surrendering aesthetics to either. Beyond the excesses of the *avant-garde* that gave rise to the charge of anarchism when *Ubu Roi* was first performed, the repetition of the motif of the spiral highlights the point at which aesthetics might mark a difference in the seemingly perpetual spiral of modernity's violence.

Unlike the setting of Jarry's France, in South Africa the play's representational field is overwhelmed by a life-and-death struggle strained by the absurdity of apartheid. Alongside Taylor's script, Kentridge's assemblages replicate this absurdity of entrapment and collision. In their specific deployment, the play traps Pa Ubu in a spiral of violence as he himself spirals out of control, uncertain about whether to confess to his crimes or downplay his role in their execution. If Pa Ubu's decaying unconscious is incapable of an *affective* strategy of problem-solving, Taylor has him face up to his actions through the mediation of technological instrumentalities to which he has become accustomed in his acts of deception. Moving images lend themselves to tragi-comic emplotments in which the subject of apartheid is destined to collide with an apparatus. The repertoire of erased and reconstructed images offers us a view of the invention of techniques of surveillance and torture, building a truth-extracting machine that forms a backdrop to the unfolding drama. The torture scenes portray techniques of interrogation, linking technical instrumentalities with techniques of extracting information. The mobile optics of film, set against the measured *techne* of the puppet as mnemotechnic prosthesis, highlight the way human emotions are constituted by the intermediation of technology and *techne*; or a cinematic form and an art of movement-making. Pa Ubu is thus

Ubu and the Truth Commission (V-7) – March 1997. A witness gives evidence at the Truth Commission (manipulated by Basil Jones [left] with assistance and voicing by Busisiwe Zokufa [right]).
Photo © Ruphin Coudyzer FPPSA.

Post-Apartheid Slapstick 149

made to confront his complicity in the spiral of violence through the interplay of puppet and moving image.

Violent Humour

To the extent that humour interrupts the process by which violence is affirmed in ideology or law, *Ubu and the Truth Commission* rethreads the heterogeneous elements of the image, fractured and rendered discontinuous by violence, from which another image of the world must be made. Unlike the instruments of law that recount violence through the discipline of forensic science, aesthetics sets its sights on the technological temporal object that mediates *a priori* images. It attends to that which sustains projections, retentions and protensions in the experience of violence. As a work rooted in the traditions of slapstick, *Ubu and the Truth Commission* demands a different attitude towards technology, one in which the underlying *techne* is retrieved from the instruments of violence.

The burden of the farcical genre which Jarry used is highlighted in an interview with Jane Taylor. She recalls lengthy debates with a student about the ethics of Charlie Chaplin's *The Great Dictator* (1940), and whether one could ever explore human rights abuses through a burlesque idiom.[16] Taylor admits that her responses are now perhaps more complex than they were then. To pre-empt her later response, we might well enquire into the work that the mobilization of humour performs in unravelling the legacies of violence.

By highlighting *techne* as a distinct and discernible aspect of technology, as opposed to mere supplement, *Ubu and the Truth Commission* provides a different view of the extended processual enfolding of the human and technology. It is from this precipice that the play seeks to recall sense and perception with an assembly of heterogeneous content, technique and performance. The resort to slapstick in the South African version of *Ubu* identifies a specific impasse in which human and machine collide. Slapstick is that order of the image which settles on the unresolved surprise in order to reclaim, redirect and rearrange a prescribed destiny by recourse to *techne*.[17] As a genre specific to the twentieth century, slapstick is discursively occasioned by a world technological shift.[18] It is distinguished from comedy by

150 Undoing Apartheid

virtue of the fact that it is not aimed at undercutting tragedy, but rather locks its interlocutors into indecision about the redemptive ends of tragedy. Like Chaplin's *The Great Dictator*, *Ubu and the Truth Commission* refuses to surrender *techne* to an inflated promise of technology. To paraphrase Taylor, our beguiled identification with the grotesque Pa Ubu is founded on our unquestioning empathy for the perpetrator's need for love. This admission occurs while the ghosts of his victims serve as a reminder of the excess of pain upon which the unconditional demand for love is premised. Slapstick places a limit on perpetrators' demands for empathy. It serves as a response to disappointments of unrequited love amidst the expectations of liberal attitudes that fail to deliver on assurances of justice and peace from conditions of *stasis*.

Neither a genre that simplistically entertains a failure of love nor one that easily proclaims a triumph of revolution *per se*, slapstick offers us an outline of the horror of irresolution in the experience of violence to which the unconscious bears witness. Put another way, slapstick does not interpellate – cannot interpellate – because its critical potential is aimed at affirming an experience of violence hitherto unanticipated by the rule of law. As a form of surprise, slapstick awakens the senses to that which might yet be recrafted if we are to plot an exit at the other end of the spiral of violence. It is against this backdrop that *Ubu and the Truth Commission* invites us to consider a mode of reconciliation that is not the prerogative of the purveyors of mythic violence represented by the hideous figure of Pa Ubu.

Recoil

Taylor and Kentridge cause us to stumble on the aesthetic repurposing of love in the face of mythic violence. As we soon learn, love has not been immune from the fraught field of national allegory.[19] Yet it is equally indispensable for a viable concept of reconciliation. By repurposing the idea of love and threading its contrived affect through the genre of slapstick, the play follows the contours of an enquiry, following Benjamin, into whether a notion of non-violent resolution to conflict is conceivable in an age of techno-modernity.[20]

How does *Ubu and the Truth Commission* respond to this Benjaminian *aporia*, or quandary, where violence reaffirms the law only to return as the circular monopolization of violence? By extension, how are we to conceive a higher-order freedom necessary for reaching the further shore of reconciliation, especially when apartheid sought to monopolize both the means and ends of violence and where mistrust haunts a non-violent resolution to conflict? Placed alongside a Benjaminian problematization of violence, reconciliation is not merely that which comes after mythic violence, but the very effort at deposing violence which blocks ethical subjectivity from achieving its goal.[21] Is there a model of reconciliation that sets forth a non-violent violence – a violence not allied to the law, but one that interrupts the teleological cycle of law and violence? Rather than that which comes after the law, for reconciliation to function as a promise of love (pure means), it must proceed not only by recalling past violence; it must also recoil from and break out of the cycle of violence.

Ubu and the Truth Commission turns its attention to the imperious fates of violence in the re-establishment of a law preserving violence, where the very contract underwriting peace is an invitation to further violence. But it also strategically mediates this slippage by means of the *techne* of the cinematic, projecting the intensity of political violence onto the screen of an interracial love affair gone awry. By resorting to the paradigm of slapstick, the play calls attention to the potential collisions that may – and do, in fact – result when the affective is diminished as a supplement in an overarching national narrative.

To this end, the play ought to be read as a reminder of Benjamin and Kracauer's cautions that the critique of fascism had fallen short of forestalling the slide into mythic violence – especially in respect of anticipating that which lies in wait at the other end of inevitable collision.[22] It bears repeating that for Benjamin, a law-giving and law-preserving violence is at the root of mythic violence. As the site of the administration and distribution of violence, mythic violence is counterposed to divine violence, which Benjamin sees as disturbing the threat of endless repetition of the mechanical inscription of the law. The introduction of the theme of divine violence serves to caution against the revolution (in technology) being given over to newer forms of mythic violence. Benjamin circumvents the tendency that results

152   Undoing Apartheid

in revolutionary violence falling prey to mythic violence by recourse to divine violence. We might understand divine violence as a name for a justice yet to come, one that presents itself as an ethical demand on the revolution.

Perhaps it is here, in the midst of that which is coming and that which has not yet arrived, that the affective will prove an indispensable resource for constituting new relations between subjects and objects. The threat that mythic violence will invariably recur compelled Benjamin to return to the question in an essay titled 'The Last Snapshot of the European Intelligentsia' (1929). Here, he rearticulated the problem of mythic violence by considering the danger that ensues when revolution loses sight of an image of freedom. Returning to the realm of aesthetic education, he noted:

> Since Bakunin, Europe has lacked a radical concept of freedom. The Surrealists have one. They are the first to liquidate the sclerotic liberal-moral-humanistic ideal of freedom, because they are convinced that 'freedom, which on this earth can only be bought with a thousand of the hardest sacrifices, must be enjoyed unrestrictedly in its fullness without any kind of pragmatic calculation, as long as it lasts.' And this proves to them that 'mankind's struggle for liberation in its simplest revolutionary form (which, however, is liberation in every respect), remains the only cause worth serving'. But are they successful in welding this experience of freedom to the other revolutionary experience that we have to acknowledge because it has been ours, the constructive, dictatorial side of revolution? In short, have they bound revolt to revolution?[23]

The turn to Bakunin is suggestive, particularly when a freedom resonant with anarchism sits uncomfortably alongside the Benjaminian recuperation of the idea of divine violence intervening in the fates of violence. It supports a simultaneously dialectical and speculative approach to freedom that bears witness to an inevitable collision between subject and object, even as it reaches beyond the horizon of such an inevitability. In the struggle to align myth, reason, fantasy and law, a condition of freedom that expresses an infinitely greater fidelity to the ambition of reconciliation must be discovered.

If slapstick approximates the absurdism that Benjamin found so alluring in the work of the Surrealists, it is perhaps because it allowed him to locate the distribution of subjects and objects

Post-Apartheid Slapstick

in the mythic qualities assigned to technological resources. Technology, he insisted, had subjected the human sensorium to a complex kind of training.[24] And the technology that had responded to the need for stimuli was exemplified by the emergence of a cinematic apparatus. In the industrialization and mechanization of memory and media, Benjamin discovered a subtle change underway in the human condition. In contrast to seeing the cinematic as a disruption of duration, as Henri Bergson had, Benjamin would retrieve the resources of *techne* from it. Rather than clinging to the romantic nostalgia established by Bergson in a philosophy of matter and memory (in which Bergson named cinematographic memory as a symptom of the fragmentation of time that disrupts duration), Benjamin would reflect on the positive element of shock in film. Shock, for Benjamin, was not only that which subtracted duration from time, but that which added a different quality to events.

The departure from Bergson can be gleaned from Benjamin's approach to the cinematic expression of slapstick. While it is evidently comic, it is thus only in the sense that 'the laughter it provokes hovers over an abyss of horror'.[25] Slapstick names that horror not only as a symptom of ideology, but also as a concern about an unquestioning belief in the incipient communism of the machine, where immaterial labour serves techno-capitalism, but also lends itself to subversion via creative potential newly freed from the drudgery and bondage of the factory system.

Wending our way through Benjamin's Chaplinesque enchantments helps to locate the sources of freedom in slapstick. For Benjamin, Chaplin approaches the incipient communism of the machine with scepticism and trepidation by presenting a deeply self-reflexive attitude towards cinematic and industrial technology in designing the fate of the human. The pantomime's filmic intervention attests to the danger of contradiction. Where others saw in the revolution in technology an opening up to greater creativity and desire, as far as Benjamin is concerned, Chaplin refuses outright such techno-optimism. Slapstick, we recall, is prognostication of the horror that awaits the human folded into the machine in a general process of the becoming technical of the human. What Benjamin brought to this scene however was the potential for inversion of this embattled relation between subject and object.

154 Undoing Apartheid

It is against this backdrop that *Ubu and the Truth Commission* shares not only in the paradigm of slapstick, but in the Benjaminian injunction to discover the sources of freedom in the intensity of the collisions of our modernity. In much the same way that fascism is thought of as more than a problem of Europe, *Ubu and the Truth Commission* locates the aftermaths of apartheid's mythic violence in the frameworks of earlier iterations of a world picture. Technological mediation was at the core of this perceptual reorientation of memory, a process that ensued with new modes of information and mass media, which converged in the cinematic experience. To the extent that the TRC recapitulates the cinematic constructions of the shock of the experience of violence, *Ubu and the Truth Commission* enables us to engage a technologically mediated virtualization of memory through the object of the theatrical prop or prosthesis.

The 1997 production returns us to an era when shifts in the image world coincided with changes in physical sciences that had altered any prospects of life being lived separately from non-living objects, and, subsequently, war on a global scale. The aesthetic encounters with technology produced a new critical attitude in the first half of the twentieth century, marking a shift from the humanistic to the machinic in the discourse of subjectivity. Borrowing from the theatre of the absurd, the later version accents the birth of a new attitude to intuition as an inexhaustible resource for reimagining post-apartheid futures. Needless to say, the performative work of Jarry, as well as in the cinematic montage of Eisenstein and the biomechanical theatre of Meyerhold are crucial references. *Ubu and the Truth Commission* is aware that dialectical thinking intensifies the experience of the cinematic apparatus – where the filmic inverts life through a process of illusory machinic projections by aligning critical and intuitive resources.

To the extent that *Ubu and the Truth Commission* partakes in this dialectical reorientation, it seeks to reach beyond the promise of the TRC by re-enacting the seemingly impossible discursive form of the South African national narrative. It condenses and displaces the testimony of human rights violations into a comedic national story of interracial love. Recoiling from the horror of the violence of apartheid enacted through translation transmitted through the puppet, the script specifically

Post-Apartheid Slapstick 155

stages arguments for and against institutionally conceived scripts of reconciliation by way of the substitutions and condensations of love and revolution. The production turns to aesthetics to resolve the indecision about whether dialectical criticism or intuitive vitalism is best suited to surpass the recurrency of mythic violence.

The method of cross-referencing in *Ubu and the Truth Commission* avails itself of an image of the spiral formed around the work of art and literature in the twentieth century.[26] From it, we learn how the aesthetic anticipates an image of the post-apartheid that exceeds the violence it references. In the case of South Africa's constitutional revolution, the effort was to keep two irreconcilable concepts of love and revolution in play. *Ubu and the Truth Commission* rearranges the terms love and revolution to open onto different horizons of the post-apartheid. The interracial union between Ma Ubu and Pa Ubu, combined in their respective entanglements with and attitudes to violence, invites us to view the mistimed encounters of weakened forms of love, which would ultimately prove inadequate to deal with apartheid's infiltration of the psychopathologies of everyday life. The image of the post-apartheid is anticipated when perception grapples with a sensory encounter with the violence of everyday life.

The image of post-apartheid freedom was thus prematurely surrendered to theological and juridical paradigms, underwritten by a weak foundational fiction of love. A shrinking world picture produced a commensurate hardening of political attitudes within national frames. It is not unsurprising that the birth of the democratic South Africa would be welcomed not only as a world historical event, but as a miracle, hailed as the most liberal constitution in the world – but not as a realization of a vitalized concept of freedom. If aesthetic judgement was largely suspended in this dispensation, it also thwarted a new attitude to technology, particularly an attitude that flipped a technological determination specific to apartheid reasoning into a condition of freedom.

This is where we might identify a politics specific to the paradigm of slapstick. Slapstick flips this biopolitical spiral by reversing its flows and extending vitality to objects. This is what we hear in Timothy Campbell's call for learning to hold things lightly. As he puts it:

156 Undoing Apartheid

> [I]f biopower (or biopolitics) works through apparatuses to capture our humanity, then a form of life that takes its cue from slapstick would be one that throws a wrench into the apparatus; that provides things, objects, and relations with an existence beyond mere aliveness.[27]

The reorientation towards the object is crucial here. This is precisely the kind of shift that *Ubu and the Truth Commission* registers as it leads us through the mediations of mnemotechnic tools and a cinematic apparatus. In both, slapstick is the result of an intensification of a world picture that transports life to what is effectively life given over to absurdity. The heightened expectation that an elusive truth is on the cusp of being revealed further recalls the experience of the cinema – or 'bioscope' in South African parlance. In this repertoire of imitation of life in biopolitics and bioscope, the paradigm of slapstick lends itself to a renewed critique of the repressed aspects of apartheid that helps to reach a revitalized concept of freedom. If the world picture thus allows us to pose the question of what is no longer the fulfilment of the promise of a world, it is to the extent that it calls attention to the way technology supercedes the universal principles of democracy and humanism which underpinned the critique of racial formations and their combined solidification in the first part of the twentieth century.

Examples of mistimed arrivals in the realms of human feeling abound in Chaplin's *The Great Dictator*. For example, a train bearing Benzino Napaloni arrives (or does not, as it turns out) to meet Hynkel (a thinly disguised Hitler).[28] In a battle over the position of the *Ur*-dictator, the inability to align the exit of the train with the welcome red carpet is shown through the cinematic illusion of the reversal and braking of the train. We glimpse through the doorway of the carriage the figure of Napaloni being tossed about. Surely this scene calls for a reading of the effort on the part of Chaplin to signal a destination at which modernity was never expected to arrive. Mistiming is a reorientation of perspective: it calls attention to the catastrophic diminishing distance in the relay of sense and perception that is conveyed by the absurd encounter with race in everyday life. Read alongside the final scene in which a Jewish barber stumbles onto a stage at a fascist rally, only to be mistaken for the dictator, we learn something about the objects with which this constriction of sense and perception are placed on a course of collision. In the introduction of sound into his filmic language, Chaplin proceeds to caution human beings against becoming machine men and machine women without feeling, announcing the potentially dangerous reach of communication and the amplification of industrial technology in idealistic constructions of the becoming technical of the human.

If *Ubu and the Truth Commission* partakes in this spirit of slapstick, it recoils from the mythic violence for which technology has simply become a means to an end. Its aesthetic choices allow speech similarly to recoil from violence. Pa Ubu, for example, is memorably confronted by a recoiling microphone as he attempts to minimize his role in apartheid violence through the usual refrain of following orders in a chain of command. Here, an instrumentalized view of the technology that sustained apartheid can no longer be relied upon to provide a concept of reconciliation as non-violent violence, that is, as reconciliation forged by aesthetic means of linking elements of the human sensorium in overcoming violence.

Rather, *Ubu and the Truth Commission* calls attention to the *techne* of the spiral, or what we might call a bioscopic biopolitics, as a way of conceiving what the post-apartheid offers to life after apartheid. To underline this imitative function at the heart of bioscope and biopolitics is to contest notions of authentic life and authentic power. In other words, to consider the notion of apartheid as intrinsic to biopolitics is to reckon with the tension that has defined analyses of apartheid on a continuum between a totalizing concept of power and an equally totalizing concept of resistance. This is where the bioscope opens a particularly productive line of enquiry about what the subject of apartheid imbibed in the encounter with the moving image. Perhaps there was something more hopeful about the moving image than the tendency for power to imitate life.

Assuming the plausibility of the hypothesis that apartheid mimicked a cinematic apparatus in which power gradually imitated life, how do we explain its use of the very instrumentality of cinema to trap the subject in loops of eternal return? The answer lies in the vulgar dialectic that is ascribed to Verwoerd's explanation of apartheid in 1948, where the question of imitation is both inscribed and presumed. Apartheid presumed that it was imitating – copying – a liberal evolutionary

158 Undoing Apartheid

sensibility in its exercise of power. It also necessarily precluded anything other than imitation (copy) in that which contested its biopolitical rationality founded on its mythic constructions of race. Race, accordingly, was *ipso facto* a politics of imitation – a bad copy – with a discourse of natural origins pseudo-intellectually claimed as a product of scientific reason. What it accomplished, to the detriment of those it placed in an order of population control, was to lock race strategically into a repertoire of images of racial and ethnic origins in machinic relays. In this way, it foreclosed protension as a distinct possibility, prohibiting a process of relinking sense and perception by intermittently disturbing the relay between the two cognitive dimensions of the psychic structure. In the process, apartheid foreclosed the work of intuition of the transcendental in the passage of aesthetics to pedagogical performance, thus thwarting the very prospect of realizing post-apartheid freedom.[29]

Spiralling Forward

The post-apartheid has fallen on the sword of the TRC's indecision about whether to name subjectivity in the idiom of violence or freedom. If we accept Maria Muhle's caution about authenticity, then the TRC's image of post-apartheid subjectivity will forever be ensnared in a perpetual struggle between authentic life and authentic power.[30] Race, in this formulation, is the order of eternal return. Rather than freedom thus constituted and constrained, post-apartheid subjectivity occasions a recrafting of freedom, beyond its imitation in nationalism and neoliberal triumphalism. If nationalism and neoliberalism appear ungenerous, the optical movement of the cinema is significantly more generous. In other words, neoliberalism needs nationalism because it is beholden to technology, to mythic violence, in which life imitates power and power imitates life. This is a biopolitical script with little room for escape. Freedom on these terms is freedom conditioned by reciprocity, or a return of the same in the form of an imitation of apartheid.

Burdened with the threat of eternal return, slapstick provokes us to set to work, yet again, on the myths by which we have come to live. Slapstick is for all intents and purposes the sound effect of modern biopolitics as the latter enlists technology to the perpetual cycle of mythic violence, sounding a misplaced (or perhaps senseless) beating to account for a mistimed encounter between subject and object as a feature of late modernity. It equally conveys the potential to surrender the subject to a perpetual cycle of violence in the collision between the human and technology. But slapstick also permits a flipping of biopolitics into a condition of freedom in a manner that might prove indispensable for a new perspective on post-apartheid subjectivity.

Brian Massumi's elaboration of a complexity effect in the chaos theory of physics enables us to distinguish an image of post-apartheid freedom from the one cast through the grids of a juridical paradigm in which that image has become ensnared. Reading over Massumi's shoulder, we gather how an image of freedom adequate to our projection and desire resides less in an *effective* freedom than in a notion of *affective* freedom. Unlike its counterpart 'effective freedom', which the American educationist John Dewey proposed as a process of self-realization, *affective freedom* is constituted in relation to the constraints in which subjectivity is discernible. *Affective freedom* is not merely the mobilization of emotions to a preconceived end, but a brush with a constraint that allows that very constraint, as Massumi says, to be flipped into a condition of freedom.[31]

There is much in the image of flipping that relates to Benjamin's critique of the spiral of violence and his snapshot of an intellectual attitude towards freedom. By sounding out biopolitics along the lines of a Benjaminian critique, slapstick gestures towards something affirmative or intuitively transcendental salvaged from the ruins of the inheritance of technology and mythic violence that constituted apartheid. The imitations are to be stretched along the passage from fascism to apartheid, and from apartheid to the post-apartheid; or from apartheid biopolitics to neoliberalism. If the critique of violence is concerned with the depleting resources of the human in the encroachments of race, the critique of apartheid is confronted with the shrinking recourse to an intellectual attitude towards freedom. Notwithstanding the efforts of Michel Foucault, reigning conceptions of biopolitics tend to ultimately privilege the reason wielded by sovereign power in adjudicating the constraints on freedom. Neoliberalism, likewise, reduces freedom to a question of economism. In response to both, critics of the twentieth

160   Undoing Apartheid

century have turned to aesthetics (albeit not aesthetic education) to open up a different horizon, one in which an image of freedom breaks through the circularity of violence. But freedom thus conceived is needlessly reduced to an unenviable choice between humanistic love and revolutionary violence and defined by an older form of consilience of art and science in which the latter is accented.

To exceed the ideological and legal scripts of apartheid would require a foundational narrative to exceed testimonies of the experience of violence mediated entirely through institutions of state and economy. Neither can it be accomplished by appeals to love alone, and certainly not a weakened concept of love traded through fantasies of interracial union. What is striking in the constellation of future images of an affirmative concept of the biopolitical is significantly altered by thinking beyond the race and class experience of violence to something more singular: the interplay of projection and protension in which the human is returned to a relationship with *techne* through an aesthetic education. Cognisant of *techne*'s indispensability to art and aesthetics, technology can no longer be conceptually reduced to mere instrument or a source of alienation of productive forces, but must itself be viewed as an apparatus invested with the competing claims of subjectivity.

Such an invested view of technology recalls Gilbert Simondon's formulation whereby *techne* must be viewed as an ensemble and invention distinct from technology,[32] and through which we can begin to discern the outlines of a post-apartheid slapstick that surprises us with the potential for making freedom rather than a surprise that results in death. It is in this rendering of *techne*, a seizing by creating or intuitive-creation (bodily knowledge in the language of the discourse of apperception), that we encounter a possible way for relinking truth and reconciliation to match the idealism of love and revolution underpinning the struggle against apartheid.[33] In a departure from a technological determinism that accompanied the militarization of states and societies of control in the twentieth century, the *techne* of arts practices that bound love and revolution as experiments of freedom might have given us a wholly different image of the post-apartheid if slapstick had been acknowledged and affirmed. The *techne* specific to a paradigm of slapstick is perhaps where the link between technology and mythic violence proves to be unsustainable. If there is a mode of theatrical politics that splits the link between technology and mythic violence, it is precisely the mode of slapstick that brings a scene of recurring violence to crisis. Slapstick reorients attention to that which might otherwise be elided in our efforts to overcome the violence by which we survive the modernity of biopolitics with its jurisdictions over life and death. Might the search for a post-apartheid image of freedom be found in the inversion possible in the mnemotechnic constellation and cinematic image that nationalism lost sight of in its eternal winter?

Exit Ubu.

6

The Double Futures of Post-Apartheid Freedom

Chorus: Take just spoils and sail at last
Out of the bad dream of your past.
                Seamus Heaney, *The Cure at Troy*

Exit Apartheid

In the setting of Richard Rive's novel, *Emergency Continued*, an account accompanying the memorial to the Trojan Horse massacre notes that on 15 October 1985, a South African Railways vehicle with gun-wielding soldiers hidden in metal crates brought a macabre scene of death and despair to the streets of Athlone. There were no consequences for those responsible for killing three local youths.

The surreptitious military tactics stunned a country already in the grip of a stalemate of civil strife. But it equally clarified what was initially unfathomable about the student protests to which the state action was a response. As an illuminating point of Rive's novel, the massacre called for an education to delve into student encounters with an uncanny return of race and to navigate the psychopathologies of a divided city. Could there be a cure adequate to the wound inflicted on that fateful day in October, as the tragedy of apartheid resonated with the mythic story of the sacking of Troy narrated in Homer's *Iliad*?

The Double Futures of Post-Apartheid Freedom   *163*

What if Mandela had encountered what the students of 1985 had accidentally discovered as he stepped into the theatre of the world on that sunny day in 1990 following his release from prison? Might he have sought a different end to the catastrophe of the senses that apartheid left in its wake, in the course of its seemingly uneventful violence and its erratic recourse to the tactics of surprise?

As with these questions, the anxious tone of Heaney's selection of the story of Philoctetes as a gift to Mandela underscores the indecision about where precisely to begin the work of undoing apartheid. Trapped in the impasse of fate and destiny, Heaney's Philoctetes is an iconoclastic subject of partition, where partition signals not merely a geopolitical condition, but a deeply sentient predisposition towards a world encumbered by partition. As a gift to Mandela, Philoctetes' predicament also illuminates what should be grasped in Verwoerd's double game, which, as I have argued, gave rise to a geopolitical partitioning of space by means of grand apartheid while infiltrating the apperceptive schema of sense-perception through the exercise of petty apartheid. Philoctetes is a reminder that partition of the kind that enveloped South Africa set feeling and thinking on a course of collision. How to avoid this inevitable scene of collision would be critical for overcoming a simple rescripting of the apperceptive schema by relinking sense and perception through a struggle that is also an aesthetic education. The gift of Philoctetes leads us to ask once again, as Monique Wittig had, what it means to live in the shadow of a Trojan Horse as it sealed the fateful script of partition at the heart of the experience of apartheid. Bearing a message of hope, one wonders whether the travails of Philoctetes may yet offer a cure for the woes of the political and subjective consequences of partition.

The subject of partition bears a wound for which there can never be a cure that is ready-to-hand. This is as true of Heaney's Philoctetes, who hedges on the promise of freedom by surrendering his bow in the war of the Trojans, as it is of Rive's students, wounded by the Trojan Horse massacre. The meaning of Philoctetes' wound, it seems, presents itself as the wound that will not heal in the story of Athlone. There a narrative about a huge wooden horse bearing a select force of men under the command of Odysseus that the Greeks used to gain entry into the city of Troy was replicated by the Civil Force of the Joint

164 Undoing Apartheid

Operations Command of the South African Defence Force in October 1985. News about the killing of Michael Miranda (age 11), Jonathan Classen (age 21) and Shaun Magmoed (age 15) by militia hidden in a wooden crate atop a flatbed vehicle was rapidly disseminated by local and international broadcasters, conveying images that replayed familiar scenes drawn from an epic tragedy. The tactic was repeated the following day in the neighbouring settlement of Crossroads, where two youth were killed by security forces. In the sprawling townships beyond the city limits, apartheid had thus struck twice. Having relocated millions from the inner city to the outskirts in a systematic programme of forced removals and relocations under the Group Areas Act, the state engaged in what appeared to be a full-scale tactic of urban warfare. In 1985, it targeted youth frustrated by the inescapable racial geographies of apartheid in a world in which technological resources conveyed the promise of mobility.

If uncertainty reigned over a future that appeared as daunting as it was horizonless, a carefully constructed judgement about the hatred of apartheid offered a standpoint in the prevailing sea of turbulence. In this explosive mix of colliding sensibilities, a rising tide of local and international anti-apartheid opinion turned towards mythic and epic descriptions, settling on an image drawn from Greek tragedy to identify the atrocity. The need for sustained study of the meaning of the event was thereby deferred by the provocation to war.

In the days, months and years that followed, the attribution of the massacre to Homer's *Iliad* confirmed how elusive the naming of a post-apartheid desire would be. Rather than transform an image of murderous violence into one of freedom and desire, the Trojan Horse massacre instead bore traces of the repressed aspects of apartheid's violence, a repression that tested the redemptive limits of Greek tragedy from which it derived its name.[1]

The Trojan Horse massacre earns its epithet from the shock produced by a televised event and its visual relay around the world that some argue garnered international condemnation of the violence of the apartheid state. Beyond the televised reports, footage of soldiers firing at protesting youth in an ambush, ordinarily reserved for the bioscope, laid bare a largely obscure experience of an apartheid of the everyday that permeated a rationality of population control.

The Double Futures of Post-Apartheid Freedom   *165*

A surreptitiously planned act of state violence that had as its reference an iconic symbol of Greek tragedy thus transported the threat of death into the heart of the divided city. The Trojan Horse massacre produced a notion of politics as an expression of a 'pure degree of intensity', which became a cynical means of presaging civic peace. Alongside the death and destruction that it wrought, the slaying of three youths on the streets of the outer edges of Cape Town was an attempt to enforce peace by appealing to 'the threat of a tear that always looms'.[2] This was a poisoned chalice from which those charged with overseeing the birth of the post-apartheid would be forced to drink; a fear that every claim to freedom would be overshadowed by the equally daunting threat of lurking catastrophe. If the TRC offered the world a face of civil peace, a kind of symmetry sought by the Greeks in the idea of *stasis*, the Trojan Horse massacre was (and remains) a reminder that beneath the thin veneer of truth and reconciliation, the unrelenting threat of civil war persisted.

The movement that culminated in the tragedy of the Trojan Horse massacre began with the demand for an end to corporal punishment in schools, and in solidarity with students who lived under a state of emergency in thirty-six magisterial districts, mainly around the Vaal Triangle of South Africa. The heady struggles waged under the banner of the Congress of South African Students had led to a near collapse of the educational system in these regions. An equally rapid spread of the movement across the Cape Flats soon resulted in pitched street battles between students and police. The eruption was aggravated by debilitating constraints on mobility resulting from hardening racial divides of urban planning in the mid-1980s.

What the historian Colin Bundy identified as 'immediatism' in his study of 'street sociology and pavement politics' is supported by evidence of the growing anxiety expressed by students who found themselves increasingly trapped by apartheid's Group Areas – but perhaps for reasons other than those proposed by Bundy.[3] The charge of 'immediatism' upheld two antithetical tendencies that appeared to have taken hold: one short-circuiting the passage from school to factory through a generalized disciplinary apparatus aimed at producing docile bodies; and the other, increased access to the cinematic image which provided recourse to the world in an otherwise immobile city.

166 Undoing Apartheid

Judging by their slogans for a better education, the students of Athlone were driven by a desire for some relief in the midst of the masochism of speed in which they found themselves, fearing being swept away by the threat that apartheid had destined them to a place from which no return was conceivable. As they set about creating an interval, the Trojan Horse massacre shattered efforts to relink sense and perception in constructing a world picture beyond the fragmentation wrought in the name of apartheid. By searching for a perceptual grasp over a world that had been set in motion by external stimuli, the students who ignited the revolt of 1985 were trapped between the divided city on the one hand, and on the other, the fear of having desire swept away by the speed of technological temporal objects of communication. In the national narrative of the political struggle against apartheid, 'the student' had too easily become a generational marker of militancy detached from the uncertain circumstances in which desire thrived.

Given all that has been written and done in memory of the students' movement in South Africa, there is surprisingly little to account for the drives and desires that underwrote an unprecedented movement of school students for a period of six months in 1985, before the Trojan Horse massacre took place. In scholarly works and documentary films, as well as memorials, poems and works of art, the Trojan Horse massacre lends itself to depictions of a divided city rather than attentiveness to what was at work in the difficulty with schooling that the students sought to overcome. As a result, we have an event that is repeatedly returned to the realms of ideology through reams of paper and memorials that re-enact a habituated memory of attachment to war and violence – as if these were the only games in town.

Cinematographic Memory

In Athlone, the school had effectively become a zone of suspension. In the midst of competing claims for liberation and education, its students desperately searched for an interval in an environment of constrictions of time and space that was increasingly resulting in an acceleration of speed in the banality of the everyday. Unlike the generation of the first state of emergency in 1960, the generation of the second emergency in 1985 stumbled

The Double Futures of Post-Apartheid Freedom   *167*

on the returns of race in the arenas of petty apartheid. The search for an adequate interval afforded an opportunity both to revisit what had been misrecognized in the encounter with race in the problematization of apartheid; and to foster a practice of post-apartheid freedom in the belly of the beast.

The interval sought by students in 1985 perhaps had much in common with the cinematic interval, which had become a point of contest in withstanding the surrender of the meaning of freedom to the industrialization of memory in emerging forms of communication technology. The cinema thus provided an education in the everyday, replete with images of the desire enabled by the interval and the phantasmagoria of race, in stark contrast to the process of apartheid schooling, which resulted in increasing fragmentation and dispersal of desire. We might say that the cinema alerted the students to the speed of the phantasmagoria that awaited them. As street and moving images folded into each other, and as films based on the epics, including films such as *Trojan Horse*, co-mingled with the proliferation of B-grade American Cold War flicks, the terrifying prospect of robots replacing gods in order to resolve seemingly insurmountable and tragic conundrums took hold. The false promise of a school overrun by the drudgery of state instrumentalization rapidly became a source of disbelief on the part of students. The cinematic interval revealed something more foreboding about the future than the racial peace promised by the institutions of apartheid schooling, with their Cold War narratives and ingrained warnings of the threats of civil and race war.

The student search for an interval was not too dissimilar to the interval associated with the language of cinematography, best articulated in the cinematic operation that Trinh T. Minh-ha develops in her study of *Cinema-Interval*.[4] She digresses to the figure of film director Dziga Vertov, especially his elaboration of the idea of cine-seeing which, Minh-ha argues, saved cinematography from the 'frightful venom of habit'.[5] Vertov's technique failed in the context of Soviet society, perhaps because he ceded too much to the more romantic vision of Sergei Eisenstein. What matters are two specific instances in Vertov's theorization of cinematography, which are important for how we read Rive's account of the students' movement in Athlone in 1985. Vertov's vision offers a different way of conceiving of the students'

168 Undoing Apartheid

movement, and with it, the work of schooling (or as he might have preferred, retooling).

Minh-ha's reading of Vertov's *Kinekos Revolution Manifesto* stresses the point that 'intervals are what cine-images, cine-documents or cine-poems are built upon ... a movement between the pieces, the frames, upon the proportions of these pieces between themselves, upon the transitions from one visual impulse to the one following it'.[6] The first point of interest relates to how Vertov rearranges relations through the device of the camera, forming the interval as the most productive instance of cinema. As Minh-ha notes: 'in his "hall of intervals" where "frames of truth" are minutely edited, all is a matter of relations: temporal, spatial, rhythmic relations; relations, as he specified, of planes, of recording speed, of light or shade, or of movement within the frame ... cinematography is in itself a multiplicity of cinema intervals'.[7] With such commitment, Vertov's determination to retheorize cinematography makes known the stakes of the becoming technical of the human. Here the fabric of the everyday is woven into the visual machine, so that film's uniqueness lies in its proximity and immediacy to an unfolding present.[8]

Crucial here is not that Vertov sought to approximate journalism, or history, or reality TV to produce what Paul Virilio calls 'virtual reality'. Carloss James Chamberlin's punning 'Dziga Vertov: The Idiot' points towards how Vertov, beyond offering a theory of cinematography, also provides an aesthetic education that reconstellates the terrains of *episteme* and *techne*, which is instructive for reading Rive's engagement with the intensities of study and revolt with which this book opens. Chamberlin notes:

> At the heart of his film, Vertov uses the steel-making process as a poetic metaphor for the transformation of both the state and the individual in socialism. This metaphor gives yet another formal layer to the structure of *Enthusiasm*. The production of steel is a process whereby pig-iron, an impure alloyed mix of several metals and therefore weak and brittle under extreme force, is shot into a converter chamber where air is forced through the metal, driving the impurities out and leaving only the 'pure' steel, which has the virtues of tensility and strength. How does a nation of backward hick [*sic*] farmers become the industrialized fulfilment of Marxist prophecy? What dynamic element can make this transformation

The Double Futures of Post-Apartheid Freedom   *169*

happen: Factories, Tractors, Machines? It is thus with the people –
the hot fiery blast of socialism and the wind of a thousand slogans
hurl away their tsarist trinkets and entertainments, their religion,
their selfishness, and their vodka – and re-tool them into supermen,
Shock Workers, Machine-Men and Machine-Women of Steel. That
is the real object of the word Stalinism and the Five-Year Plan. The
steelification – the Stalinization – of the human being.[9]

The interval, I suggest, is that interlude within which the slide
into a fateful destiny is potentially redirected; not only by
dislodging technology as a means to an end, but by finding in
it the circumstances for an education sought in the composite
arena of an aesthetic education adequate to a world being coded
as global. If cinema had the sort of consequence that I attribute
to its development in Athlone, it ought to be read not as a means
to an end, but as a phase – an interval – in the technological
milieu that gave us the memory of the students' movement and
the meaning of schooling. To return to the scene of Athlone
with Vertov is to ask for a fresh attentiveness to the human and
technology that awakened students in 1985 by attending to the
very concept of education that could not be adequately elaborated amid the growing indistinction developing between school
and factory. What the students confronted was how neither
was available for plotting a future in the midst of apartheid's
isolation and economic decline.

While many attributed the upsurge of student protests in the
1980s to the economic plight that awaited youth under apartheid
– where they faced a future of being transformed into 'hewers
of wood and drawers of water', a biblical phrase that did the
rounds in pamphlets at the time – there was something else latent
in their agency.[10] Ordinarily this latency would be commonly
spoken about as a function of thought, but that would not
be helpful simply because it dialectically pits thought against
action, in which thought is once more jettisoned as a site of
politics. Neither could the upsurge in Athlone be explained only
as a response to the repressive atmosphere of authoritarianism
and corporal punishment in schools. Nor was it a simple act of
solidarity with the despair that faced students elsewhere in South
Africa under a state of emergency. What drove the students
to action was precisely that upon which they acted: namely,
schooling and the fate of the becoming technical of the human.

170   Undoing Apartheid

Perhaps a better way to think about the generative energy unleashed by the students is through the notion of a memory of the future, a formulation with which I hope to rename the activity that thousands of students embarked upon in 1985. To this end, a shift is called for: from a designation of the upsurge of 1985 expressed in terms such as 'schools boycott' and 'mass movement', towards something that disaggregates and relinks the relation between student and movement in the co-constituting couplet 'students' movement'. Such a move seeks to substitute the common understanding of the students as prone to violence and militancy in their responses, with an agency that could be read as apparently more passive, with something more thoughtful and studied; and which together resulted in the erasure of the interval by the speed with which the events surrounding the upsurge of 1985 unfolded.

A CBS film crew was alerted to something about to unfold in Thornton Road on the day of the shootings. Chris Everson, Nicola Della Casa (in charge of sound recording) and John Rubythorn recorded the shocking events in Athlone on the day.[11] Describing the footage as explosive, they called *Cape Times* journalist Tony Weaver, who selected three frames from the footage for an article under the headline 'Trojan Horse massacre', to be published in the newspaper. In the meantime, the CBS journalists chartered a plane to Nairobi, and 'microwaved' the footage to New York. Broadcast on television around the world, the Trojan Horse massacre was a place-keeper for a movement, the potential of which was lost to the immediacy and urgency demanded by the act of state violence and the gathering storms of technological determination. The story of the Trojan Horse had been given over to the technics of communication, through boxes, in which the televisual was synchronized by the death carried in a railway truck turned into a war machine; not unlike the fateful gift of the Greeks to the unsuspecting Trojans.

But in all the ways the Trojan Horse has been memorialized, what is not clear is how the killings resulted in a scene of political drives that became detached and disconnected from desire. The idea of the school that had been problematized in the students' movement had resulted in a further fetishization of school as ideological state apparatus, leaving no language for a memory of the future that the desire for schooling had kindled in the students' movement of 1985.

Partitioning Sense and Perception

The partitioning of sense and perception, as suggested through the preceding pages, established patterns of behaviour by measuring image reactions taken at accelerated speeds in the conduct of controlled psychotechnic experiments. Shattering the very image by which a subject might negotiate the object world, apartheid in its supposedly minor key led to a scene of devastating collision. The corrosive psychic consequences infantilized, humiliated, belittled and caricatured the very psychic structure it identified as vulnerable under the strain of its experiments. Under these circumstances, race frequently functioned as a source of superstition and paranoia, especially in a contest over who was better equipped at making political, as opposed to aesthetic, judgements. This game was rigged in favour of determining racial outcomes in advance. Experimental psychology, that marginal discipline that carried the ironic title of a benevolent intervention known as social work, and with which Verwoerd was associated, infiltrated the very depths of the psychic structure in order to train memory to abide by nondescript objects of desire.

In the bid to limit horizons, a statist project led to the establishment of Group Areas and a system of Bantu Education through which memory and desire were spatially isolated, rather than linked through education, in an overarching effort to control and influence behaviour. Apartheid was a mechanism that not only thrived on the notion of the divided city, but was in hindsight a faltering early version of a paradigm of neoliberalism. To that end, it was a mechanism that took its ill-fated passengers on a rapidly accelerating journey that would result in a collision of the subject with the edifice of race it had constructed. Wittingly or unwittingly, apartheid produced an efficient mode of transporting the psyche to the depths of despair so that none of those being careered towards an inevitable collision could remain unscathed.

On this side of the grave, hope and history can only be scoured from among the remains of the objects and images strewn across the landscape, not unlike the efforts by Aby Warburg's *Mnemosyne Atlas* from 1924. Warburg created a constellation of images to map the afterlife of antiquity that reappears in later

172 Undoing Apartheid

times and places, a montage of seemingly unconnected images that Georges Didi-Huberman describes as follows:

> The Warburgian atlas is an object thought on a bet. It is the bet that images, collected in a certain manner, would offer us the possibility – or better still, the inexhaustible resource – of a rereading of the world. To reread the world is to link the disparate pieces differently, to redistribute the dissemination, which is a way of orienting and interpreting it, no doubt, but also of respecting it, of going over it again or re-editing and piecing it together again without thinking we are summarizing or exhausting it.[12]

While Warburg pursued a wordless *Nachleben* (afterlife) of *Pathosformel* (pathos formula) in Renaissance art and cosmology, Freud set out in search of the meaning of the psychopathology of everyday life, and Benjamin's *Passagen-Werk*, or *Arcades Project*, set to work by way of the *flâneur* of the Parisian arcades in a shared disbelief in the promise of peace founded on a shift from virulent to benevolent ideas of race. At issue was the search for peace after World War I that brought together ideas about 'holism' and evolution espoused by Jan Smuts, South African Prime Minister at the time. Smuts's influence in the making of a European peace can easily be detected in the sentiments of benevolent racism that peppered the transfer of the estate of European empires to a league of modern (read European) nation-states.[13] Along with the prevailing suspicion and trepidation among intellectuals of the Black Atlantic, Warburg, Freud and Benjamin shared a mistrust of a European peace, electing instead to work towards reconstituting the shattered fragments of memory from which fascism was rising, and upon which an emboldened capitalism was feasting. The rise of apartheid was a further sign that the mistrust that had gathered around race had created a predicament of *stasis* from which an exit appeared unlikely. *Stasis* was clearly no antidote for apartheid, which had already usurped this rationality as the basis for its justification.

Returning to Athlone

Nicole Loraux's *The Divided City* alerts us to the complications that arise when the idea of *stasis* is reduced to the symmetry of parts, a complication that is especially pertinent when we

The Double Futures of Post-Apartheid Freedom   *173*

consider it in relation to what is specific to the name apartheid shares with a strand of *Gestalt* psychology forged in Leipzig between the 1890s and the 1920s.[14] She argues for reorienting the meaning of the notion of *stasis* so that it is adequate to the demands of watching over the repression of violence and warfare in the pursuit of civic peace.[15] Several crucial moves in the overarching argument of her *The Divided City* are indispensable for relating how such an extension of meaning could be achieved. Loraux genealogically disaggregates the notion of *stasis*, a word that enters the Greek lexicon as a term associated not only with motionlessness, but more specifically with *kinesis*: movement, or agitation.[16] In other words, for the Greeks, *stasis* bore a double meaning, which ultimately cohered around the idea of movement at rest. Loraux suggests that we take one step beyond this political and philosophical rendering of the idea of *stasis* by extending it to account for the symmetry sought by the Greeks, rather than the explosive qualities often intended by the habits of dialectical reason in more recent times. To inaugurate such a meaning, she asks us to consider how it was that the further notion of division operated in the Greek political and philosophical lexicon; first as a form of warfare against the foreigner or stranger (the Persian mainly); and second, as an arena of thought in which the ambivalence of the first produced a sense of what was shared, although not held in common. Loraux's attempt to overcome the impasse of the city constructed by historians and anthropologists recalls an aspect of Freud's *Interpretation of Dreams* written at the turn of the twentieth century, as psychoanalysis stumbles upon the public sphere.[17]

The reading of how reconciliation, harmony, conflict and division played out in the Greek city state, by analogy, helps to place Athlone beyond a history of space internally divided into zones of exclusion and inclusion in the city. In fact, we are introduced to a context where that narrative breaks through *stasis*, that is, provides another way of thinking that breaches the limits imposed by the city. It is not surprising that the psychic repair that was promised through the TRC should return repeatedly to the motif of 'shattering' to describe the essence of apartheid's violence.[18] While it is unclear whether such shattering resides in the disfiguring of the psychic structure of the subject or with the divided city, apartheid, as also Athlone, conjures images of the

174 Undoing Apartheid

fate of the slave – and the reinscription of the remains of slavery in a generalized process of the becoming technical of the human.

Apartheid, in short, is the name given to the shattering that results in distributing the shards of sense and perception to what Lorraine Daston calls the idea of the 'merely mechanical'.[19] Daston argues that the instrumentalities that promote the idea of the 'merely mechanical' emerge from the seventeenth to the nineteenth centuries in Europe to produce a form of docility lodged in slavish and repetitious rule-bound reflexive consciousness that eschews freedom, judgement, creativity and imagination – while configuring all these as natural offshoots of modernity. If apartheid is a continuation of this process, it is to the extent that it consummates the onset of immaterial labour at the end of slavery in the direction of a facile neoliberal subjectivity reincarnated as an entrepreneur of the self. Apartheid, in its disguise as petty apartheid, achieves what capital in its normal progression was incapable of achieving: a partition of sense and perception that drove the subject of race towards the becoming technical of the human.

The monuments scattered across the expanse of settlements that arose as a result of the dreaded system of forced removals are grim reminders of a period of the intermittent eruption of violence. They are markers of memory that conceal the myth of violence that is repressed in the interest of preserving a tenuous peace in the present. What then lurks behind the violence of a massacre that bears the name of a catastrophe in a far-off land and a far-away time, of a war that knew no end? More precisely, what is being preserved in the present through the image of civil war conjured by the Trojan Horse massacre? These questions initially lead in divergent directions: one to the past and the other to the future – not unlike the difference established by the fall of Troy and the painful homecoming of Odysseus, disguised as a beggar, to the island of Ithaca, ten years after the defeat of the Trojans.[20] Upon closer scrutiny, the question of what is being preserved converges in the defensiveness indicated in attitudes to the past and the future, partly because the TRC framed the event of apartheid in the cloaks and daggers of civil war. The TRC's rationality was no doubt pitted against apartheid's enforced peace, rather than reflecting the post-World War II Nuremberg model, as is all too commonly believed in the familiar laying out of a miraculous triumph of redemption over retribution.

The Double Futures of Post-Apartheid Freedom   *175*

This self-narration that was accepted by an exhausted people encountered a limit when pitted against heinous acts of violence such as the Trojan Horse massacre. For the TRC, such events were precisely ones that masked the threat of civil war, and from which South Africa was desperately seeking to withdraw. By the same token, apartheid was also ironically claimed by its ideologues as the very justification for avoiding the inevitable slide into race war.[21] By this logic, the TRC presented itself as a new model of anti-colonial humanism grounded in law that was more effective in averting race war than apartheid's trickery, which had promised civil peace under the cover of a dangerous proposition of turning everyday life into a laboratory of endless turmoil. The evil lurking in the detail of a new politics of race after World War II can be heard in Verwoerd's grandstanding on the eve of the National Party victory in 1948, under the banner of apartheid:

> South Africa has to deal here with one of her greatest problems, and one of the most serious problems, which any country in the world could be called upon to deal with. The question of war and peace is no more serious to other countries than the problem of finding a solution for a possible clash between white and black is for South Africa. In other countries of the world, where there is a move towards apartheid, sometimes merely towards apartheid between Whites and Whites, where the present Opposition's former ally, Russia, is merely another European race within its borders, then it seeks to apply apartheid which has to be paved with bloodshed and misery. An example is Palestine, where the Jew and the Arab are up against one another, and stand for apartheid, but mainly in this sense that each of the two parties wants the whole country for itself alone. Where we are prepared to accord to non-Europeans the right to their own opportunities of development, where we bring it about not by means of the sword, but through the benevolent hand of the Europeans who are in the country, then do not arouse suspicions of the world outside, where there are so many difficulties. Do not arouse suspicion that there is oppression, but show them that there is a policy which seeks rights and justice towards all.[22]

If *stasis* masks the threat of civil war, Verwoerd's limitless arrogance and cynicism was folded into it as an instance of the cunning reorientation of the idea of race in light of the defeat of fascism in Europe. Beneath the veneer of claiming to remake politics by modifying the rule of race to chime with the tenor of

176   Undoing Apartheid

a national and global peace in a grand gesture of apartheid, an equally cunning (if not even more pernicious, because protracted) effort at constituting a mechanism in which the psychic apparatus enfolded the infinite process of the becoming technical of the human was set in motion.

The TRC was later tasked with unravelling this knot as it grappled with the psychopathologies of apartheid and the topology of apartheid's divides. If the pursuit of separate strands was doomed from the start, it was to the extent that apartheid was the ultimate act of political trickery: one that might better be understood as a game of parts and wholes. Apartheid, according to this account, was a precursor of later paradigms of neoliberalism, in which the state linked power and population through a meandering discourse for which there was no end other than *stasis*. It is not surprising then that the TRC set out to probe individual experiences of violence, but ended with a somewhat futile effort at identifying the sources of violence in the legal discourse of grand apartheid. Unfortunately, by so doing, it cast an emergent nation's collective eye over the aims of a legal apparatus upon which it sought to establish a legal instrument capable of forestalling a push into civil war.

The discursive frame through which the post-apartheid was conceived by the TRC was rooted in jurisprudence. However, events such as the Trojan Horse massacre were also the source of its most glaring indecision about whether to grasp the nettle of apartheid by tackling the fallacies sustained by its grand design or by its intrusions into everyday life, the points at which *stasis* was enforced or civil war fostered. Might the Trojan Horse massacre not signal a ceaseless and persistent threat of violence bought about by divisions premised on the idea of race articulated through petty apartheid? Might it offer a glimpse of the shared fates of the slave and the subject of neoliberalism in the becoming technical of the human?

Apartheid's subtle redirection of the concept of apperception, as suggested in the pages of this book, reflected a late-nineteenth-century extension of the project of experimental psychology. Taking hold of the sensory and perceptual dimensions of the subject by mnemotechnic means, apartheid created the infra-structure for which the divided city became emblematic of what Freud called everyday life. In addition to Bergson, it is Freud who ultimately offers us a vantage point from which to think

The Double Futures of Post-Apartheid Freedom   *177*

about the consequences of the false problem on which apartheid was conceived.

John Mowitt has shown how Freud's attempts to orient psychoanalysis towards the task of the interpretation of dreams amounted to an affirmation of the public commitments of his discourse. Psychoanalysis, Mowitt argues, was forged in the interval between *Project for a Scientific Psychology* (1895) and *Interpretation of Dreams* (1900). Everyday life in the construction of this Freudian interval is not merely a countervailing discourse to that of the town planner or minor bureaucrat. Rather, it is a search for the sources of division internal to the *mind* of the city. Apartheid by this reckoning is not primarily a programme of grand social engineering, but also a mnemotechnic experiment that takes hold of relations between sense and perception, and orchestrates a partition at the core of their meaning for a liveable life. Everyday life, to be unambiguous, becomes another name for the exercise of petty apartheid. As such, it is precisely the symptom formed by a division that acts as a dynamic internal to the city, from which there is little room to escape other than through surrender to civil war.

There can be no future in this conception of the everyday, one that has become contested terrain in the city of the historian and anthropologist, for overcoming the divided city. In fact, the settling of scores between the city of the historian and that of the anthropologist answers to the terrifying prospect for which civil war was created, and for which race war provided a costly mechanism of release. This is perhaps what Mowitt means in his rereading of Freud's correspondence with Fleiss, in which the former notes, in an exasperated tone, that 'otherwise, Vienna is Vienna, that is to say extremely revolting'. 'What makes Vienna be Vienna', asks Mowitt, or, 'what makes this fact – the fact of Vienna being Vienna – extremely revolting?'[23] In the bungling and missteps through which Freud makes common cause with ordinary lives, the revolting feeling must surely conjure a spectre of race — or anti-Semitism in Freud's case – that makes encounters with the everyday, well, terrifying.

Athlone presents us with a different problem to Freud's Vienna, in which the psychopathologies of everyday life are bent towards objects of consumption. Linking politics in the aftermath of a threat of civil war appears to have suffered a similar fate to that foreseen by Loraux in the *stasis* of the

178 Undoing Apartheid

ancient Greek city. What makes *Athlone be Athlone* – that is, as revolting as that which makes *Vienna be Vienna* – is that it trips over the interval that Freud reserved for the relinking of the mind and the city. But how then to break out of *stasis* without falling prey to civil war?

Whereas Freud's Vienna calls for a process of political interweaving of the city, and Loraux for instituting a movement at the heart of *stasis*, Vincent Azoulay suggests a different approach. In his reading of Loraux, he asks whether it is appropriate 'to simply ensure and maintain its unity through harmony and friendship'.[24] As Azoulay notes in his assessment of Loraux's stirring of the peace established between the historians and anthropologists in the study of democracy in ancient Athens, exceeding the city – perhaps, we might add, through an education into the unknown as opposed to one that is beholden to a model of trusteeship for training citizens – might allow us to find a new way of linking politics to life.[25]

This is a pertinent reminder of how we think Athlone. Apartheid proved considerably more intractable as a problem, not least because of its grafting onto a discourse of culture and psychology forged in the *Gestaltist* forays of Wundt. In the realms of petty apartheid, a simple lesson drawn from Wundt appeared to offer an analogous reference: that a psychological response does not exist when the subject is treated merely as a passive responder to externally imposed conditions. Psychological responses depend on the excitation of the senses. It is the capacity of this submerged layer of the infiltration of objects in everyday life to trigger psychological responses that became a consistent strand of petty apartheid. Petty apartheid tests the limits of sensory excitation, a limit that when breached results in unprecedented violence.

The Trojan Horse massacre likewise thwarted any futurity beyond the orders of race bequeathed by apartheid. It was a proverbial nail in the coffin, a wedge driven into the sensory and perceptual apparatus on which petty apartheid was founded, sustained and extended. The TRC overlooked this level of apartheid in the interests of securing an eternal peace against the threat to return the city to a state of civil war. In this uneasy peace, the Trojan Horse massacre falls short of the transitional mechanism of truth and reconciliation, especially since it approximates the same order of *stasis*, albeit by other

The Double Futures of Post-Apartheid Freedom   *179*

means. As Danby's artwork discussed in Chapter 2 presaged, the act of restoration merely reinserted the slave in desublimated relays of capital and the project of making modern political institutions.

However, when the massacre is placed in a larger frame of the debate about liberation and education, a potential relinking of sense and perception is availed for the purposes of revitalizing questions of freedom unanticipated by the purveyors of mythic violence. By attending to the psychic missteps in the process of traversing a city held captive by the threat of civil war, might it be possible to effect such a shift through an intervention that would short-circuit apartheid's operation as a self-perpetuating machine? What could a future possibly entail at the level of the psychic, collective and technical dimensions of apartheid beyond the repetition of history calling twice, as tragedy and as farce? The answer perhaps resides in the way we apprehend the competing temporalities necessary for conceiving of revolution that defies apartheid's grand and petty designs, and how we educate the sensory equipment for duration as distinct from overdetermined event. If retiming is what matters in overcoming petty apartheid, its features can best be recounted anecdotally by returning to the confluence of image and sound in Athlone. This is where we learn something about surviving apartheid by living through competing temporalities in the 'features' and 'futures' that were spoken and left unspoken for the thousands who frequented the cinemas, or bioscopes, of a divided city.

Abdullah Ibrahim, the renowned jazz pianist, recounted how everyday talk about the experience of going to the bioscope for a cinematic overload of a '*double feature*' was charmingly referred to by locals as 'going to watch a *double future*'. If the '*double feature*' provided for a future of abundance, the '*double future*', at the very least, proved ominous. Rather than signifying a sense of multiplied despair, the '*double future*' placed the bioscope in a peculiarly productive relationship of hope to the biopolitics of apartheid, coming both before and after that mechanism by which apartheid orchestrated its relationship to racialized discourses of population and individual life. The bioscope seemingly nurtured an illusion of what it might mean to live free of the strictures of life rationalized by the small-minded and petty dictates of apartheid's administrative rule.

180   Undoing Apartheid

Stumbling in Athlone

As the divided city leads us to the inevitability of civil war, might there be a way to conceive of the post-apartheid that produces an alternative concept of technology – one that presents itself as different to the experience of accompanying psychotechnics on a proverbial death drive? I believe there is, if we are prepared to thread Athlone through the cinematic memory in which it was primarily produced. Consider Abdullah Ibrahim's meditation on memory, moving image and music in the critique of apartheid conveyed in Chris Austin's 1987 film, *A Brother with Perfect Timing*. Ibrahim reflects on Manenberg, both the name of a place in Athlone (and a legacy of apartheid's forced removals) and one that inspired a jazz composition, which replays a discourse on the repressed aspects of the critique of apartheid with which I opened this book. Speaking from exile, he tells us:

> Duke had perfect timing. Timing is arriving at the right point at the right time, with a minimum of effort. In Manenberg, Basil Coetzee, the tenor saxophone player, told us a story: Imagine a Saturday morning in the township ... I mean you've never seen so many children anywhere in your life than a Saturday morning in the township ... children, people going shopping, cats, dogs, chickens. So here these two guys ambling down the road, have a little ... whiff ... taste. Now these brothers have perfect timing. The moment of perfect timing crystallises in everyone focusing on this moment ...

In the film clip that accompanies Ibrahim's meditation on the scene, we are drawn to a cutaway of two 'brothers' walking down a dusty Cape Flats street, sharing in the pleasure of what appears to be a joint in a joint that is out of time. As they amble along, a little girl enters the frame skipping, passing them from behind and moving directly into the path of an oncoming car. Ibrahim explains that without losing a beat, '[one brother] just scoops the girl up, puts her down on this side (on the right), takes the joint from the other hand and back in front and there we go ... perfect timing man, master musicians'.

Let us rewind. Duke, as in Duke Ellington (not Duke Ngcukana, the renowned saxophonist from Langa township who may be named in honour of the first), had perfect timing only insofar as his movement and timing arrived at a point

The Double Futures of Post-Apartheid Freedom   *181*

with minimum effort. At the very least, two predicaments are overcome in this space of effortlessness. First, the entire scene of Basil Coetzee's story, as recounted by Ibrahim, is destined to result in a collision at the point of arrival. The perspective formed around three seemingly discrete movements – approaching motor vehicle, skipping girl and ambling brothers – each deliberately slowed by corresponding speeds to produce the conditions for an inevitable collision. As the movement of the image decelerates, the car accelerates beyond the girl skipping as she passes the ambling brothers. Rather than seeing these as discrete instances of movement, we are given access to a sense of duration underscored by a rendition of 'Mannenberg – "is where it is happening"', a jazz composition through which Abdullah Ibrahim, Basil Coetzee and Robbie Jansen became crucial to a generation of anti-apartheid activists in and beyond Cape Town. Duration leads us to a sense of the convergence of sound, image and movement into a whole that opens onto another plane through which Athlone – and apartheid – might be anticipated. Rather than *stasis*, Ibrahim's 'Mannenberg' offers us duration. And while Ibrahim adopts Islam and martial arts as techniques of his self-styling, these choices underline what it means to hold onto composition, and by extension, duration.

Edmund Husserl's phenomenology may have been better served by the world out of which 'Mannenberg' is composed. In the phenomenology of memory as retention, or what he terms 'primary memory', perfect timing may be taken to function in his schema, and that of Austin's film, as an effortless unfolding of time as duration – from New York to the dusty streets of Athlone, from sound to image. But as an instance of recollection, or secondary memory, the filmic rendering of car, girl and ambling brothers catapults us towards a memory of the future that is hurtling towards collision. Husserl's recourse to melody effectively separates perception from imagination, so that primary memory – or retention – is pure perception, while secondary memory, or recollection, is dependent on imagination. This is precisely where we might identify a playing out of a concept of *stasis* as civil war; and *stasis* as movement at rest.

As a film conscious of its anti-apartheid commitments, *A Brother with Perfect Timing* reaches beyond opposing primary memory with secondary memory, dissolving the difference

182 Undoing Apartheid

between perception and imagination as distinct operations in Husserl's phenomenology. It achieves this by drawing the viewer out of the wager between history and apocalypse, and into that which underscores a memory of what we forget in the constellation of sound and image in Athlone. Put differently, what underscores duration is the interval of the 'whiff' in Ibrahim's recounting of a Saturday morning in Manenberg. Replaying the scene, the enduring memory is that which extends beyond the focal point of collision, swapping the point of arrival for arriving effortlessly. While we all expect arrival to be consummated at a point of collision, duration produces a place elsewhere. If Manenberg is the name of a place in which collision is destined, its elsewhere resides in the composition of 'Mannenberg', with its subtle doubling of a geminated consonant '*n*' which can be heard enunciated at 12"44' on the 1974 recording.

The dominant motif in this overlaying of sound and image in *A Brother with Perfect Timing* is composition convened through re-sensing temporalities of the everyday. Ibrahim tells of the formation of the melody but with no indication of why or how it became a signature tune of opposition to apartheid for many across South Africa and beyond. He recalls stepping out of a rehearsal studio that was kitted with a grand piano, and finding himself in front of an upright piano. He tells how a melody appeared to him, plausible because the upright piano pushes sound back at the pianist. He invited Basil Coetzee to play out a sequence on the horn and, finally, they decided on a bridge that would lead them out of the melody. All along, the technical temporal objects of sound and sight colluded to produce a consciousness that took on the form of cinematographic memory performed in the idiom of a brother with perfect timing.

Stressing the political pedigree of 'Mannenberg' has meant that the composition is too hastily associated with national or cosmopolitan political influences. It too readily falls to the sides of the divide between history and apocalypse, or the opposition between the city of the anthropologist and the city of the historian, in which post-apartheid freedom is increasingly seen as a dwindling promise. In a review of *A Brother with Perfect Timing* in *The New York Times* in 1987, Jon Pareles writes about the expansive reach of Ibrahim's music, but does not sufficiently stress how its multivocal foundations make it function as a statement against apartheid:

The Double Futures of Post-Apartheid Freedom   *183*

When he left South Africa in the 1960's, Abdullah Ibrahim took Cape Town with him. The city's mixture of African, Arabic, Oriental and European cultures echoes in the music he writes for his septet, Ekaya; there are spirituals, slow-rolling South African marabi rhythms, American jazz (especially Thelonious Monk and Duke Ellington), African traditional melodies, even the samba rhythms that Mr. Ibrahim traces to Africa.

This may indeed be the case if the composition is recalled in respect of Ibrahim's religious and eclectic musical sensibilities. Surprisingly though, this range of intersecting influences omits the ways in which Ibrahim's composition might be thought to function as filmic soundtrack. It was, after all, produced in the era of the so-called 'spaghetti Western' soundtracks of Ennio Morricone, which could be heard in the bioscopes of the Cape Flats that Ibrahim inhabited.[26] The cinematic formed a particular temporal object that mediated relations of sound and image. How else do we explain an early composition by Ibrahim titled 'Liberation Dance (When Tarzan Met the African Freedom Fighter)' from the album *Africa: Tears and Laughter* (1979) except by assigning to Athlone the flux of the cinematic?

Despite claims made about 'Mannenberg' as unofficial anthem of the liberation movement, its impulse is only explicitly revealed against the backdrop of the cinematic montage of Chris Austin's 1987 film.[27] This is where musical notes and accompanying images converge most cogently in the relation they are assigned in the filmic text. The point I wish to drive home here is one in which Manenberg/'Mannenberg', the names of both a place and a composition, brings us circling back to the need to consider the memory of apartheid in terms of what Stiegler calls tertiary memory, and which he marks as a specific development in Edmund Husserl's forays into the phenomenology of consciousness. Let us pause at Stiegler's insistence on the specificity of the concept of tertiary memory as it is distinguished from primary and secondary retention in Husserl's phenomenology. Perhaps a tertiary memory that intrudes into the domains of recollection provides the resources for relinking the divided city by constellating relations of sense and perception detached from a Wundtian paradigm of apperception that sustained apartheid. I have already pointed out why everything is inscribed in advance within the retentional finitude of consciousness: the fact that

184 Undoing Apartheid

memory is originally a process of selection and forgetting. Stiegler notes that in all remembering of a past temporal object, 'there is a necessary process of *dérushage*, of montage, a play of special effects, of slowing down, accelerating and even freezing an image: this is the time of reflection that Husserl analyzes precisely as such – a moment of the analysis of memory, of recollection's decomposition'.[28]

But given that we have also seen that this selection first affects primary retention itself, we then have to acknowledge that consciousness is always in some fashion a montage of overlapping primary, secondary and tertiary memories. We must, suggests Stiegler, thus mark as tertiary retentions all forms of 'objective' memory: 'cinematogram, photogram, writing, paintings, sculptures – but also monuments and objects in general, since they bear witness, for me, say, of a past that I enforcedly did not live'.[29] The distinction from Husserl is subtle, but consequential here. Ordinarily, he tells us, consciousness is constructed around two poles: one drawn from the proverbial melody where each note is heard as a perceptual act of retention that makes the object of melody endure; and a secondary memory, born of recollection that is the domain of imagination.

Stiegler wants us to rethink this bifurcation at the heart of phenomenology, to place in the midst of its operation a tertiary memory in which technology is integral to consciousness. In other words, consciousness is that 'post-production room' where the flows of primary, secondary and tertiary memory are assembled. As a cutting room, consciousness provides for a scene of projection and screening that has hitherto had the effect of demarcating the world into an apartheid of sense and perception.

To the extent that Athlone is a name for what we select to forget in recollections of apartheid, we could say that its memory is entirely given over to the flux of the temporal object of cinema of the kind encountered in *A Brother with Perfect Timing*. What is presented here is the technical becoming of the human where, as Stiegler reminds us, 'the cinematic *effect* ceaselessly produces particular consciousness'.[30] Tertiary memory establishes a retentional finitude, the locus of a memory which cannot contain itself and is thus reliant on a technical temporal object – in this case the cinema. Stated succinctly, Athlone's consciousness is, for better or for worse, cinematic. If the cinema defines the structure of memory in Athlone, it does so at the expense of the opposition

The Double Futures of Post-Apartheid Freedom   *185*

between a memory that is discretely melodic and one that is insulated by the photographic image. As *A Brother with Perfect Timing* reminds us, Athlone is a memory that we forget only so that it can be revealed in the mode of the cinematic.

Perhaps soundtrack, rather than anthem or multicultural context, gives us an opening to think about the industrialization of memory that made 'Athlone be Athlone'. To stumble upon Athlone is to discover the cinematographic qualities of its individual and collective consciousness reverberating in its political and religious repertoires. To stumble upon this Athlone is also to brush up against the possibilities of a concept of the post-apartheid that is more than the sum of the techniques of apartheid. In the becoming technical of the human an interval is availed in which the potential for rethinking the relation between the human and technology offers itself as an instance of recuperating *stasis* as a supplement to movement, rather than mortality. The question is whether it is possible to traverse the space of Athlone's cinematographic memory, not to harness nostalgia and violence, but to locate points where the instabilities of race on which apartheid rested enable a push towards post-apartheid freedom.

To achieve this, we might indeed need to learn from stumbling upon what in Athlone appears as a troubling distortion of the apperceptive schema. Let us recall that in the Wundtian framework, apperception referred to the difference in clarity of a group of phenomena given in consciousness. This required a method that would produce psychological order out of chaos. The aim of the experiments in apperception were to determine the point at which greatest clarity is reached in the activation of the senses that finds a reciprocal expression in perception. I have argued that petty apartheid was a derivative discourse that mediated the experience and consciousness of race by privileging sensation over perception. If Athlone names this apperceptive dissonance, it is not because it recalls the memory of apartheid's techniques of subjection, but the *technogenesis* that once flickered across the screens of the bioscope in a choreography of becoming technical of the human, or the passing of race from one technical system to another.

How then can we reconstitute the relations of sense and perception to grant another lease on post-apartheid freedom? How can we inscribe a post-apartheid sensibility, in this full or

186   Undoing Apartheid

robust sense, into our understanding of the work of public arts, rather than public parts? How might this sensibility function precisely as a mode of schooling that reveals another script of *technogenesis*, one that places the human in a more proximate relation to life and art, rather than the nostalgia enveloping war?[31] Premised on a specific understanding of everyday life as that where the present is non-identical with itself – of double-future – I suggest that to 'get lost in Cape Town' (as suggested by Zoë Wicomb's novel *You Can't Get Lost in Cape Town*) is to stumble upon that which gives to the post-apartheid its most enduring claim to be a discourse that extends beyond apartheid. To select this reorientation, we might reread Wicomb's novel as an injunction to lose one's way by traversing the passage of race that ensued after slavery – if only to offer the post-apartheid as a specific concept for which an aesthetic education may prove its most powerful supplement.

The name for this supplement may very well be Athlone – a name that is more than a place-keeper for a local geography, but one that Rive's *Emergency Continued* reworks to signify a memory of the future. That memory is not only one related to local memories of racial domination, forced removals and economic control that went by the name APARTHEID; rather, a memory of the future relates to the unconscious ways in which apartheid operated and was potentially eclipsed, even tricked, in the everyday. It is that memory which is now unfortunately unavailable and illegible in the wake of apartheid.

Yet, Athlone also serves as a name for the non-identity between the past and present, where apartheid passes without the post-apartheid coming into its own, and where, if we take our cue from *Emergency Continued*, a post-apartheid sensibility was closer to hand than what followed in its aftermath. Athlone here is the name for a memory that we select to forget in the interest of a civic peace, and which the memorial to atrocity fails to memorialize because it detaches the event of violence from the desire for schooling. Rive paves one way out of this circularity. His revision of the meaning of schooling will prove indispensable for understanding how race is being sustained by a re-grammatization of the world through technological means.

The convergence of race and technology produces a mode of *technogenesis* of which we need to remain fearful. For the human thus folded into the machine is only ever a compression

The Double Futures of Post-Apartheid Freedom 187

of movement, of uncontrollable speed, and undulating sadness and *stasis*. The students of 1985 realized that in the institutions of apartheid schooling they faced the prospect of a future worse than that of earlier generations. In the generational conflicts that a discourse of race fostered, they understood clearly how apartheid had dragooned their forebears into factories with little prospect of escaping capital's addiction to the racial myths of apartheid. What the students intuitively foresaw was that their future lay elsewhere. The images they garnered from the cinema were good reason to take fright. In the latter, they caught a glimpse of a future destined to a life of immaterial labour, disciplinary power and repeated collision. A devastating story rehearsed over two centuries awaited the students as they accidentally discovered a model of race that prescribed the modernity of apartheid. Unfortunately, what they failed to see was that an aesthetic education would prove indispensable to retraining the senses towards perception and imagination in light of such a diabolical script.

For it was largely because of the intensifying assault on the senses that the students of 1985 encountered the complexity surrounding the second term in the coupling of truth and reconciliation that would later define South Africa's transition to democracy. What lay at the heart of their discovery was the element of surprise brought about by traversing the consiliences across the physical and biological sciences, the human and technology, and knowledge and power, upon which truth of race came to settle in a lesser form of petty apartheid. The novelty was not so much in the synthesis of the unity of knowledge, but in the surprise of discovering an undetected problem of race in petty apartheid lodged in consilience. Only a process of study of the element of surprise could potentially deliver a more pronounced, revitalized and equally surprising concept of reconciliation with which to end the threat of ongoing civil war. The reconciliation of a difference based on a concept of race that was foundational to apartheid thwarted this potential from the outset. Undoing apartheid thus requires setting to work on a lesser, more malleable, minor key in apartheid's operationalization of difference where art and aesthetics are given equal claim to crafting a workable concept of reconciliation, one capable of relinking sense and perception and staking a claim to truth content on its own terms. Dismissals of the concept

188 Undoing Apartheid

of reconciliation as the fiction of mere 'rainbowism' ultimately fail to grasp its profound consequence for bringing the history of the senses to bear on the burden of truth. More than apartheid's stain on the conscience of our modernity, post-apartheid freedom may be an opportunity to seize the moment by creating, and in the process making race unavailable to conjuring, new forms of mythic violence.

This is perhaps the backdrop against which to imbibe the lesson of Willie Bester's 'Trojan Horse' sculpture, which memorialized those who were killed and traumatized by the massacre: as a sentient object which reveals the operation that folds the human into technology, making technics a part of the figuring of the industrialization of memory and a hardening of sensibilities. Like the Greeks who folded the human into a war machine with which a premature peace is made, Bester's work warns against a practice of remembering the past in a manner that merely reassembles modern technics, with surveillance, threat, control, mobility and death rolled into a scene of unending battle with the self.

Returning to the interval that connects the urgency of liberation and the duration of education, consider an event four years after the Trojan Horse killings, in which Coline Williams and Robert Waterwitch were ambushed by the state security apparatus. As the record indicates, they were killed while attempting to plant explosives at a magistrates' court in the central business district of Athlone. The story of their deaths has become legendary on the Cape Flats, not least because their killing was brought about by the same surreptitious kind of dirty tricks and ambush that had delivered the Trojan Horse to the streets of Athlone and Crossroads. As the TRC was to reveal, their deaths resulted from a zero-timed explosive device, issued via the covert state apparatus through the agency of a security police informer who had infiltrated an underground cell. The aim of this infiltration was to ensure that the two operatives were killed.

In their memory, the space beyond the magistrates' court today holds a statue of Robbie and Coline as they have been popularly inscribed into a public imaginary. Coline glances over her shoulder nervously, as if recognizing the scene of interpellation, while Robbie walks confidently abreast.

The magistrates' court has become the target of their attention in descriptions of their deaths – like a scene from Kafka's 'Before

The Double Futures of Post-Apartheid Freedom 189

the Law' ('*Vor dem Gesetz*'), where the law reveals itself as also the very condition for violence. Like Kafka, the memorial cautions us never to be complacent before the law. Yet, in a broader optic, the space of the memorial brings into view the bioscope that once stood immediately across the street from where the sculpture stands. Today that building houses the government department of Communication and Information; but it was once home to the Kismet bioscope, a name that when translated gives us recourse to that which remains to be said about the collisions orchestrated by apartheid. It is a word that has its beginnings in Arabic (the root *Qasama* means to divide), becoming *Qisma* (meaning division, portion, or lot), and, with the rise of the Ottoman Empire, the word entered the Turkish language as *kismet* (meaning fate or destiny). From here it was deposited into Hindi and Urdu, retaining its Turkish inflection, before travelling to Athlone where it simply came to mean 'the bioscope'. That, at least, is what is left of the memory of the future, a scene of desire that shares in the fate and destiny of the cure of reschooling, and in the process, retooling.

The students' movement of 1985 was not of the order of a schools boycott. It was a desire for a return to an interval, in a space of intensity in which compression of time diluted and dilated space, giving the students a mode of communication with little prospect of advance, let alone retreat. What the bioscope shared with the desire for schooling was a different conception of the interval: one that promised a non-sectarian future in place of the difference marked out by the strangulating experiments of apartheid.

Perhaps, from within this newly conceived interval, from the long silence that has fallen onto the double futures of a theatrocracy, echoes from *The Cure at Troy* rise from beneath the din of history and beckon us to hope again:

(*Chorus ritually clamant*, as HERCULES)
I have opened the closed road
Between the living and the dead
To make the right road clear to you.
This is the voice of Hercules now.

Here on earth my labours were
The stepping-stones to upper air:

190   Undoing Apartheid

Lives that suffer and come right
Are backlit by immortal light.

So let my mind light up your mind.
You must see straight and turn around.
You must complete your oath-bound course.
You cannot yet return to Scyros.

Go, Philoctetes, with this boy,
Go and be cured and capture Troy.
Asclepius will make you whole,
Relieve your body and your soul.

Go, with your bow. Conclude the sore
And cruel stalemate of our war.
Win by fair combat. But know to shun
Reprisal killings when that's done.

Then take just spoils and sail at last
Out of the bad dream of your past.
Make sacrifice. Burn spoils to me.
Shoot arrows in my memory.

And, Neoptolemus, you must be
His twin in arms and archery.
Marauding lions on that shore,
Troy's nemesis and last nightmare.

But when the city's being sacked
Preserve the shrines. Show gods respect.
Reverence for the gods survives
Our individual mortal lives.
...

Now it's high watermark
And floodtide in the heart
And time to go.
The sea-nymphs in the spray
Will be the chorus now.
What's left to say?

Suspect too much sweet talk
But never close your mind.
It was a fortunate wind

The Double Futures of Post-Apartheid Freedom   *191*

That blew me here. I leave
Half-ready to believe
That a crippled trust might walk

And the half-true rhyme is love.

Seamus Heaney, *The Cure at Troy*

Notes

Chapter 1: Introduction: Apartheid's Double-binds

1 Richard Rive, *Emergency Continued* (Cape Town: David Philip Publishers, 1990).
2 Heidi Grunebaum, *Memorializing the Past: Everyday Life in South Africa after the Truth and Reconciliation Commission* (New Brunswick, NJ: Transaction Publishers, 2011).
3 Richard Rive, *Emergency* (Springfield, OH: Collier Books, 1970).
4 Adam Sitze, 'Study and Revolt', *Safundi: The Journal of South African and American Studies*, 17: 3 (2016), 271–95.
5 See Henri Bergson's critique of Wilhelm Wundt's attempts to designate an organ of apperception and the traces of images on the substance of the brain. Henri Bergson, *Matter and Memory*, translated by Nancy Margaret Paul and W. Scott Palmer (New York: Dover Publications, 2004), 164.
6 Monique Wittig, 'The Trojan Horse', *Feminist Issues*, 4 (1984), 45.
7 John Bellamy Foster and Paul Burkett, 'Ecological Economics and Classical Marxism: The "Podolinsky Business" Reconsidered', *Organization and Environment*, 17: 1 (March 2004), 32–60; Jochen Fahrenberg, *Wilhelm Wundt: 1832–1920* (Freiburg: Albert-Ludwigs-Universität, 2019), 107; Wan-chi Wong, 'Retracing the Footsteps of Wilhelm Wundt: Explorations in the Disciplinary Frontiers of Psychology and in *Völkerpsychologie*', *History of Psychology*, 12: 4 (2009).

Notes to pp. 11–13 193

8 For a differentiation between technology and machine, see Thomas Pringle, 'The Ecosystem is an Apparatus', in Gertrud Koch, Bernard Stiegler and Thomas Pringle (eds.) *Machine* (Lüneburg: Meson Press, 2019), 50.

9 Norbert Wiener, *The Human Use of Human Beings* (Boston: Da Capo Press, 1950), 77. Wiener's broader project of connecting informational and messaging functions of human and machine interaction serves as an enabling discourse for my forays into the effects of petty apartheid.

10 Petty apartheid could be thought of as the inverse of Bergsonism, which proposes a model of sense-impression in which images as things are correlated with thought that is a movement. Bergson, *Matter and Memory*, 156–9.

11 The reinvention of race that followed the abolition of slavery has been the subject of an expansive historiography in and of South Africa. See, for example, Pumla Gqola, *What is Slavery to Me? Postcolonial/ Slave Memory in Post-Apartheid South Africa* (Johannesburg: Wits University Press, 2010); Kirk Sides, 'Precedence and Warning: Global Apartheid and South Africa's Long Conversation on Race with the United States', *Safundi: The Journal of South African and American Studies*, 18: 3 (2017), 221–38; Nigel Worden and Clifton Crais (eds.), *Breaking the Chains: Slavery and its Legacy in the Nineteenth Century Cape Colony* (Johannesburg: Wits University Press, 1994); Pamela Scully, *Liberating the Family? Gender and British Slave Emancipation in the Rural Western Cape, South Africa 1823–1853* (Portsmouth, NH: Heinemann, 1997).

12 Valmont Layne, 'The Sonic Cape', unpublished doctoral dissertation, University of the Western Cape, 2019. See also Aidan Erasmus, 'The Sound of War: Apartheid, Audibility, and Resonance', unpublished doctoral dissertation, University of the Western Cape, 2018.

13 Donald Moodie (ed.), *The Record: Or, a Series of Official Papers Relative to the Condition and Treatment of the Native Tribes of South Africa* (Cambridge: Cambridge University Press, 2011 – 1838 1st edition). See also Fiona Vernal, 'Discourse Networks in South African Slave Society', *African Historical Review*, 43: 2 (2011), 1–36; Premesh Lalu, 'Sara's Suicide: History and the Representational Limit', *Kronos*, 26 (August 2000), 89–101.

14 Premesh Lalu, *The Deaths of Hintsa: Post-Apartheid South Africa and the Shape of Recurring Pasts* (Cape Town: HSRC Press, 2009).

15 Leslie Witz, *Apartheid's Festival* (Bloomington: Indiana University Press, 2003). See also Ciraj Rassool and Leslie Witz, 'The 1952 Jan van Riebeeck Tercentenary Festival: Constructing and Contesting Public National History in South Africa', *Journal of African History*, 34 (1993), 447–68; and Crain Soudien, 'New Accents

194 Notes to pp. 14–20

on the Social: Thinking on South Africa's History at UWC', *South African Historical Journal*, 70: 3 (2018), 603–18.

16 For an example of reference to the Homeric plays in South Africa, see Njabulo Ndebele, *The Cry of Winnie Mandela* (Cape Town: Pan Macmillan, 2003).

17 The mythic denotes the 'bundles of relations' by which apartheid came to be sustained as a discourse of race. The study of the mythic precursors of apartheid's political rationality and its precepts of race takes its cue from Claude Lévi-Strauss and Roland Barthes. Lévi-Strauss, 'The Structural Study of Myth', *Journal of American Folklore*, 68: 270 (October–December 1955), 431; Roland Barthes, *Mythologies*, translated by Annette Lavers (New York: Hill and Wang, 1957). Uncovering the patterned structure of myth ought to be placed alongside a consideration of the creation of myths proposed by Paul Veyne, *Did the Greeks Believe in Their Myths? An Essay on the Constitutive Imagination*, translated by Paula Wissing (Chicago: University of Chicago Press, 1988).

18 Samuel Weber, *Theatricality as Medium* (New York: Fordham University Press, 2004), 36.

19 Weber, *Theatricality as Medium*, 37.

20 Seamus Heaney, *The Cure at Troy: A Version of Sophocles' 'Philoctetes'* (London: Faber and Faber, 1991).

21 Lorna Hardwick, interview with Seamus Heaney, September 2007, Open University. Heaney tested the moral and political consequences of ready-to-hand political settlements privileged by contemporary elaborations of nationalism at the end of the Cold War. Stephen Rea and Bob Crowley note that Heaney insisted on the Philoctetes story even though his peers encouraged him to create a modern version of *Antigone*. A high political voltage attached to the figure of *Antigone* in Ireland meant that the play had become too recognizable in civil rights and feminist movements to offer room for fresh reinterpretation. As an alternative, the story of Philoctetes confirmed that the gift was carefully selected in relation to the fresh circumstances that had arisen in Ireland and South Africa in 1990.

22 Eugene O'Brien, *Seamus Heaney as Aesthetic Thinker: A Study of the Prose* (Syracuse, NY: Syracuse University Press, 2016), 179.

23 George Morgan, 'Interview with Seamus Heaney', *Cycnos*, 15: 2 (2008). For a response to critiques of Heaney's pastoral politics, see Jahan Ramazani, 'Seamus Heaney's Globe', *Irish Pages*, 9: 1 (2014), 190–6.

24 Joshua Billings, *The Philosophical Stage* (Princeton, NJ: Princeton University Press, 2021), 131.

25 Simon Goldhill, *Sophocles and the Language of Tragedy* (Oxford: Oxford University Press, 2012), 46.

Notes to pp. 23–34   *195*

26 Weber, *Theatricality as Medium*, 143.
27 For the contestations surrounding the idea of apartheid, see Saul Dubow, 'Afrikaner Nationalism, Apartheid and the Conceptualization of "Race"', *Journal of African History*, 33: 2 (1992), 224.
28 Elizabeth Stewart, *Catastrophe and Survival: Walter Benjamin and Psychoanalysis* (London: Bloomsbury, 2009), 23.
29 Deborah Posel, *The Making of Apartheid, 1948–1961* (Oxford: Oxford University Press, 1991). See also Deborah Posel, 'Truth? The View from South Africa's Truth and Reconciliation Commission', in Ali Benmakhalouf et al. (eds.) *Keywords: Truth* (New York: Other Press, 2004), 17–18.
30 Christoph Marx, *Trennung und Angst: Hendrik Verwoerd und die Gedankenwelt der Apartheid* (Berlin: De Gruyter Oldenbourg, 2020).
31 See Dubow, 'Afrikaner Nationalism'.
32 The post-Aristotelian deconstructive move must be grasped in this formulation. See Frank Lentricchia, 'Derrida, History and Intellectuals', *Salmagundi*, 50/51 (Fall 1980–Winter 1981), 284–301.
33 Aletta Norval, *Deconstructing Apartheid Discourse* (London: Verso, 1996), 188; and Jamie Miller, *An African Volk: The Apartheid Regime and its Search for Survival* (Oxford: Oxford University Press, 2016), 8–10.
34 Importantly, the final report of the TRC makes special mention of psychological work by Verwoerd and his mentor, R.W. Wilcocks, as well as E.G. Malherbe, in lending justification to conceptions of race that affected policies governing everyday life. *Truth and Reconciliation Commission of South Africa Report, Volume 4* (Cape Town: Government Publishers, 1998), 139. For discussions about the TRC as theatre, see Catherine Cole, *Performing South Africa's Truth Commission: Stages of Transition* (Bloomington: Indiana University Press, 2010); and Rustom Bharucha, *Terror and Performance* (London: Routledge, 2014).

Chapter 2: Apartheid's Mythic Precursors

1 Leonard Thompson, *The Political Mythology of Apartheid* (New Haven, CT: Yale University Press, 1985).
2 The erosion of the origin myth has been the subject of important critique. See André du Toit, 'No Chosen People: The Myth of the Calvinist Origins of Afrikaner Nationalism and Racial Ideology', *American Historical Review*, 88 (1983), 920–52; Isabel Hofmeyr,

'Popularising History: The Case of Gustav Preller', *Journal of African History*, 29: 3 (1988). On the persistence and political consequences of this mythology, see Saul Dubow, 'Afrikaner Nationalism, Apartheid and the Conceptualization of "Race"', *Journal of African History*, 33: 2 (1992), 224.

3 For an Afrikaner nationalist rendering of this mythic narrative, see C.F.J. Muller, *500 Years: A History of South Africa* (Pretoria: Academia, 1969); on the post-apartheid reckoning with the anti-colonial nationalist narrative of the killing of Hintsa, see Premesh Lalu, *The Deaths of Hintsa: Post-Apartheid South Africa and the Shape of Recurring Pasts* (Cape Town: HSRC Press, 2009).

4 Steven Ruskin, *John Herschel's Cape Voyage: Private Science, Public Imagination and the Ambitions of Empire* (London: Routledge, 2004). See also Lalu, *The Deaths of Hintsa*.

5 William Ashworth, 'John Herschel, George Airy, and the Roaming Eye of the State', *History of Science*, 36: 2 (1998), 152.

6 Leigh Davin Bregman, '"Snug Little Coteries": A History of Scientific Societies in Early Nineteenth-Century Cape Town, 1824–1835', unpublished doctoral dissertation, University College London, 2003, 208.

7 Steven Fuller, *Thomas Kuhn: A Philosophical History for our Times* (Chicago: University of Chicago Press, 2000), 80.

8 John Herschel, *A Preliminary Discourse on the Study of Natural Philosophy* (London: Longman, Brown, Green, 1830), 143.

9 David Wilson, 'Herschel and Whewell's Version of Newtonianism', *Journal of the History of Ideas*, 35: 1 (1974), 85.

10 Wilson, 'Herschel and Whewell's Version of Newtonianism', 95.

11 Joseph Agassi, 'Sir John Herschel's Philosophy of Success', *Historical Studies in Physical Sciences*, 1 (1969), 14.

12 Agassi, 'Sir John Herschel's Philosophy of Success', 14.

13 Joseph Agassi, 'Sensationalism', *Mind*, 75: 297 (January 1966), 4.

14 Herschel, *A Preliminary Discourse*, 63.

15 Agassi, 'Sir John Herschel's Philosophy of Success', 16.

16 Agassi, 'Sir John Herschel's Philosophy of Success', 23.

17 Jules Verne, *From the Earth to the Moon* (New York: Scribner, Armstrong and Co., 1865).

18 Henry Cowles, 'On the Origin of Theories: Charles Darwin's Vocabulary of Method', *American Historical Review*, 122: 4 (2017), 1086.

19 An expanding market in art helped to fund industries formed by new technologies. Brett sold the Danby painting when lucrative prospects of investing in telegraphic ventures for speculative investments in railways and communication technologies were encouraged by the state. The birth of submarine electric telegraphy introduced

Notes to pp. 50–61

a mode of communication by telegraphic means from the British Isles across the Atlantic Ocean to Nova Scotia, as well as other colonies and Europe. Brett's invention of a telegraphic infrastructure connecting Africa, Asia and Europe to the Americas enabled a new transoceanic communication network that resulted in the spatio-temporal constriction of the world picture.

20 Michael Crowe, *The Extraterrestrial Life Debate, 1750–1900* (Cambridge: Cambridge University Press, 1986).

21 Kevin Young, *Bunk: The Rise of Hoaxes, Humbug, Plagiarists, Phonies, Post-facts, and Fake News* (Minneapolis: Graywolf Press, 2017).

22 Michel Foucault, *Society Must be Defended*, translated by David Macey (New York: Picador, 2003).

23 Larry Schaaf, 'John Herschel, Photography and the Camera Lucida', *Transactions of the Royal Society of South Africa*, 49: 1 (1994), 87–102; Omar Nasim, 'The "Landmark" and "Groundwork" of Stars: John Herschel, Photography and the Drawing of the Nebulae', *Studies in History and Philosophy of Science*, 42: 1 (2011), 67–84.

24 Siegfried Kracauer, *Theory of Film: The Redemption of Physical Reality* (Princeton, NJ: Princeton University Press, 1997), 28.

25 Sarah Alexander, *Victorian Literature and the Physics of the Imponderable* (New York: Routledge, 2015), 94.

26 Srinivas Aravamudan, *Enlightenment Orientalism: Resisting the Rise of the Novel* (Chicago: University of Chicago Press, 2012), 122.

27 Silas Modiri Molema, *The Bantu: Past and Present* (Edinburgh: W. Green and Son, 1920), 328.

28 See Jane Starfield, 'A Dance with the Empire: Modiri Molema's Glasgow Years, 1914–1921', *Journal of Southern African Studies*, 27: 3 (September 2001).

29 Garland Allen, 'Mechanism, Vitalism, and Organicism in Late Nineteenth and Twentieth-Century Biology', *Studies in History and Philosophy of Biological and Biomedical Science*, 36: 2 (July 2005), 280.

30 Thozama April, 'Theorising Women: The Intellectual Contributions of Charlotte Maxeke to the Struggle for Liberation in South Africa', unpublished doctoral thesis, University of the Western Cape, 2009.

31 Molema, *The Bantu*, 366.

32 Molema, *The Bantu*, 367.

33 Jacqueline Jenkinson, 'Black Sailors on Red Clydeside: Rioting, Reactionary Trade Unionism and Conflicting Notions of "Britishness" Following the First World War', *Twentieth Century British History*, 19: 1 (July 2007).

34 Molema, *The Bantu*, 190.

35 Jane Starfield, '"A Member of the Race": Dr Modiri Molema's

198   Notes to pp. 61–77

Intellectual Engagement with the Popular History of South Africa, 1912–1921', *South African Historical Journal*, 64: 3 (2012), 434–49.

36 J.E. Inikori suggests that the wealth generated by slavery was not merely to be seen at the level of generating private profits, but in more subtle transformations enabled in the consolidation of a division of labour and institutional transformation. Joseph E. Inikori, *Africans and the Industrial Revolution in England* (Cambridge: Cambridge University Press, 2002).

37 Molema, *The Bantu*, 276.
38 Molema, *The Bantu*, 277.
39 Molema, *The Bantu*, 278.
40 Molema, *The Bantu*, 328.
41 Molema, *The Bantu*, 233.
42 Molema, *The Bantu*, 351.
43 Molema, *The Bantu*, 352.
44 Molema, *The Bantu*, 355.
45 Molema, *The Bantu*, 355.
46 Molema, *The Bantu*, 335.
47 Norbert Wiener, *The Human Use of Human Beings* (Boston: Da Capo Press, 1950), 128.
48 Wiener, *The Human Use of Human Beings*, 129.

Chapter 3: The Return of Faust: Rats, Hyenas and other Miscreants

1 John Noyes, 'Goethe on Cosmopolitanism and Colonialism: *Bildung* and the Dialectic of Critical Mobility', *Eighteenth-Century Studies*, 39: 4 (2006), 443–62.
2 Gabriel Trop, 'Goethe's *Faust* and the Absolute of *Naturphilosophie*', *Germanic Review*, 92 (2017), 396.
3 Katharina Keim, 'Contemporary African and Brazilian Adaptations of Goethe's *Faust* in Postcolonial Context', in Lorna Fitzsimmons (ed.) *International Faust Studies: Adaptation, Reception, Translation* (New York: Continuum, 2008), 253.
4 James Hutson, *Gallucci's Commentary on Dürer's 'Four Books on Human Proportion'* (Cambridge: Open Book Publishers, 2020).
5 See Richard Bernheimer, 'Theatrum Mundi', *Art Bulletin*, 38: 4 (1956), 228.
6 Ruby Cohn, '*Theatrum Mundi* and Contemporary Theater', *Comparative Drama*, 1: 1 (Spring 1967), 28–35.
7 William Kentridge, 'Faustus in Africa', *Contemporary Theatre Review*, 9: 4 (1999), 45–82.

Notes to pp. 77–88

8 Jane Taylor (ed.), *The Handspring Puppet Company* (Cape Town: David Krut Publishing, 2009), 23.
9 For a discussion of vitalism and the philosophy of life, see Donna Jones, *The Racial Discourses of Life Philosophy: Négritude, Vitalism, and Modernity* (New York: Columbia University Press, 2010), 141. Jones offers a careful reading of the way the subject and object are positioned in debates surrounding negritude, which is another interpretive frame for the Kentridge and Handspring production.
10 David Levering Lewis, *W.E.B. Du Bois: A Biography, 1868–1963* (New York: Henry Holt and Co., 1993); Dickson Bruce, 'W.E.B. Du Bois and the Idea of Double Consciousness', *American Literature*, 64: 2 (June 1992), 299–300.
11 Jones, *The Racial Discourses of Life Philosophy*, 129.
12 Jones, *The Racial Discourses of Life Philosophy*, 28.
13 Sara Munson Deats, *The Faust Legend: From Marlowe and Goethe to Contemporary Drama and Film* (Cambridge: Cambridge University Press, 2019), 80.
14 B.W. Wells, 'Goethe's "Faust"', *Sewanee Review*, 2: 4 (August 1894).
15 Wells, 'Goethe's "Faust"', 408.
16 On the speculative dynamics of slavery, see Ian Baucom, *Specters of the Atlantic: Finance Capital, Slavery, and the Philosophy of History* (Durham, NC: Duke University Press, 2005).
17 Carl Hammer, 'Goethe's Astronomical Pursuits', *South Central Bulletin*, 30: 4 (Winter 1970), 197–200.
18 Trop, 'Goethe's *Faust*', 395.
19 Trop, 'Goethe's *Faust*', 390.
20 Karl Marx, *Grundrisse*, translated by Martin Nicolaus (New York: Penguin Books, 1973), 623.
21 David McNally, *Monsters of the Market: Zombies, Vampires and Global Capitalism* (Chicago: Haymarket Books, 2012), 133.
22 Michael Hardt and Antonio Negri, *Empire* (Cambridge, MA: Harvard University Press, 2000), 292.
23 Jacques Derrida, *Paper Machine*, translated by Rachel Bowlby (Stanford, CA: Stanford University Press, 2005), 170. Derrida notes that the German language seemed to have a special elective affinity for philosophy, especially its speculative element; easily distrusted in the West as dangerously unclear – and not entirely without justification.
24 See Premesh Lalu, 'Thinking across Hemispheres: Further Notes on Oversights and Blind Spots in Disciplinary African Studies', *Africa Focus*, 32: 1 (2018).
25 McNally, *Monsters of the Market*, 133.

200 Notes to pp. 88–101

26 McNally, *Monsters of the Market*, 134.
27 Thomas Kemple, *Reading Marx Writing: Melodrama, the Market and the 'Grundrisse'* (Stanford, CA: Stanford University Press, 1995), 28.
28 Kemple, *Reading Marx Writing*, 30.
29 Kemple, *Reading Marx Writing*, 32.
30 Kemple, *Reading Marx Writing*, 42.
31 Harry Magdoff, 'The Meaning of Work: A Marxist Perspective', *Monthly Review*, 58: 5 (October 2006).
32 Marx cited in Kemple, *Reading Marx Writing*, 43.
33 Karl Marx, 'The Eighteenth Brumaire of Louis Bonaparte', in Karl Marx and Frederick Engels, *Collected Works, Vol. 11* (New York: International Publishers, 1979), 106.
34 Noyes, 'Goethe on Cosmopolitanism and Colonialism', 443–62.
35 For a later articulation of this idea of idle resources, see the South African contribution to the Mont Pelerin Society. William Harold Hutt, *The Theory of Idle Resources* (Auburn, AL: Ludwig von Mises Institute, 2011).
36 Trop, 'Goethe's *Faust*', 388–406.
37 Mauro Scalercio, 'Dominating Nature and Colonialism: Francis Bacon's View of Europe and the New World', *History of European Ideas*, 44: 8 (2018), 1076–91.
38 Joseph Lawrence, 'Schelling and the Meaning of Goethe's Faust', *Analecta Hermeneutica*, 5 (2013), 3.
39 Susanna Lindberg, 'The Remains of the Romantic Philosophy of Nature: Being as Life, or the Plurality of Living Beings?', *New Centennial Review*, 10: 3 (Winter 2010), 41.
40 Lindberg, 'The Remains of the Romantic Philosophy of Nature', 42.
41 Karen Koehler, 'More than Parallel Lines: Thoughts on Gestalt, Albers and the Bauhaus', in Vanja Malloy (ed.) *Intersecting Colors: Josef Albers and his Contemporaries* (Amherst, MA: Amherst College Press, 2015).
42 Anne Harrington, 'Metaphoric Connections: Holistic Science in the Shadow of the Third Reich', *Social Research*, 62: 2 (Summer 1995), 366.
43 Harrington, 'Metaphoric Connections', 374.
44 Abiola Irele, *The African Imagination: Literature in Africa and the Black Diaspora* (Oxford: Oxford University Press, 2001), 71.
45 Jane Brown asks us to consider how the theatre is linked to the processes of scientific experiment that provides a basis for the renewal of a theatre of modernity, first plotted in Goethe's 1798 essay on 'Experience and Science' (*Erfahrung und Wissenschaft*). A specifically European identity is sealed by the theatrical linking of art and science. The theatre gives form to the chaos of unstable identities, or, as Brown puts it, 'to accumulate perceptions and

Notes to pp. 105–111 *201*

observations to reveal a pattern implicit in them'. Jane Brown, 'Theatricality and Experiment: Identity in Faust', in Hans Schulte, John Noyes and Pia Kleber (eds.) *Goethe's Faust: Theatre of Modernity* (Cambridge: Cambridge University Press, 2011), 326.

Chapter 4: Woyzeck and the Secret Life of Apartheid's Things

1 Hermann Giliomee, 'The Making of the Apartheid Plan, 1929–1948', *Journal of Southern African Studies*, 29: 2 (June 2003), 373–92.
2 See Saul Dubow, 'Racial Irredentism: Ethnogenesis, and White Supremacy in High-Apartheid South Africa', *Kronos: Southern African Histories*, 41 (November 2015).
3 Christoph Marx, 'Hendrik Verwoerd's Long March to Apartheid: Nationalism and Racism in South Africa', in Manfred Berg and Simon Wendt (eds.) *Racism in the Modern World: Historical Perspectives on Cultural Transfer and Adaptation* (New York: Berghahn, 2017).
4 Maurits van Bever Donker, *Texturing Difference: Black Consciousness Philosophy and the Script of Man* (forthcoming).
5 Judith Butler, *The Psychic Life of Power: Theories in Subjection* (Stanford, CA: Stanford University Press, 1997), 113.
6 See Pierre Macherey, 'Out of Melancholia: Notes on Judith Butler's *The Psychic Life of Power: Theories in Subjection*', *Rethinking Marxism*, 16: 1 (2004), 7–17.
7 Butler, *The Psychic Life of Power*, 130.
8 Étienne Balibar, 'Althusser's Dramaturgy and the Critique of Ideology', *Differences: A Journal of Feminist Cultural Studies*, 26: 3 (2015), 1–21.
9 Balibar, 'Althusser's Dramaturgy', 4.
10 Balibar, 'Althusser's Dramaturgy', 14.
11 Pierre Macherey, 'Figures of Interpellation in Althusser and Fanon', *Radical Philosophy*, 173 (May–June 2012), 1–12.
12 Stuart Hall, 'The Problem of Ideology', *Journal of Communication Inquiry*, 10: 2 (1986), 28–44.
13 Jean-Luc Nancy, 'The Two Secrets of the Fetish', *Diacritics*, 31: 2 (Summer 2001), 3–8.
14 Étienne Balibar, *The Philosophy of Marx*, translated by Chris Turner (London: Verso, 2007), 42.
15 Nancy, 'The Two Secrets of the Fetish', 7.
16 Sander Gilman, 'Alban Berg, the Jews, and the Anxiety of Genius', in Ronald Radano and Philip Bohlman (eds.) *Music and the Racial Imagination* (Chicago: University of Chicago Press, 2000), 484.

202 Notes to pp. 111–123

17 J.L. Crighton, 'Anatomy and Subversion: 150th Anniversary of Georg Büchner's Death', *British Medical Journal*, 294 (21 February 1987).

18 Victor Price, 'Introduction', in Georg Büchner, *Danton's Death, Leonce and Lena, Woyzeck*, translated by Victor Price (Oxford: Oxford University Press, 1971), ix.

19 Gilman, 'Alban Berg', 492.

20 Karl Marx, *Capital I*, translated by Ben Fowkes (London: Penguin, 1990), 548.

21 Stephen Dowden, 'Nietzsche, Büchner, and the Blues', in Stephen Dowden and Thomas Quinn (eds.) *Tragedy and the Tragic in German Literature, Art, and Thought* (Rochester, NY: Camden House, 2014), 128.

22 Robert Tucker (ed.), *The Marx–Engels Reader* (New York: Norton & Co., 1978), 207.

23 Fredric Jameson, *Representing Capital* (London: Verso, 2011), 31.

24 A good overview of this complex emerging field is provided by Edward B. Titchener, 'Wilhelm Wundt', *American Journal of Psychology*, 32: 2 (April 1921), 161–78. See also Alan Kim, 'Wilhelm Maximilian Wundt', in Edward Zalta (ed.) *Stanford Encyclopedia of Philosophy* (Fall 2016 edition).

25 Bill Brown, *Other Things* (Chicago: University of Chicago Press, 2015), 22.

26 Deborah Posel, 'Race as Common Sense: Racial Classification in Twentieth-Century South Africa', *African Studies Review*, 44: 2 (2001), 105.

27 In Berg's early-twentieth-century operatic rendering of the work, Woyzeck takes his own life.

28 James Crighton, *Büchner and Madness: Schizophrenia in Georg Büchner's 'Lenz' and 'Woyzeck'* (New York: Edwin Mellen Press, 1998).

29 Ute Holl, *Cinema, Trance and Cybernetics* (Amsterdam: Amsterdam University Press, 2017), 46.

30 Walter Cannon, 'John Herschel and the Idea of Science', *Journal of the History of Ideas*, 22: 2 (1961), 223.

31 David Richards, *Georg Büchner's Woyzeck: A History of its Criticism* (Rochester, NY: Camden House, 2001), 23.

32 Richards, *Georg Büchner's Woyzeck*, 23.

33 This has also been the case elsewhere. See Daniel Kopp, 'Cultural Continuity and National Emasculation: Werner Herzog's and Dariush Mehrjui's Cinematic Adaptations of Georg Büchner's Woyzeck', *Journal of Adaptation in Film and Performance*, 11: 1 (2018), 27–39. See also Richard Gray, 'The Dialectic of Enlightenment in Büchner's Woyzeck', *German Quarterly*, 61: 1 (1998), 78–96.

34 In recent years, this neglect has been addressed by Keith Breckenridge

Notes to pp. 123–130 203

in *The Biometric State* (Cambridge: Cambridge University Press, 2014); also, Antina von Schnitzler, 'Infrastructure, Apartheid Technopolitics, and Temporalities of "Transition"', in Nikhil Ananda et al. *The Promise of Infrastructure* (Durham, NC: Duke University Press, 2018).

35 We should be careful not to establish guilt by mere association. Other visitors to Wundt's laboratory included psychologists, philosophers and anthropologists such as James Mark Baldwin, Franz Boas, Émile Durkheim, Bronislaw Malinowski and Edmund Husserl. Wundt himself was a co-founder of the Association of German Workers and had a life-long interest in workers' education.

36 Samuel Weber, *Theatricality as Medium* (New York: Fordham University Press, 2004), 320.

37 Stanley Uys, 'Dr. Hendrik Frensch Verwoerd, Prime Minister of South Africa', *Africa South*, 3: 2 (January–March 1959).

38 Roberta Balstad Miller, 'Science and Society in the Early Career of H.F. Verwoerd', *Journal of Southern African Studies*, 19: 4 (December 1993), 634–61. See also T. Dunbar Moodie, *The Rise of Afrikanerdom: Power, Apartheid, and the Afrikaner Civil Religion* (Berkeley: University of California Press, 1975), 154; T.R.H. Davenport, *South Africa: A Modern History* (London: Macmillan, 1991), 288.

39 Miller, 'Science and Society', 640.

40 Miller, 'Science and Society', 644.

41 Kurt Danziger, 'Origins and Basic Principles of Wundt's *Völkerpsychologie*', *British Journal of Social Psychology*, 22: 4 (1983), 303. Danziger, one of the most crucial voices to reclaim Wundt for a critical posture of the discipline of psychology, notes that Wundt combined experimental psychology with an interest in *Völkerpsychologie*, seeing the latter as a necessary endpoint of his work on psychic causality, in which individual and community relations are properly and scientifically accounted for. The history of psychology narrated by Danziger holds that *Völkerpsychologie* was dispensed with by Wundt's successors and replaced by a much greater emphasis on experimental psychology.

42 Garland Allen, 'Mechanism, Vitalism and Organicism in Late Nineteenth and Twentieth-Century Biology', *Studies in History and Philosophy of Biological and Biomedical Science*, 36: 2 (July 2005), 261–83.

43 Wilhelm Wundt, *Elements of Folk Psychology*, translated by Edward Leroy Schaub (New York: Macmillan, 1916), 29.

44 Saul Dubow suggests that Verwoerd's faith in the socially transformative powers of science, as the basis for informed rational planning, was nurtured during his years as an academic. See Saul

204 Notes to pp. 131–139

Dubow (ed.), *Science and Society in Southern Africa* (New York and Manchester: Manchester University Press, 2000), 127.

45 Ross Truscott and Michelle Smith, 'Aftershocks: Psychotechnics in the Wake of Apartheid', *Parallax*, 22: 2 (May 2016), 252.

46 On Münsterberg, see Arthur Blumenthal, 'Wilhelm Wundt: Psychology as the Propaedeutic Science', in Claude Buxton (ed.) *Points of View in the Modern History of Psychology* (New York: Academic Press, 1985), 70. The idiographic pointed to individuated subjectivity, while the nomothetic to general rules of specific groups. On Münsterberg's importance for labour relations in South Africa, see Ronald Legg, 'A History of the Professionalisation of Human Resource Management in South Africa, 1945–1995', unpublished MA thesis, University of KwaZulu-Natal, 2004, 38.

47 Wundt, *Elements of Folk Psychology*, 464.

48 This is a point that Norbert Wiener argues: 'The nervous system and the automatic machine are fundamentally alike in that they are devices which make decisions on the basis of decisions they have made in the past.' Norbert Wiener, *The Human Use of Human Beings* (Boston: Da Capo Press, 1950), 33.

49 Henning Schmidgen, 'Time and Noise: The Stable Surroundings of Reaction Experiments, 1860–1890', *Studies in History and Philosophy of Biological and Biomedical Sciences*, 34 (2003), 245.

50 Schmidgen, 'Time and Noise', 293.

51 Henri Bergson, *Matter and Memory*, translated by Nancy Margaret Paul and W. Scott Palmer (New York: Dover Publications, 2004), 121. For discussion of Bergson's notion of intuition as method, see Elizabeth Grosz, 'Bergson, Deleuze and the Becoming of Unbecoming', *Parallax*, 1: 2 (2005), 9–10.

52 Lydia Liu, *The Freudian Robot* (Chicago: University of Chicago Press, 2010), 224.

53 Liu, *The Freudian Robot*, 265.

Chapter 5: Post-Apartheid Slapstick

1 Jonathan Beller's understanding of a world-historical restructuring of the image has been crucial for this formulation. See Jonathan Beller, *The Cinematic Mode of Production: Attention, Economy and the Society of the Spectacle* (Hanover, NH: Dartmouth College Press, 2006).

2 Albie Sachs (ed.), *Spring is Rebellious: Arguments about Cultural Freedom* (Cape Town: Buchu Books, 1990).

3 Martin Esslin, *The Theatre of the Absurd* (New York: Double Day, 1961).

Notes to pp. 141–150   *205*

4 Alastair Brotchie, *Alfred Jarry: A Pataphysical Life* (Cambridge, MA: MIT Press, 2011), 169.

5 Siegfried Kracauer, *Theory of Film: The Redemption of Physical Reality* (Oxford: Oxford University Press, 1960).

6 Miriam Bratu Hansen, *Cinema and Experience: Siegfried Kracauer, Walter Benjamin, and Theodor W. Adorno* (Berkeley: University of California Press, 2012), 163.

7 Hansen, *Cinema and Experience*, 166.

8 Miriam Bratu Hansen, 'Room-for-Play: Benjamin's Gamble with Cinema', *Canadian Journal of Film Studies*, 13: 1 (Spring 2004), 2–27.

9 Hansen, *Cinema and Experience*, 341.

10 Wole Soyinka, *King Baabu* (London: Methuen, 2002).

11 Brotchie, *Alfred Jarry*, 170. It is important to note that while Ubu has been resurrected to represent Idi Amin, Ceausescu, Mugabe, and any number of tyrants, Jarry insisted that Ubu was Everyman (p. 160).

12 Steve McCaffery, *Prior to Meaning: The Protosemantic and Poetics* (Evanston, IL: Northwestern University Press, 2001), 22.

13 Nico Israel, *Spirals: The Whirled Image in Twentieth-century Literature and Art* (New York: Columbia University Press, 2015).

14 Israel, *Spirals*, 2.

15 Erman Kaplama, *Cosmological Aesthetics through the Kantian Sublime and Nietzschean Dionysian* (Lanham, MD: Rowman & Littlefield, 2013), 167.

16 Jane Taylor, *Ubu and the Truth Commission* (Cape Town: University of Cape Town Press, 1998), v.

17 The shift in emphasis from technology to *techne* recasts the lack of promise in Agamben's formulation of the relationship between the state of exception and decision. See Giorgio Agamben, *Homo Sacer: Sovereign Power and Bare Life*, translated by Daniel Heller-Roazen (Stanford, CA: Stanford University Press, 1998).

18 The technological shift inaugurates shifts in both cinema and psychoanalysis, in which the force of the development of electricity propelled into being new mediations, meditations and concerns about the altered relationship between perception and memory anticipated in Freud's discourse on the mystic writing pad. *Techne* is what is shared and deferred in the co-evolution of the human and technology that is given as potential.

19 See Doris Sommer, *Foundational Fictions: The National Romances of Latin America, Vol. 8* (Berkeley: University of California Press, 1991). See also John Mowitt, *Radio: Essays in Bad Reception* (Berkeley: University of California Press, 2011), 148.

20 Anne-Lise François, '". . . and will do none": *Gewalt* in the Measure

206   Notes to pp. 151–160

of a Parenthesis', *Critical Times*, 2: 2 (2019), 285–95. François notes that in translations of Benjamin's interpretation of *Einigung*, the idea of non-violent agreement 'can be found wherever the culture of the heart has placed pure means of accord in human hands'. 'Pure means', François tells us, refers to the constitution of ethical subjectivity towards the goal of reconciliation. Only now we are called to unblock the passage from subjectivity towards an ethical goal.

21 See, for example, Pablo Oyarzún, 'Law, Violence, History: A Brief Reading of the Last Paragraph of Walter Benjamin's "Toward the Critique of Violence"', *Critical Times*, 2: 2 (2019), 330–7.

22 See, for example, Laura Mulvey, *Death 24x a Second* (London: Reaktion, 2006); Owen Hatherley, *The Chaplin Machine: Slapstick, Fordism and the Communist Avant-Garde* (London: Pluto, 2016); Eli Friedlander, 'The Only Angel of Peace Suited to this World: Walter Benjamin on Charlie Chaplin', Lecture, School of Criticism and Theory, Cornell University, Ithaca, NY, 15 September 2015.

23 Walter Benjamin, 'Surrealism: The Last Snapshot of the European Intelligentsia', in Lawrence Rainey (ed.) *Modernism: An Anthology* (Malden, MA: Blackwell, 2005), 1093.

24 Walter Benjamin, *Charles Baudelaire: A Lyric Poet in the Era of High Capitalism*, translated by Harry Zohn (London: Verso, 1997), 312.

25 Miriam Bratu Hansen, 'Benjamin, Cinema and Experience: "The Blue Flower in the Land of Technology"', *New German Critique*, 40 (1987), 222.

26 Samuel Beckett enables us to connect Jarry to Chaplin, in part because of his attention to both in his theatrical work. See also Esther Leslie, *Hollywood Flatlands* (London: Verso, 2002).

27 Timothy Campbell, 'Fearless Speech, Slapstick and the Neoliberal Academy', *Social Dynamics*, 38: 1 (March 2012), 38.

28 Charlie Chaplin (director), *The Great Dictator* (New York: United Artists, 1940).

29 Gayatri Spivak, *An Aesthetic Education in the Era of Globalization* (Cambridge, MA: Harvard University Press, 2012), 125.

30 Maria Muhle, 'A Genealogy of Biopolitics: The Notion of Life in Canguilhem and Foucault', in Vanessa Lemm and Miguel Vatter (eds.) *The Government of Life: Foucault, Biopolitics, and Neoliberalism* (New York: Fordham University Press, 2014), 80.

31 Brian Massumi, *The Power at the End of the Economy* (Durham, NC: Duke University Press, 2014), 79. See also Mary Zournazi, *Hope: New Philosophies for Change* (London: Routledge, 2002), 222.

32 Gilbert Simondon, *The Mode of Existence of Technical Objects*,

Notes to pp. 160–173

translated by Cécile Malaspina and John Rogove (New York: Univocal Publishing, 2017), 65.
33 See, for example, Adam Sitze, *The Impossible Machine* (Ann Arbor: Michigan University Press, 2013).

Chapter 6: The Double Futures of Post-Apartheid Freedom

1 Heidi Grunebaum, *Memorializing the Past: Everyday Life in South Africa after the Truth and Reconciliation Commission* (New Brunswick, NJ: Transaction Publishers, 2011).
2 See Azoulay's analysis of Nicole Loraux's *Divided City*, in Vincent Azoulay, 'Repoliticising the Ancient Greek City, Thirty Years Later', translated by Angela Krieger, *Annales. Histoire, Sciences Sociales*, 64: 3 (2014), 476.
3 Colin Bundy, 'Action Comrades, Action! Street Sociology and Pavement Politics in Cape Town in 1985', in Mary Simons and Wilmot James (eds.) *The Angry Divide: Social and Economic History of the Western Cape* (Cape Town: David Philip Publishers, 1989).
4 Trinh T. Minh-ha, *Cinema-Interval* (New York: Routledge, 1999).
5 Minh-ha, *Cinema-Interval*, vii.
6 Minh-ha, *Cinema-Interval*, iv.
7 Minh-ha, *Cinema-Interval*, 252.
8 We should recall here Kracauer's reference to Herschel's predictions about the moving image discussed in Chapter 2.
9 Carloss James Chamberlin, 'Dziga Vertov: The Idiot', *Senses of Cinema*, 41 (November 2006).
10 South African Democracy Education Trust, *The Road to Democracy in South Africa: Volume 2, 1970–1980* (Pretoria: Unisa Press, 1990), 880.
11 Conversation with Tony Weaver, *Cape Times* opinions editor, 20 August 2014; also CBS producer Michael Gavshon, cameraman Chris Everson and photographer Rashid Lombard.
12 Georges Didi-Huberman, *Atlas, or the Anxious Gay Science*, translated by Shane Lillis (Chicago: University of Chicago Press, 2018), 11.
13 See, for example, George Steinmetz, *Sociology and Empire* (Durham, NC: Duke University Press, 2013); George Curry, 'Woodrow Wilson, Jan Smuts, and the Versailles Settlement', *American Historical Review*, 66: 4 (July 1961), 970.
14 Nicole Loraux, *The Divided City: On Memory and Forgetting in*

208   Notes to pp. 173–186

Ancient Athens, translated by Corinne Pache and Jeff Fort (New York: Zone Books, 2006), 104.

15 Loraux, *The Divided City*, 105.

16 Loraux, *The Divided City*, 104.

17 John Mowitt, 'Stumbling on Analysis: Psychoanalysis and Everyday Life', *Cultural Critique*, 52 (Autumn 2002), 61–85.

18 Ross Truscott, Maurits van Bever Donker, Premesh Lalu and Gary Minkley (eds.), *Remains of the Social: Desiring the Post-Apartheid* (Johannesburg: Wits University Press, 2017).

19 Lorraine Daston and Peter Galison, 'The Image of Objectivity', *Representations*, 40 (Autumn 1992), 83.

20 See, for example, Thomas Dilworth, 'The Fall of Troy and the Slaughter of the Suitors: Ultimate Symbolic Correspondence in "The Odyssey"', *Mosaic*, 27: 2 (June 1994), 1–24.

21 See Saul Dubow, 'Afrikaner Nationalism, Apartheid, and the Conceptualization of "Race"', *Journal of African History*, 33: 2 (1992), 209–37.

22 H.F. Verwoerd, 'The Policy of Apartheid', Speech to the Parliament of South Africa, Hansard, 3 September 1948.

23 Mowitt, 'Stumbling on Analysis', 61–85.

24 Azoulay, 'Repoliticising the Ancient Greek City', 475.

25 Azoulay, 'Repoliticising the Ancient Greek City', 475.

26 See, for example, Charles Leinberger, *Ennio Morricone's 'The Good, the Bad and the Ugly'* (Lanham, MD: Scarecrow Press, 2004).

27 John Edward Mason, '"Mannenberg": Notes on the Making of an Icon and Anthem', *African Studies Quarterly*, 9: 4 (Fall 2007), 25–46.

28 Bernard Stiegler, *Technics and Time, Volume 3*, translated by Stephen Barker (Stanford, CA: Stanford University Press, 2011), 27.

29 Bernard Stiegler, *The Fault of Epimetheus, Volume 1*, translated by Richard Beardsworth and George Collins (Stanford, CA: Stanford University Press, 1998), 28.

30 Stiegler, *Technics and Time, Volume 3*, 15.

31 For a discussion of the concept of affirmative biopolitics, see Timothy Campbell, *Improper Life: Technology and Biopolitics from Heidegger to Agamben* (Minneapolis: University of Minnesota Press, 2011).

Select Bibliography

Joseph Agassi, 'Sir John Herschel's Philosophy of Success', *Historical Studies in the Physical Sciences*, 1 (1969).

Sarah Alexander, *Victorian Literature and the Physics of the Imponderable* (New York: Routledge, 2015).

Garland Allen, 'Mechanism, Vitalism and Organicism in Late Nineteenth and Twentieth-Century Biology', *Studies in History and Philosophy of Biological and Biomedical Sciences*, 36: 2 (July 2005).

Srinivas Aravamudan, *Enlightenment Orientalism: Resisting the Rise of the Novel* (Chicago: University of Chicago Press, 2012).

William Ashworth, 'John Herschel, George Airy, and the Roaming Eye of the State', *History of Science*, 36: 2 (1998).

Étienne Balibar, *The Philosophy of Marx*, translated by Chris Turner (London: Verso, 2007).

Étienne Balibar, 'Althusser's Dramaturgy and the Critique of Ideology', *Differences: A Journal of Feminist Cultural Studies*, 26: 3 (2015).

Roland Barthes, *Mythologies*, translated by Annette Lavers (New York: Hill and Wang, 1957).

Ian Baucom, *Specters of the Atlantic: Finance Capital, Slavery, and the Philosophy of History* (Durham, NC: Duke University Press, 2005).

Jonathan Beller, *The Cinematic Mode of Production: Attention,*

Economy and the Society of the Spectacle (Hanover, NH: Dartmouth College Press, 2006).

Walter Benjamin, *Charles Baudelaire: A Lyric Poet in the Era of High Capitalism*, translated by Harry Zohn (London: Verso, 1997).

Walter Benjamin, 'Surrealism: The Last Snapshot of the European Intelligentsia', in Lawrence Rainey (ed.) *Modernism: An Anthology* (Malden, MA: Blackwell, 2005).

Henri Bergson, *Matter and Memory*, translated by Nancy Margaret Paul and W. Scott Palmer (New York: Dover Publications, 2004).

Rustom Bharucha, *Terror and Performance* (London: Routledge, 2014).

Joshua Billings, *The Philosophical Stage* (Princeton, NJ: Princeton University Press, 2021).

Arthur Blumenthal, 'Wilhelm Wundt: Psychology as the Propaedeutic Science', in Claude Buxton (ed.) *Points of View in the Modern History of Psychology* (New York: Academic Press, 1985).

Alastair Brotchie, *Alfred Jarry: A Pataphysical Life* (Cambridge, MA: MIT Press, 2011).

Bill Brown, *Other Things* (Chicago: University of Chicago Press, 2015).

Jane Brown, 'Theatricality and Experiment: Identity in Faust', in Hans Schulte, John Noyes and Pia Kleber (eds.) *Goethe's Faust: Theatre of Modernity* (Cambridge: Cambridge University Press, 2011).

Dickson Bruce, 'W.E.B. Du Bois and the Idea of Double Consciousness', *American Literature*, 64: 2 (June 1992).

Colin Bundy, 'Action Comrades, Action! Street Sociology and Pavement Politics in Cape Town in 1985', in Mary Simons and Wilmot James (eds.) *The Angry Divide: Social and Economic History of the Western Cape* (Cape Town: David Philip Publishers, 1989).

Judith Butler, *The Psychic Life of Power: Theories in Subjection* (Stanford, CA: Stanford University Press, 1997).

George Caffentzis, 'The End of Work or the Renaissance of Slavery? A Critique of Rifkin and Negri', *Common Sense*, 24 (December 1999).

Timothy Campbell, *Improper Life: Technology and Biopolitics from Heidegger to Agamben* (Minneapolis: University of Minnesota Press, 2011).

Select Bibliography

Carloss James Chamberlin, 'Dziga Vertov: The Idiot', *Senses of Cinema*, 41 (November 2006), http://sensesofcinema.com/2006/feature-articles/dziga-vertov-enthusiasm/ (accessed 12 August 2014).

Ruby Cohn, '*Theatrum Mundi* and Contemporary Theater', *Comparative Drama*, 1: 1 (Spring 1967).

Catherine Cole, *Performing South Africa's Truth Commission: Stages of Transition* (Bloomington: Indiana University Press, 2010).

Henry Cowles, 'On the Origin of Theories: Charles Darwin's Vocabulary of Method', *American Historical Review*, 122: 4 (2017).

James Crighton, *Büchner and Madness: Schizophrenia in Georg Büchner's 'Lenz' and 'Woyzeck'* (New York: Edwin Mellen Press, 1998).

Kurt Danziger, 'Origins and Basic Principles of Wundt's *Völkerpsychologie*', *British Journal of Social Psychology*, 22: 4 (1983).

Lorraine Daston and Peter Galison, 'The Image of Objectivity', *Representations*, 40 (Autumn 1992).

Sara Munson Deats, *The Faust Legend: From Marlowe and Goethe to Contemporary Drama and Film* (Cambridge: Cambridge University Press, 2019).

Jacques Derrida, *Paper Machine*, translated by Rachel Bowlby (Stanford, CA: Stanford University Press, 2005).

Georges Didi-Huberman, *Atlas, or the Anxious Gay Science*, translated by Shane Lillis (Chicago: University of Chicago Press, 2018).

Saul Dubow, 'Afrikaner Nationalism, Apartheid and the Conceptualization of "Race"', *Journal of African History*, 33: 2 (1992).

Saul Dubow (ed.), *Science and Society in Southern Africa* (New York and Manchester: Manchester University Press, 2000).

Saul Dubow, 'Racial Irredentism: Ethnogenesis, and White Supremacy in High-Apartheid South Africa', *Kronos: Southern African Histories*, 41 (November 2015).

André du Toit, 'No Chosen People: The Myth of the Calvinist Origins of Afrikaner Nationalism and Racial Ideology', *American Historical Review*, 88 (1983).

Martin Esslin, *The Theatre of the Absurd* (New York: Double Day, 1961).

212 Select Bibliography

Jochen Fahrenberg, *Wilhelm Wundt: 1832–1920* (Freiburg: Albert-Ludwigs-Universität, 2019).

John Bellamy Foster and Paul Burkett, 'Ecological Economics and Classical Marxism: The "Podolinsky Business" Reconsidered', *Organization and Environment*, 17: 1 (March 2004).

Michel Foucault, *Society Must be Defended,* translated by David Macey (New York: Picador, 2003).

Steven Fuller, *Thomas Kuhn: A Philosophical History for our Times* (Chicago: University of Chicago Press, 2000).

Hermann Giliomee, 'The Making of the Apartheid Plan, 1929–1948', *Journal of Southern African Studies*, 29: 2 (June 2003).

Sander Gilman, 'Alban Berg, the Jews, and the Anxiety of Genius', in Ronald Radano and Philip Bohlman (eds.) *Music and the Racial Imagination* (Chicago: University of Chicago Press, 2000).

Simon Goldhill, *Sophocles and the Language of Tragedy* (Oxford: Oxford University Press, 2012).

Pumla Gqola, *What is Slavery to Me? Postcolonial/Slave Memory in Post-Apartheid South Africa* (Johannesburg: Wits University Press, 2010).

Richard Gray, 'The Dialectic of Enlightenment in Büchner's Woyzeck', *German Quarterly*, 61: 1 (1998).

Heidi Grunebaum, *Memorializing the Past: Everyday Life in South Africa after the Truth and Reconciliation Commission* (New Brunswick, NJ: Transaction Publishers, 2011).

Stuart Hall, 'The Problem of Ideology', *Journal of Communication Inquiry*, 10: 2 (1986).

Miriam Bratu Hansen, 'Benjamin, Cinema and Experience: "The Blue Flower in the Land of Technology"', *New German Critique*, 40 (1987).

Miriam Bratu Hansen, 'Room-for-Play: Benjamin's Gamble with Cinema', *Canadian Journal of Film Studies*, 13: 1 (Spring 2004).

Miriam Bratu Hansen, *Cinema and Experience: Siegfried Kracauer, Walter Benjamin, and Theodor W. Adorno* (Berkeley: University of California Press, 2012).

Michael Hardt and Antonio Negri, *Empire* (Cambridge, MA: Harvard University Press, 2000).

Anne Harrington, 'Metaphoric Connections: Holistic Science

Select Bibliography 213

in the Shadow of the Third Reich', *Social Research*, 62: 2 (Summer 1995).

Owen Hatherley, *The Chaplin Machine: Slapstick, Fordism and the Communist Avant-Garde* (London: Pluto, 2016).

Seamus Heaney, *The Cure at Troy: A Version of Sophocles' 'Philoctetes'* (London: Faber and Faber, 1991).

John Herschel, *A Preliminary Discourse on the Study of Natural Philosophy* (London: Longman, Brown, Green, 1830).

Isabel Hofmeyr, 'Popularising History: The Case of Gustav Preller', *Journal of African History*, 29: 3 (1988).

Ute Holl, *Cinema, Trance and Cybernetics* (Amsterdam: Amsterdam University Press, 2017).

William Harold Hutt, *The Theory of Idle Resources* (Auburn, AL: Ludwig von Mises Institute, 2011).

Abiola Irele, *The African Imagination: Literature in Africa and the Black Diaspora* (Oxford: Oxford University Press, 2001).

Nico Israel, *Spirals: The Whirled Image in Twentieth-century Literature and Art* (New York: Columbia University Press, 2015).

Fredric Jameson, *Representing Capital* (London: Verso, 2011).

Donna Jones, *The Racial Discourses of Life Philosophy: Négritude, Vitalism, and Modernity* (New York: Columbia University Press, 2010).

Erman Kaplama, *Cosmological Aesthetics through the Kantian Sublime and Nietzschean Dionysian* (Lanham, MD: Rowman & Littlefield, 2013).

Katharina Keim, 'Contemporary African and Brazilian Adaptations of Goethe's *Faust* in Postcolonial Context', in Lorna Fitzsimmons (ed.) *International Faust Studies: Adaptation, Reception, Translation* (New York: Continuum, 2008).

Thomas Kemple, *Reading Marx Writing: Melodrama, the Market and the 'Grundrisse'* (Stanford, CA: Stanford University Press, 1995).

Siegfried Kracauer, *Theory of Film: The Redemption of Physical Reality* (Princeton, NJ: Princeton University Press, 1997).

Premesh Lalu, *The Deaths of Hintsa: Post-Apartheid South Africa and the Shape of Recurring Pasts* (Cape Town: HSRC Press, 2009).

Claude Lévi-Strauss, 'The Structural Study of Myth', *Journal of American Folklore*, 68: 270 (October–December 1955).

214   Select Bibliography

David Levering Lewis, *W.E.B. Du Bois: A Biography, 1868–1963* (New York: Henry Holt and Co., 1993).

Susanna Lindberg, 'The Remains of the Romantic Philosophy of Nature: Being as Life, or the Plurality of Living Beings?', *New Centennial Review*, 10: 3 (Winter 2010).

Lydia Liu, *The Freudian Robot* (Chicago: University of Chicago Press, 2010).

Nicole Loraux, *The Divided City: On Memory and Forgetting in Ancient Athens*, translated by Corinne Pache and Jeff Fort (New York: Zone Books, 2006).

Pierre Macherey, 'Out of Melancholia: Notes on Judith Butler's *The Psychic Life of Power: Theories in Subjection*', *Rethinking Marxism*, 16: 1 (2004).

Pierre Macherey, 'Figures of Interpellation in Althusser and Fanon', *Radical Philosophy*, 173 (May–June 2012).

Harry Magdoff, 'The Meaning of Work: A Marxist Perspective', *Monthly Review*, 58: 5 (October 2006).

Christoph Marx, 'Hendrik Verwoerd's Long March to Apartheid: Nationalism and Racism in South Africa', in Manfred Berg and Simon Wendt (eds.) *Racism in the Modern World: Historical Perspectives on Cultural Transfer and Adaptation* (New York: Berghahn, 2017).

Christoph Marx, *Trennung und Angst: Hendrik Verwoerd und die Gedankenwelt der Apartheid* (Berlin: De Gruyter Oldenbourg, 2020).

Karl Marx, *Grundrisse*, translated by Martin Nicolaus (New York: Penguin Books, 1973).

Karl Marx, 'The Eighteenth Brumaire of Louis Bonaparte', in Karl Marx and Frederick Engels, *Collected Works, Vol. 11* (New York: International Publishers, 1979).

John Edward Mason, '"Mannenberg": Notes on the Making of an Icon and Anthem', *African Studies Quarterly*, 9: 4 (Fall 2007).

Brian Massumi, *Parables for the Virtual* (Durham, NC: Duke University Press, 2002).

Brian Massumi, *The Power at the End of the Economy* (Durham, NC: Duke University Press, 2014).

Steve McCaffery, *Prior to Meaning: The Protosemantic and Poetics* (Evanston, IL: Northwestern University Press, 2001).

David McNally, *Monsters of the Market: Zombies, Vampires and Global Capitalism* (Chicago: Haymarket Books, 2012).

Jamie Miller, *An African Volk: The Apartheid Regime and its Search for Survival* (Oxford: Oxford University Press, 2016).

Roberta Balstad Miller, 'Science and Society in the Early Career of H.F. Verwoerd', *Journal of Southern African Studies*, 19: 4 (December 1993).

Trinh T. Minh-ha, *Cinema Interval* (New York: Routledge, 1999).

Silas Modiri Molema, *The Bantu: Past and Present* (Edinburgh: W. Green and Son, 1920).

Donald Moodie (ed.), *The Record: Or, a Series of Official Papers Relative to the Condition and Treatment of the Native Tribes of South Africa* (Cambridge: Cambridge University Press, 2011 – 1838 1st edition).

T. Dunbar Moodie, *The Rise of Afrikanerdom: Power, Apartheid, and the Afrikaner Civil Religion* (Berkeley: University of California Press, 1975).

George Morgan, 'Interview with Seamus Heaney', *Cycnos*, 15: 2 (2008).

John Mowitt, 'Stumbling on Analysis: Psychoanalysis and Everyday Life', *Cultural Critique*, 52 (Autumn 2002).

John Mowitt, *Radio: Essays in Bad Reception* (Berkeley: University of California Press, 2011).

Maria Muhle, 'A Genealogy of Biopolitics: The Notion of Life in Canguilhem and Foucault', in Vanessa Lemm and Miguel Vatter (eds.) *The Government of Life: Foucault, Biopolitics, and Neoliberalism* (New York: Fordham University Press, 2014).

C.F.J. Muller (ed.), *500 Years: A History of South Africa* (Pretoria: Academia, 1969).

Jean-Luc Nancy, 'The Two Secrets of the Fetish', *Diacritics*, 31: 2 (Summer 2001).

Omar Nasim, 'The "Landmark" and "Groundwork" of Stars: John Herschel, Photography and the Drawing of the Nebulae', *Studies in History and Philosophy of Science*, 42: 1 (2011).

Aletta Norval, *Deconstructing Apartheid Discourse* (London: Verso, 1996).

John Noyes, 'Goethe on Cosmopolitanism and Colonialism: *Bildung* and the Dialectic of Critical Mobility', *Eighteenth-Century Studies*, 39: 4 (2006).

Eugene O'Brien, *Seamus Heaney as Aesthetic Thinker: A Study of the Prose* (Syracuse, NY: Syracuse University Press, 2016).

Pablo Oyarzún, 'Law, Violence, History: A Brief Reading of the

Last Paragraph of Walter Benjamin's "Toward the Critique of Violence"', *Critical Times*, 2: 2 (2019).

Deborah Posel, *The Making of Apartheid, 1948–1961* (Oxford: Clarendon Press, 1991).

Deborah Posel, 'Race as Common Sense: Racial Classification in Twentieth Century South Africa', *African Studies Review*, 44: 2 (2001).

Deborah Posel, 'Truth? The View from South Africa's Truth and Reconciliation Commission', in Ali Benmakhalouf et al. (eds.) *Keywords: Truth* (New York: Other Press, 2004).

Victor Price, 'Introduction', in Georg Büchner, *Danton's Death, Leonce and Lena, Woyzeck*, translated by Victor Price (Oxford: Oxford University Press, 1971).

Thomas Pringle, 'The Ecosystem is an Apparatus', in Gertrud Koch, Bernard Stiegler and Thomas Pringle (eds.) *Machine* (Lüneburg: Meson Press, 2019).

Jahan Ramazani, 'Seamus Heaney's Globe', *Irish Pages*, 9: 1 (2014).

Ciraj Rassool and Leslie Witz, 'The 1952 Jan van Riebeeck Tercentenary Festival: Constructing and Contesting Public National History in South Africa', *Journal of African History*, 34 (1993).

David Richards, *Georg Büchner's Woyzeck: A History of its Criticism* (Rochester, NY: Camden House, 2001).

Richard Rive, *Emergency Continued* (Cape Town: David Philip Publishers, 1990).

Steven Ruskin, *John Herschel's Cape Voyage: Private Science, Public Imagination and the Ambitions of Empire* (London: Routledge, 2004).

Mauro Scalercio, 'Dominating Nature and Colonialism. Francis Bacon's View of Europe and the New World', *History of European Ideas*, 44: 8 (2018).

Larry Schaaf, 'John Herschel, Photography and the Camera Lucida', *Transactions of the Royal Society of South Africa*, 49: 1 (1994).

Henning Schmidgen, 'Time and Noise: The Stable Surroundings of Reaction Experiments, 1860–1890', *Studies in History and Philosophy of Biological and Biomedical Sciences*, 34 (2003).

Pamela Scully, *Liberating the Family? Gender and British Slave Emancipation in the Rural Western Cape, South Africa 1823–1853* (Portsmouth, NH: Heinemann, 1997).

Select Bibliography

Kirk Sides, 'Precedence and Warning: Global Apartheid and South Africa's Long Conversation on Race with the United States', *Safundi: The Journal of South African and American Studies*, 18: 3 (2017).

Gilbert Simondon, *The Mode of Existence of Technical Objects*, translated by Cécile Malaspina and John Rogove (New York: Univocal Publishing, 2017).

Adam Sitze, *The Impossible Machine* (Ann Arbor: Michigan University Press, 2013).

Adam Sitze, 'Study and Revolt', *Safundi: The Journal of South African and American Studies*, 17: 3 (2016).

Crain Soudien, 'New Accents on the Social: Thinking on South Africa's History at UWC', *South African Historical Journal*, 70: 3 (2018).

South African Democracy Education Trust, *The Road to Democracy: Volume 2, 1970–1980* (Pretoria: Unisa Press, 1990).

Gayatri Spivak, *An Aesthetic Education in the Era of Globalization* (Cambridge, MA: Harvard University Press, 2012).

Jane Starfield, '"A Member of the Race": Dr Modiri Molema's Intellectual Engagement with the Popular History of South Africa, 1912–1921', *South African Historical Journal*, 64: 3 (2012).

George Steinmetz, *Sociology and Empire* (Durham, NC: Duke University Press, 2013).

Elizabeth Stewart, *Catastrophe and Survival: Walter Benjamin and Psychoanalysis* (London: Bloomsbury, 2009).

Bernard Stiegler, *The Fault of Epimetheus, Volume 1*, translated by Richard Beardsworth and George Collins (Stanford, CA: Stanford University Press, 1998).

Bernard Stiegler, *Technics and Time, Volume 3*, translated by Stephen Barker (Stanford, CA: Stanford University Press, 2011).

Jane Taylor, *Ubu and the Truth Commission* (Cape Town: University of Cape Town Press, 1998).

Jane Taylor (ed.), *The Handspring Puppet Company* (Cape Town: David Krut Publishing, 2009).

Leonard Thompson, *The Political Mythology of Apartheid* (New Haven, CT: Yale University Press, 1985).

Edward B. Titchener, 'Wilhelm Wundt', *American Journal of Psychology*, 32: 2 (April 1921).

218 Select Bibliography

Gabriel Trop, 'Goethe's *Faust* and the Absolute of *Naturphilosophie'*, *Germanic Review*, 92: 4 (2017).

Ross Truscott and Michelle Smith, 'Aftershocks: Psychotechnics in the Wake of Apartheid', *Parallax*, 22: 2 (May 2016).

Maurits van Bever Donker, Ross Truscott, Gary Minkley and Premesh Lalu (eds.), *Remains of the Social: Desiring the Post-Apartheid* (Johannesburg: Wits University Press, 2017).

Truth and Reconciliation Commission of South Africa Report, Volume 4 (Cape Town: Government Publishers, 1998).

Robert Tucker (ed.), *The Marx–Engels Reader* (New York: Norton & Co., 1978).

Jules Verne, *From the Earth to the Moon* (New York: Scribner, Armstrong and Co., 1865).

H.F. Verwoerd, 'The Policy of Apartheid', Speech to the Parliament of South Africa, Hansard, 3 September 1948.

Paul Veyne, *Did the Greeks Believe in Their Myths? An Essay on the Constitutive Imagination*, translated by Paula Wissing (Chicago: University of Chicago Press, 1988).

Samuel Weber, *Theatricality as Medium* (New York: Fordham University Press, 2004).

B.W. Wells, 'Goethe's "Faust"', *Sewanee Review*, 2: 4 (August 1894).

Norbert Wiener, *The Human Use of Human Beings* (Boston: Da Capo Press, 1950).

David Wilson, 'Herschel and Whewell's Version of Newtonianism', *Journal of the History of Ideas*, 35: 1 (1974).

Monique Wittig, 'The Trojan Horse', *Feminist Issues*, 4 (1984).

Leslie Witz, *Apartheid's Festival* (Bloomington: Indiana University Press, 2003).

Wan-chi Wong, 'Retracing the Footsteps of Wilhelm Wundt: Explorations in the Disciplinary Frontiers of Psychology and in *Völkerpsychologie'*, *History of Psychology*, 12: 4 (2009).

Nigel Worden and Clifton Crais (eds.), *Breaking the Chains: Slavery and its Legacy in the Nineteenth Century Cape Colony* (Johannesburg: Wits University Press, 1994).

Wilhelm Wundt, *Elements of Folk Psychology*, translated by Edward Leroy Schaub (New York: Macmillan, 1916).

Kevin Young, *Bunk: The Rise of Hoaxes, Humbug, Plagiarists, Phonies, Post-facts, and Fake News* (Minneapolis: Graywolf Press, 2017).

Index

aesthetic
    education, 6, 7, 10, 64, 138, 152, 160, 163, 168, 169, 187
    in *Faustus in Africa*, 71, 98
    in *Ubu and the Truth Commission*, 143
    theory, 93, 100, 143
Afrikaner nationalism, 33–4, 35, 64
apartheid,
    origins 11, 23–4, 29, 128, 135, 157–8, 176
    political mythologies of 14–15, 33–5, 66, 104–5
    psychic dimensions 28, 124, 171, 173, 176
    as *Trauerspiel* 24, 25
    see also Afrikaner nationalism; grand apartheid; petty apartheid; post-apartheid freedom
apocalyptic sublime, 45, 49
apperception, 116, 160, 163, 176, 185
applied psychology, 129, 131, 132

astronomy, 41, 42, 44, 45, 56, 83–4
Athlone, 2, 5, 163–4, 166, 169, 173, 178, 184–5, 186

Babbage, Charles, 36, 38, 40
Bergson, Henri, 135, 140, 153
biopolitics, 28, 120, 156, 157, 158, 159, 160
bioscope *see* cinema
A Brother with Perfect Timing (film) (Chris Austin), 180, 181–2, 183, 185
Büchner, Georg, 8, 106, 111, 112, 113, 118

capital, 42, 66, 73, 83, 85, 87, 89, 104, 110, 174
    speculation 79, 90
Chaplin, Charlie, 144, 149, 150, 153,
    The Great Dictator, 156–7
cinema, 156, 157, 179, 184, 185
cinematic form *see* slapstick
cinematic interval, 166, 167–9

220 Index

cinematic/cinematographic
memory *see under* memory
civil war 15, 18, 19, 165, 174,
175, 176, 177, 178, 179,
181
comedy, 138
and tragedy, 139 *see also* theatre
of the absurd; slapstick
commodity fetishism, 109–10,
117–18
commodity and human traits,
116 *see also* apperception
communication
and control, 11, 15, 26, 28,
66, 117, 132, 135
scientific revolution in, 48, 53,
57
technologies, 54, 66, 73, 87,
96, 127
Congress of South African
Students, 165
consilience
of arts and sciences, 66, 97,
160, 187
of inductions 7, 40, 46
The Cure at Troy (Seamus
Heaney), 14, 15, 16, 17,
31, 163, 189–91
deception plot, 19–20
cybernetics, 11, 64, 65

Danby, Francis *The Opening of
the Sixth Seal*, 46–50
myth and reason in 46, 47, 50
slave in 47–8, 49
deductive methods/reason 41, 45,
98, 132
divided city, 4, 5, 165, 166, 173,
176, 179
divine violence, 151, 152
see also mythic violence; *see also*
under the everyday; *see*
also under memory
Du Bois, W.E.B., 80

education
and liberation, 2–5, 6, 20, 29,
167
protests 2, 3, 165–6, 169, 170,
187
see also aesthetic education
Emergency (Richard Rive), 3
Emergency Continued (Richard
Rive), 2–6, 31, 186
energy 8, 10, 11, 130
see also stasis
Ehrhardt, Adolf, 105
ethnographic psychology *see*
Völkerpsychologie
the everyday, 5, 6, 96, 97
Freud and 172, 176, 177
and race 11, 98, 108, 117
and science 25
as reflected in theatre 7, 21,
106
time and space in 96, 182
violence of 155, 164
see also trivial things; mythic
violence; revolutionary
violence
exchange value, 117
experimental psychology, 28, 96,
123, 127–8, 129, 130–1,
135, 171, 178

farce, 79, 149
fascism, 71, 143, 144, 145, 175
Faust (Goethe, Johann Wolfgang
von)
cellar rat in 85, 87, 88, 93
plot 81
themes 75, 76, 79, 81, 82, 83,
84
see also Marx, Karl
Faust II (Goethe, Johann
Wolfgang von)
compared to *Faustus in Africa*
99
themes 83, 93, 98

Index

Faust (character) 68, 69, 75, 76, 79, 82
Faust (legend) 68–9, 81–2, 101
Faustus (character in *Faustus in Africa*) 31, **68**, 76, 99
Faustus in Africa (William Kentridge) 8, 68
  aesthetic(s) in 94, 98, 99–100
  Africa, significance in, 92, 93, 94
  compared to *Faust II*, 99
  hyena in 77–8, 95, 96, 100
  plot 69, 76, 81
  psychoanalytic reading 76, 79–80
  props 71
  puppet in **68**, 77–8, 95
  themes 25, 30, 69, 71–3, 74, 75, 79, 94, 97, 99, 100–1
  see also Naturphilosophie; experimental psychology
fetish object, 123
freedom *see* education and liberation; post-apartheid freedom
Freud, Sigmund 76, 172, 173 176, 177

Gestalt psychology, 128, 129, 133, 135, 173, 178
Gestalt theory, 96, 97, 98, 128, 133
Gestaltism, 96, 97, 81, 82, 83, 128
Goethe, Johann Wolfgang von, 8,
  and colonialism, 68, 91
  and cosmopolitanism, 68, 91, 100, 101
  and Romanticism, 79, 80, 82, 83
grand apartheid, 1, 15, 26, 27, 163 *see also* apartheid; petty apartheid

The Great Dictator (film) (Charlie Chaplin), 156–7
The Great Moon Hoax, 46, 50–3, **52**
  as an allegory of race, 51
  science in 53

The Handspring Puppet Company *see Faustus in Africa*; *Ubu and the Truth Commission*; *Woyzeck on the Highveld*
Heaney, Seamus
  The Cure at Troy, 14, 15, 16, 17, 31, 163, 189–91
  deception plot, 19–20
Herschel, John, 40, 51, 121
  political viewpoints, 36–8
  role in scientific development, 36, 39, 45, 53
  see also consilience (of inductions)
Herschel, William, 84
holism, 98, 172

Ibrahim, Abdullah, 179, 181, 182, 183 *see also* 'Mannenberg'
immaterial labour, 31, 73, 83, 85, 86, 87, 89, 90, 101, 121, 187
  precarities of, 86
immateriality, 25, 30, 90, 110
indecision, 3, 6, 35, 77, 79, 139, 143, 150, 155, 158, 143, 163, 176
inductive methods/reason, 38, 40, 41, 42, 43, 44, 45, 98
industrial revolution
  (first), 42, 59, 80
  (second), 60
industrialization, 35, 50
  and slavery, 40
intergenerational conflict, 4–5, 18

Index

interpellation
 conflicting, 7
 scene of, 103, 104, 106, 107, 108, 109, 114, 120, 121
interval *see* cinematic interval

Jarry, Alfred, 8, 138, 141, 146, 147

Kentridge, William, 77 *see also Faustus in Africa; Ubu and the Truth Commission; Woyzeck on the Highveld*
kinaesthetic learning, 145
kinetic object, 30, 105
King Baabu (Wole Soyinka), 146
Kismet bioscope, 189
Krueger, Felix, 128

labour
 unalienated, 87, 88
 see also immaterial labour
liberalism, 35, 50, 51, 52, 56, 58, 59, 61, 62, 63
liberation and education, 2–5, 20, 29, 167
life philosophy, 28, 80–1

Mandela, Nelson 12, 13, 14, 16, 17, 18, 31
Manenberg (place), 180
'Mannenberg' (jazz composition), 181, 182–3
Marx, Karl
 use of cellar rat in 'Fragments...' 85–8, 89, 90–1, 93
 on idleness 91
 and science 90
 slavery 115–16, 117
memory, 15, 154, 174, 188–9
 cinematic/cinematographic 140, 153, 180, 182

of the future, 186, 189
instruments of, 75, 129–30
primary, 181
secondary, 181, 184
tertiary, 183, 184
of violence, 75, 145
Mickey Mouse, 144
migrant labour system, 102, 103, 122, 124
mnemotechnics, 7, 25–6, 30, 75, 109, 118, 122–3, 156
Molema, Silas Modiri, 56
 on race, 56–64
 in Scotland and Britain, 58
 in South Africa, 56–8, 61, 63
 on colonized subject 59
 on education 62
Münsterberg, Hugo, 131
myth
 and post-apartheid freedom, 6, 9, 10, 66, 94
 and reason 34, 35, 36, 45–6, 47, 50, 55, 57, 66
 and theatre, 23–4
 see also political mythologies
mythic violence, 139, 145, 150, 151–2, 155, 174, 188
 and slapstick, 160–1
 see also divine violence; mythic violence; revolutionary violence; *see also under* memory

nationalism, 59, 158, 161 *see also* Afrikaner nationalism
natural history, 57
natural philosophy, 36, 39, 42, 53, 70, 83–4, 96
Naturphilosophie, 70, 76, 79, 83, 84, 93, 94, 96
Nazism, 98, 122
Negritude, 98
neoliberalism, 134, 158, 159, 171, 176

Index

object theatre 7, 9
The Opening of the Sixth Seal
(Francis Danby), 46–50, 17
myth and reason in 46, 47, 50
slave in 47–8, 49

Pa Ubu (character), 139, 148, 150, 155, 157
perception, 42, 98, 185
experimental apparatus, 97
learned, 97
petty apartheid, 2, 6–7, 8, 10, 11, 15, 35, 94, 97, 118, 124, 129, 177
derivation 11, 117, 185
dynamic of 11, 26–8, 97, 106, 178
and the everyday 11, 26, 176
puppet and 106
Philoctetes (Sophocles), 15, 21
see also 'The Cure of Troy'
physics 36, 83, 97, 155 see also energy; thermodynamics
physiological psychology, 133–4
Podolinsky, Sergei, 10
poetry, 18, 56
political mythologies (of apartheid), 33–6
post-apartheid freedom, 8, 10, 11, 32, 64, 155, 158, 185
conditions, 30, 32
desire for, 6–7, 101, 170
vocabulary of, 27
primary memory see under memory
prosthetic objects, 29, 30, 78, 120, 154
psychotechnics, 8, 28, 126, 130
puppet
function of, 29–30, 77, 98, 105, 106, 135
Hyena in *Faustus in Africa*, 77–8
in *Woyzeck on the Highveld*,

106, 109–10, 120, 121, 122
see also mnemotechnics

race
as biology 60, 105, 127
and class 35, 104, 160
and culture 60, 105, 132, 134
modern concept of 27, 29, 30, 40, 45–6, 53–4, 66, 85,
origin 8, 35, 41, 43, 56
recasting of discourse 56, 57, 59, 60, 80
return 2, 7, 57, 66, 71, 76, 101, 125, 158
as an unstable idea 15, 27, 65, 97, 115, 123, 132, 136, 185
see also *The Opening of the Sixth Seal*; *Faustus in Africa*
Ranschburg memory apparatus
see under memory
reason 43, 50, 81
deductive 41, 45, 98, 132
experimentation on 94
inductive 38, 40, 41, 42, 43, 44, 45, 98
myth and 34, 35, 36, 45–6, 47, 50, 55, 57, 65–6
reconciliation, 51–2, 165, 173, 178, 187–8
see also Truth and Reconciliation Commission; *Ubu and the Truth Commission;*
revolutionary violence 151, 160
see also divine violence; mythic violence; see also under the everyday; see also under memory
Rive, Richard
Emergency, 3
Emergency Continued, 2–6, 31, 186

224 Index

Romanticism, 75, 79, 82, 83, 94, 101
Royal Commission of Aboriginal Peoples of 1835, 59

science
political choices in name of, 37, 38, 39, 40, (60)
professionalization, 36, 38, 39, 53,
see also reason
scientific method 38–40, 41, 42, 43, 45, 53, 57, 60–1
empiricism, 128
observation in, 43, 44
and speculation 38, 39, 41, 53, 83
scientific revolution, 37, 42,
sense-perception, 26, 27–8, 125, 129, 136, 155
partitioning, 105, 171, 174, 177
relinking, 158, 179, 183, 187
stimulation 134
theatrical devices 78
see also apperception; perception
sensorium, 25, 103, 131, 153, 157 *see also* sense-perception
shock, 10, 25, 31, 64, 116, 130, 144, 145, 153, 154, 164
slapstick, 141, 143–5, 149, 152, 153, 154, 155–6, 158–9, 160–1
slave, 41, 45, 55, 60, 61, 114, 115
and machine 65, 66, 114
and race, 8, 22, 29, 65, 115, 117
slavery,
abolition of 28, 34, 40, 42, 51, 54, 60, 64, 65, 90
re-establishment of, 63, 77

reinscription of, 174
see also The Opening of the Sixth Seal; The Great Moon Hoax
social psychology, 132
Sophocles *see Philoctetes*
spiral, 64–5, 118, 145–7, 155, 157
Kentridge on, 146
stasis, 172, 173, 176, 178
as civil war, 181
as movement at rest, 173, 181
surplus value, 115

Taylor, Jane, 149 see also *Ubu and the Truth Commission*
techne, 7, 20, 71, 79, 99, 101, 147, 149, 157
technogenesis, 185, 186
technological resources, 6, 8, 15, 46, 51, 74, 86, 113, 132, 143, 153, 164
tertiary memory, *see under* memory
theatre, resource, 18, 20, 22, 30, 74–5, 78–9
theatre of the absurd 139, 141, 147–8
theatricality, role of, 29, 73, 108
theatrocracy, 16, 23, 31, 108
Theatrum Mundi (Giulio Camillo), 75
thermodynamics *see* energy
tragedy, 10, 24, 25, 28–9, 71, 74, 78, 79, 82, 119, 139, 164
and song 73
Trauerspiel, 24
trivial things, 117, 118, 135
'Trojan Horse' (sculpture) (Willie Bester), 188
Trojan Horse massacre, 5, 162, 163–4, 166, 170, 178
aftermaths of, 31
Trojan Horse myth, 5, 6, 9–10, 30, 163

Index 225

Troy, fall of, 174
Truth and Reconciliation
Commission (TRC) 28,
143, 144, 145, 158,
165, 174–5, 176 *see also*
reconciliation

Ubu (Jarry's) (character), 141
Ubu (Taylor's) (character), 32,
141
Ubu and the Truth Commission
(Jane Taylor) 8, 138
plot, 139–40
puppet, 140, **141**, 147, 148,
154
themes, 25, 30, 138–9, 141,
142–3, 144, 145, 146,
150, 151, 153, 154, 156,
157
see also mythic violence;
slapstick
Ubu Roi (King Ubu) (character),
138, **142**
uncanny return, 76–7 *see also*
under race

Verne, Jules 44–5
Verwoerd, Hendrik 25, 117, 123,
157
academic career 126, 127, 128
anti-apartheid representations
of 125–6, 127
and apartheid (in1948) 175
laboratory technician 127
in Leipzig 126
and petty apartheid 129, 132
as state official 132
at Stellenbosch 126
violence *see* divine violence;

mythic violence;
revolutionary violence; *see*
under the everyday; *see*
under memory
Völkerpsychologie, 25, 127, 129,
131, 133, 134

Waterwitch, Robert, 188
Whewell, William, 36, 39, 40
Wiener, Norbert, 64–5
Williams, Coline, 188
Wittig, Monique, 9–10
wound, 14, 15, 17, 18, 19, 22,
26, 27, 28, 163
potential for healing, 79, 100
Woyzeck (Georg Büchner), 106,
111–13
themes, 112–14, 119–20
Woyzeck, Franz (character in
Woyzeck (Büchner))
Woyzeck, Harry, (character
in *Woyzeck on the*
Highveld), 31–2, 103,
106, 109, 110, 114,
119–20, 122, 125
character emblematic of
mechanization, 103
Woyzeck, Johann Christian, 106,
110
Woyzeck on the Highveld
(William Kentridge) 8, 103
plot, 103
puppet, 105, 106, 109–10,
(118), 121, 122
themes 25, 30, 104, 107, 108,
122, 124, 125, 135, 147
Wundt, Wilhelm, 10–11, 97, 106,
116–17, 123, 129, 132,
133